I0828046

IMAGES
of America

BELMONT

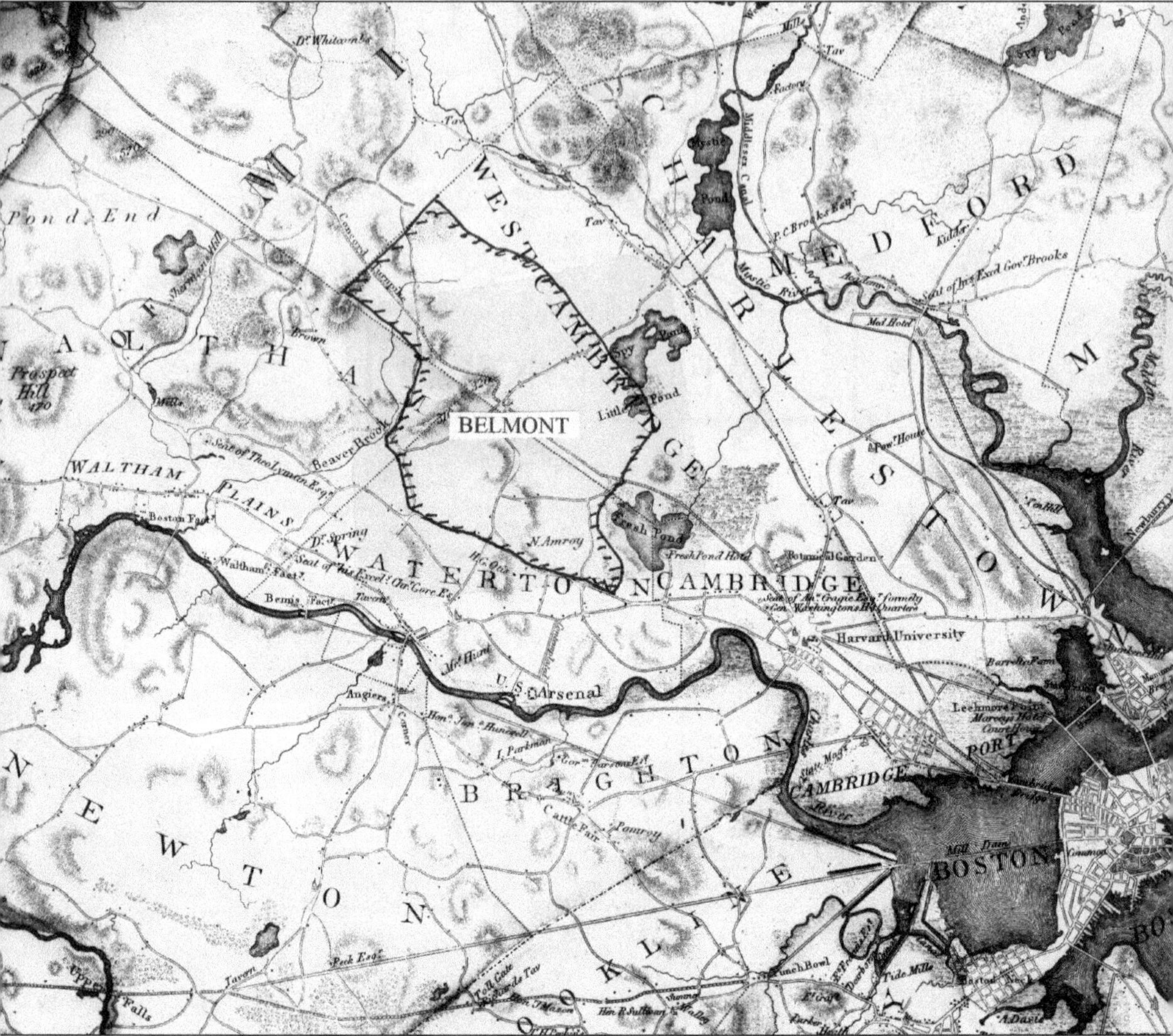

This 1819 map by Jonathan Hale shows Watertown, Waltham, and West Cambridge with present-day Belmont superimposed in the center of the map.

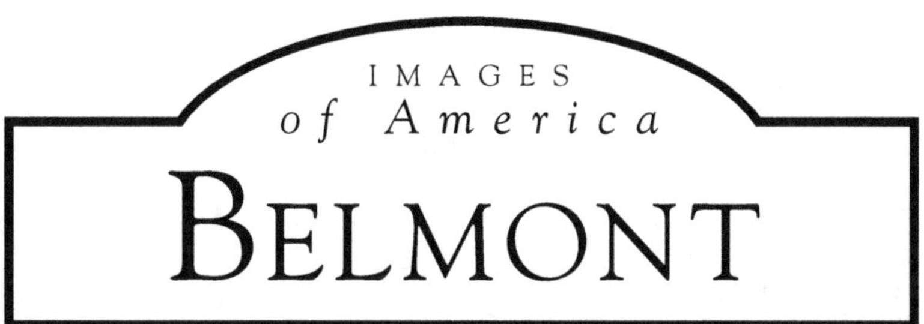

Belmont Historical Society

Richard B. Betts, Town Historian
Victoria Haase, Historical Society President
Norma A. Marsh, Associate Curator
Alfred D. Shea, Claflin Room Curator

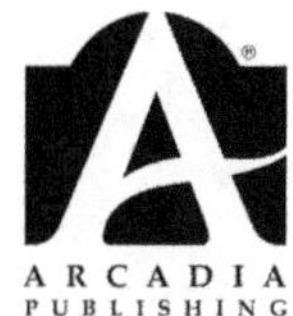

ISBN 978-1-5316-0289-5

Published by Arcadia Publishing
Charleston, South Carolina

Library of Congress Catalog Card Number: 00-104055

For all general information contact Arcadia Publishing at:
Telephone 843-853-2070
Fax 843-853-0044
E-mail sales@arcadiapublishing.com
For customer service and orders:
Toll-Free 1-888-313-2665

Visit us on the Internet at www.arcadiapublishing.com

Contents

Acknowledgments

This book would not have been possible without the individual talents and team efforts of Richard Betts, Norma Marsh, and Al Shea. The Belmont Historical Society extends its overwhelming gratitude to these members, whose countless hours of compiling both photographs and text, made possible this pictorial history of Belmont from conception to centennial.

The Belmont Historical Society is forever grateful for the many members and friends whose donations over the years have added to the files bits of nostalgia, letters, photographs, and family memorabilia, creating the inventory from which we gathered. Thanks is also extended to those of you already acknowledged individually throughout the book for allowing items from your own private collections to be included, and to Jefferson Haase for his photograph-copying work to make these images camera ready.

We would also like to thank our editor Amy Sutton for accepting our initial proposal and bringing to completion this project with both enthusiasm and excellence.

Finally, we would like to thank the citizens of Belmont, whose unique and diverse interests and accomplishments have laid the foundations on which we continue to build a rich history for future generations.

—Victoria Haase, coauthor and Belmont Historical Society President

INTRODUCTION

The story of Belmont begins in the 1630s, when a group of Englishmen ventured up the River Charles to an area now called Fresh Pond, settling there on land occupied by the Pequosette Native Americans and known as Pequosette Plantation. In search of good soil, those men were rewarded with abundant crops, which could be carried from field to market on horseback. The colony thrived despite the increasing discontent with its relationship with England. At the battle of Lexington and Concord in 1775, local residents-turned-patriots entered into full conflict until the Revolution ended. A time of general peace and prosperity followed.

Belmont, however, soon turned its attention to another struggle. Despite fierce opposition from its originators in Waltham, Watertown, and West Cambridge, incorporation was finally realized when little "Belle" became the 338th town in the Commonwealth on March 18, 1859. Waltham conceded 0.67 of a square mile, Watertown 2.25 square miles (a third of its total area and a third of its tax property) and West Cambridge 2.75 square miles (a third of its total area and a quarter of its tax property). A new town had been born, and the five-year battle for independence had been won.

With an already significant 200-year history, much of Belmont's 19th-century growth and success continued on the foundations of its prominent citizens, early businessmen, and original farmers. Influences such as the railroad and trolley car lines brought an ever-expanding population to this area already known for its market gardens and country estates. Sometimes referred to as the Town of Homes, Belmont includes a diversity of architectural styles represented by modest farmhouses, historic mansions, and multiple family dwellings.

Among its many prominent citizens were John P. Cushing, China trade merchant and owner of the 50-room mansion Bellmont, which means "beautiful mountain," from which the town took its name. William J. Underwood, whose company's work included pioneering the art of preserving food in canisters, later called "cans," also made Belmont home. His family-owned business held the oldest registered food trademark in the country. Frederick Tudor, "the Ice King of New England," transported ice cut on Fresh Pond by rail to his wharf in Boston. In 1806, the Tudor Ice Company delivered the first shipment of ice to a port outside the United States.

Belmont has been home to various businesses. The Parry Brothers brick manufacturing business, whose clay was known as the very best in this section of New England, merged with the New England Brick Company and produced 15 million bricks a year at the Belmont yard. The Tower Piano Key Factory, founded in 1897 was said to be the most completely equipped plant of its kind in the United States. Belmont Garden's ten greenhouses were owned and operated by Walter Lenk, who applied for and received one of the first patents ever issued on plants. He shipped on average 8,000 gardenias per day worldwide. The Highland Stock Farm was operated by Winthrop Chenery, who imported the breed of Holstein cattle into the United States. His best cow produced 40 quarts of milk a day. The oldest continuous business is Belmont Springs Water Company, incorporated in 1876. During World War II, the company supplied 10,000 gallons of water a week, canned for naval and merchant vessels. McLean Hospital, a world famous psychiatric facility, opened in 1895 on the largest piece of real estate in Belmont. Landscaping of the 240-acre grounds was based on a design by Frederick Law Olmstead.

Early farm families, both numerous and noteworthy, grew and brought by horse and wagon much of the best produce to the Farmers Market at Faneuil Hall in Boston. Wellington Farm occupied the land now known as Belmont Center and was managed by family descendants of Roger Wellington, an original settler in 1636. The Hittinger Farm in 1849 produced fruit trees, berries, and vegetables in 20 greenhouses on 40 acres. The Shaw Farm grew a large variety of vegetables. The Hill and Richardson families owned the last working farm in Belmont on land granted by King Charles I of England to Abraham Hill in 1633.

Belmontians have taken a great interest in leisure and recreation. Artist Winslow Homer, nephew of William Flagg Homer, spent many summers in Belmont, the inspiration for several of his paintings, including *The Croquet Scene*, and *Boys in a Pasture*. The Underwood Pool (a gift of the Underwood Family) was the first outdoor swimming pool in the United States in 1912. The Belmont Tennis Club was established in 1884 and incorporated in 1889. The Belmont Country Club, one of greater Boston's oldest golf clubs, was remodeled from a former residence in 1908. It began with a 9-hole course and quickly grew to an 18-hole course. The Highland Farm racetrack, established in 1886 by Mr. Chenery, drew Sunday afternoon crowds of up to 3,000 people.

The railroad made the purely agricultural town of Belmont more accessible by extending its tracks from Fresh Pond to Waverley Square in 1843. As can be expected with growth, Belmont became a town filled with residential neighborhoods, schools, playgrounds, and parks. Various religious orders and many clubs and organizations found in Belmont a suburb in which to reside. The first 100 years brought much expansion and continuing change, as agriculture gave way to technology; by 1959, the town resembled other affluent suburban communities close to Boston. Today, Belmont has become a bedroom community for a diverse blend of people whose contributions remain an important part of its continuing history.

One

A Town Is Born

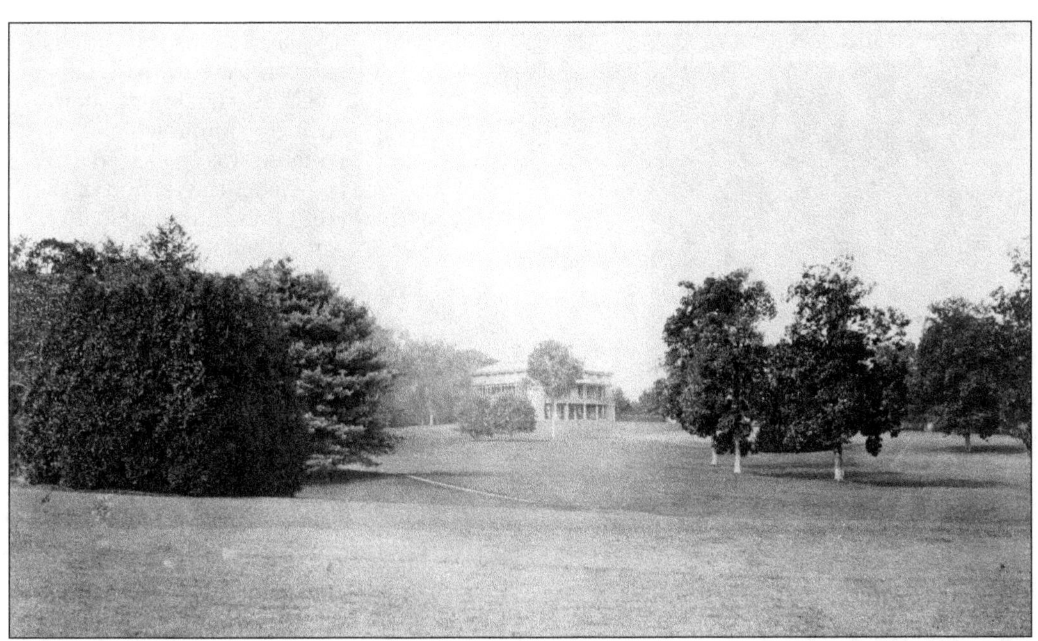

After making his fortune in the China trade, John Perkins Cushing returned to Boston and eventually acquired 200 acres in what was then Watertown. In about 1840, he erected Bellmont, a 50-room mansion. His wealth and influence greatly aided in the battle to create a new town. When incorporated in March 1859, Belmont took its name from the Cushing estate, with one *l* dropped.

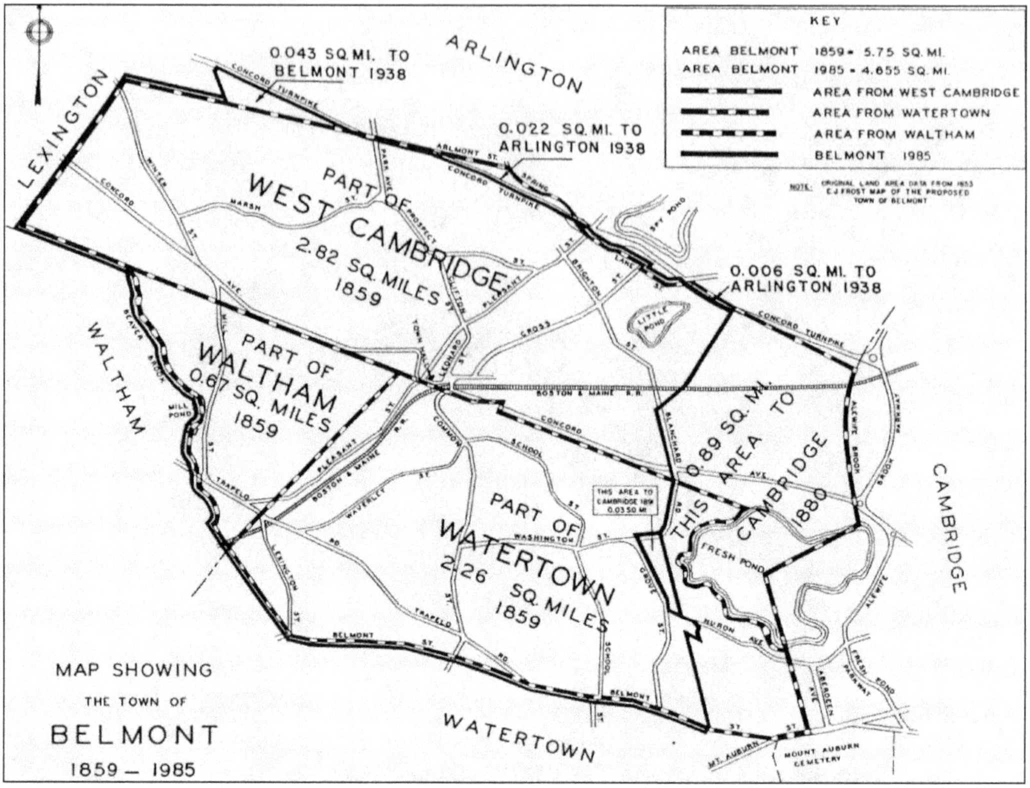

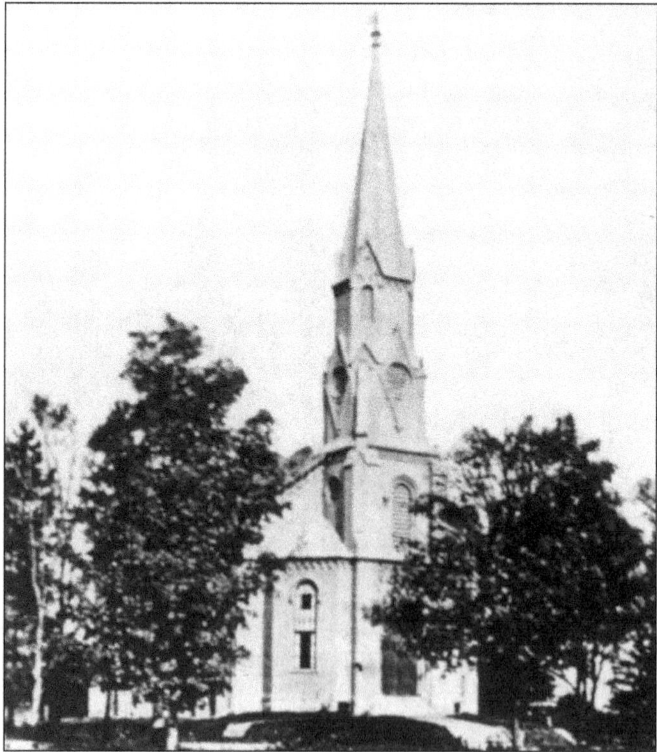

This map shows the various parts of Watertown, Waltham, and West Cambridge (now Arlington) from which Belmont was created in 1859. It includes the section of the Fresh Pond area, originally part of Belmont but reannexed to Cambridge in 1880.

One argument against incorporation was that the proposed town did not have a church. In defense of that accusation, the would-be people of Belmont in 1857 erected the First Church of Belmont (Unitarian). It was located on the north side of Concord Avenue on the site of the present day post office. The First Church was destroyed by fire in 1890 and was replaced by the present stone building across the street.

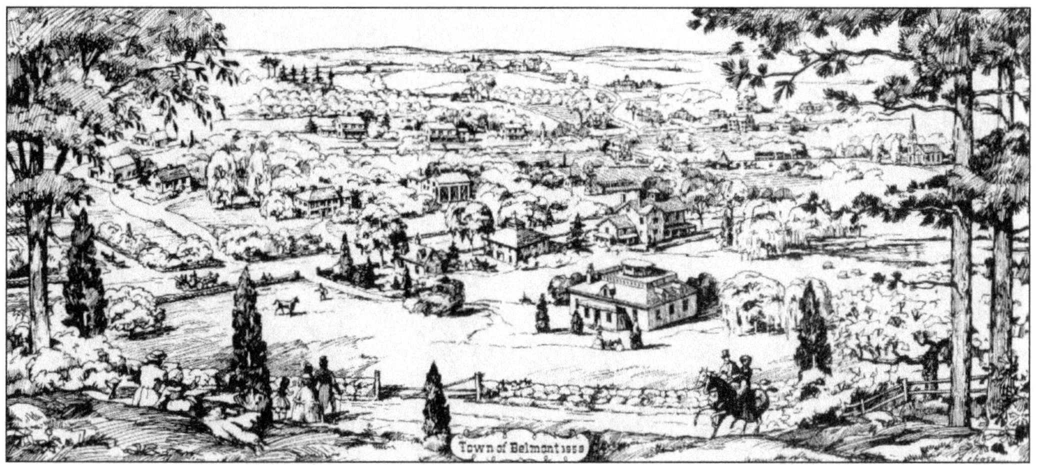

Looking toward Belmont Center from School Street near Common Street, one would have seen the vista captured by artist Winslow Homer's sketch *The New Town of Belmont, Massachusetts*. Several of the houses that show in the foreground are still standing on the Underwood Estate.

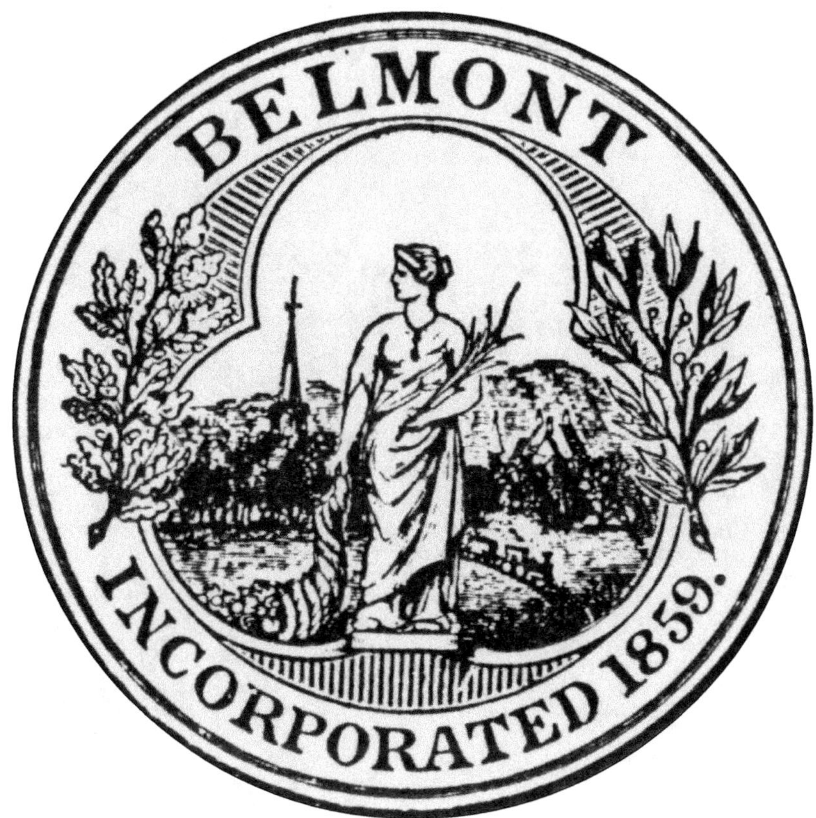

In 1882, a town seal was adopted. The design represents a statue of Pomona, the goddess of fruits and gardens. Also shown is the spire of the original First Church, the town hall, and the railroad. The scene is drawn on a trefoil to symbolize the three towns from which Belmont took its territory. The whole is encircled by two rings, between which is engraved the words "Belmont Incorporated 1859."

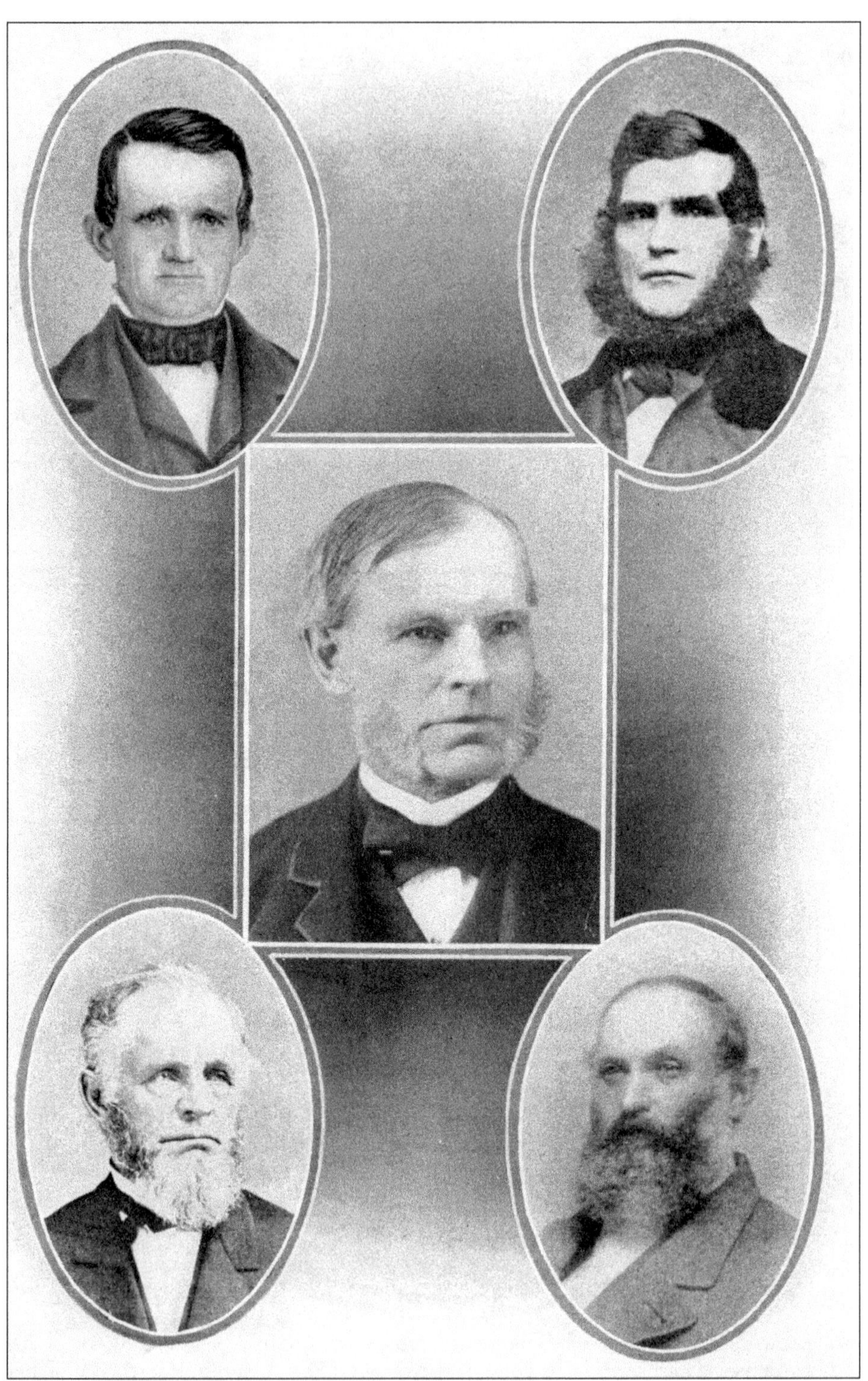

Members of the first Belmont Board of Selectmen were, counterclockwise from top left, Joseph Hill, Jonas B. Chenery, Jacob Hittinger, Mansur W. Marsh, and J. Varnum Fletcher, center, who was also the first state senator from Belmont.

TOWN MEETING.

Commonwealth of Massachusetts.

MIDDLESEX, ss.

To Jonas B. Chenery, an Inhabitant of Belmont, in said County:

You are hereby required, in the name of the Commonwealth of Massachusetts, to notify and warn the Inhabitants of Belmont qualified to vote in elections of town officers, to meet at the Vestry of the Belmont Congregational Meeting House, on

Monday, the 28th day of March, instant, at 3 o'clock, P.M.,

to act upon the following Articles, viz:

1st. To make choice of a Moderator, to preside at said Meeting.

2d. To see if the said Inhabitants will accept the Act entitled, "An Act to incorporate the town of Belmont." Approved March 18th, 1859.

3d. To make choice of all Town Officers for the ensuing year—such as towns are by law authorized and required to choose at their annual meetings.

Given under my hand, this nineteenth day of March, 1859.

SAMUEL O. MEAD,
Justice of the Peace.

This is a copy of the notice of the first town meeting in the new town of Belmont. Sent out by Samuel O. Mead on March 19, 1859, the notice lists three items on the agenda: selecting a moderator, accepting "An Act to incorporate the town of Belmont," and choosing all town officials. (Courtesy of the Wellington Family.)

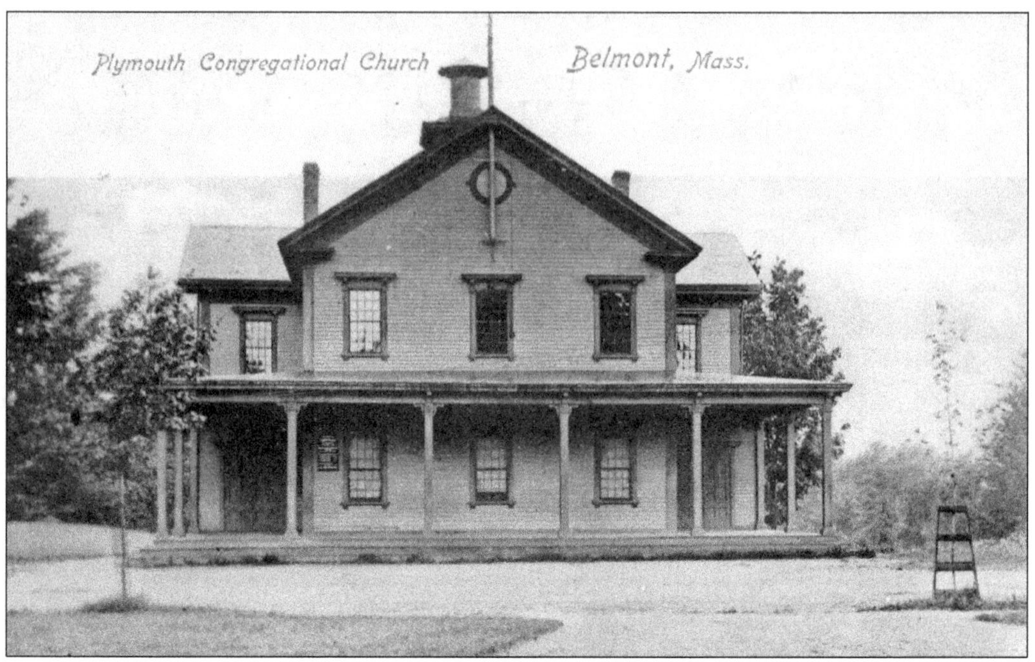

Erected in 1867 as the town's first high school, this building also served as the town hall and public library. The Plymouth Congregational Church met there for several years, as did the Belmont Masonic Lodge. Later, the building was used as an elementary school. It was closed in 1904 and torn down in 1908.

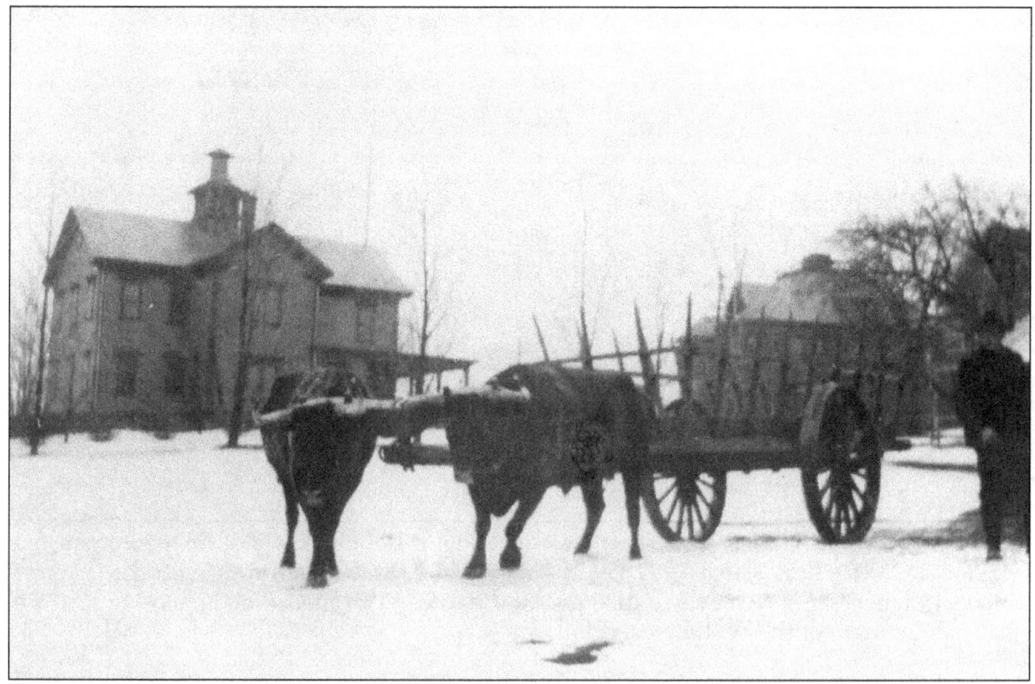

A view of oxen and cart on the Underwood Estate depicts a typical scene of a gentleman farmer. The 1867 high school and town hall building on School Street can be seen in the background.

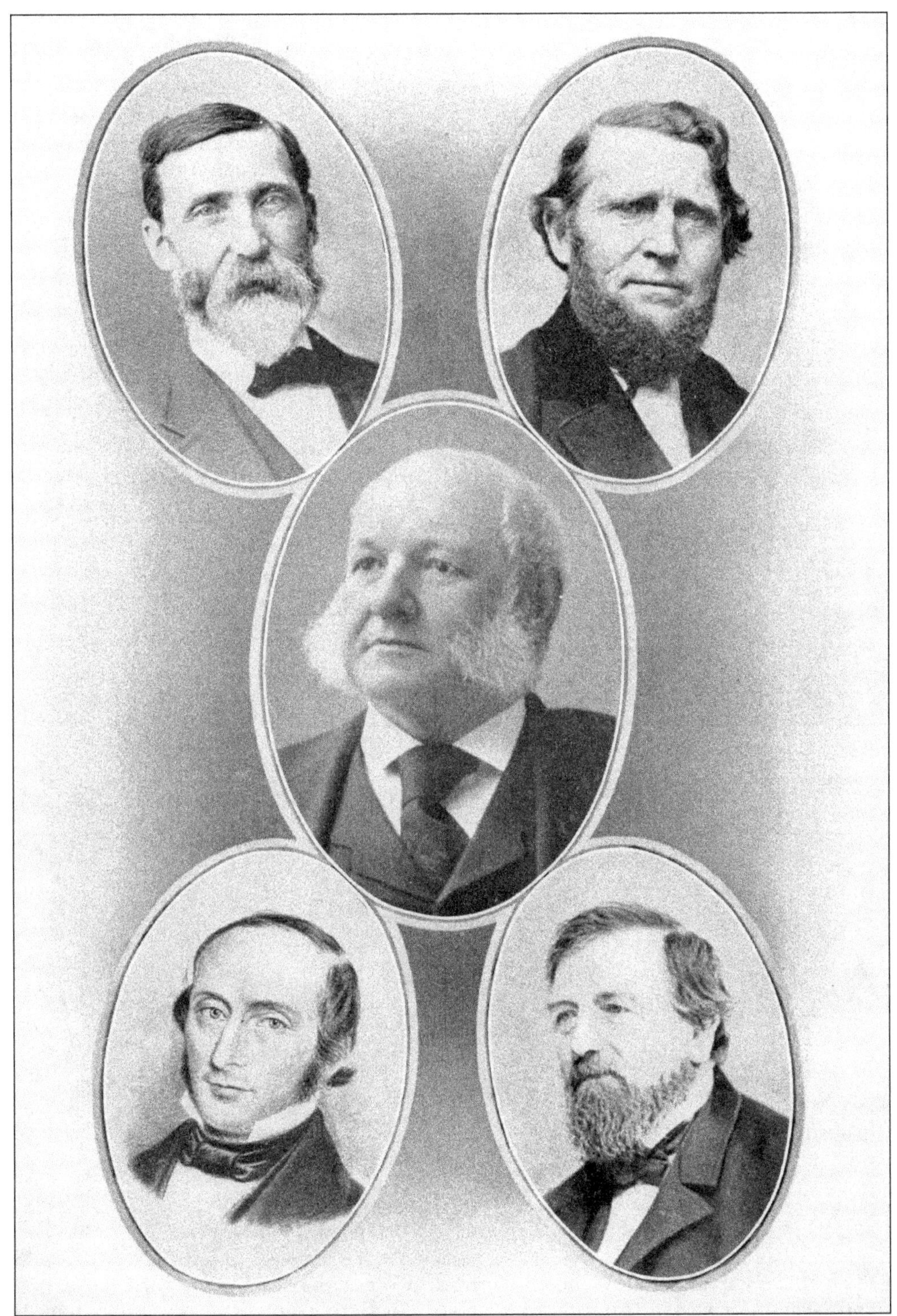

The first town officers were, clockwise from top left, Samuel P. Hammatt, town clerk; George S. Adams, town treasurer; J. Oliver Wellington, board of assessors chair; Rev. Amos Smith, school committee chair; and William J. Underwood, center, library trustees chair.

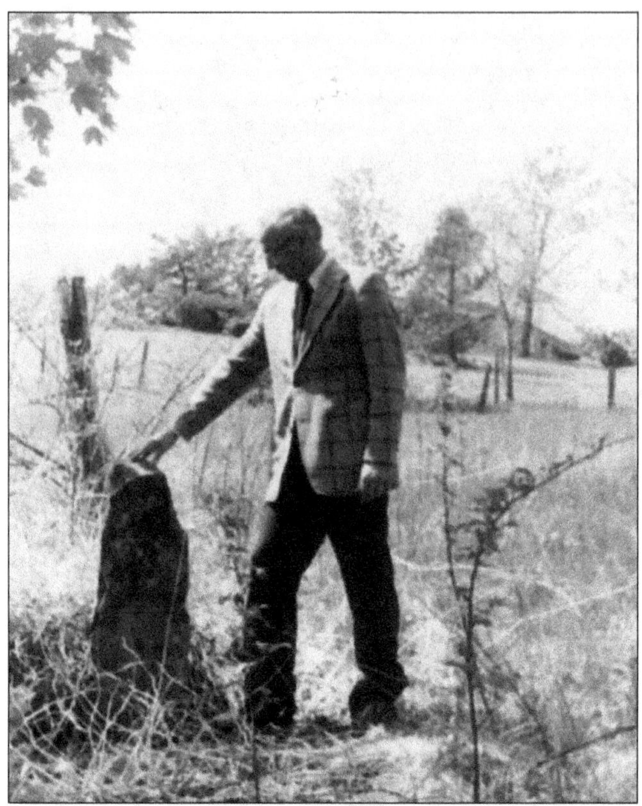

Town historian Richard Betts stands by the original boundary stone marking the junction of Waltham, Watertown, and West Cambridge (now Arlington), the three towns from which Belmont was created in 1859. Set in 1738, the boundary stone is still in place.

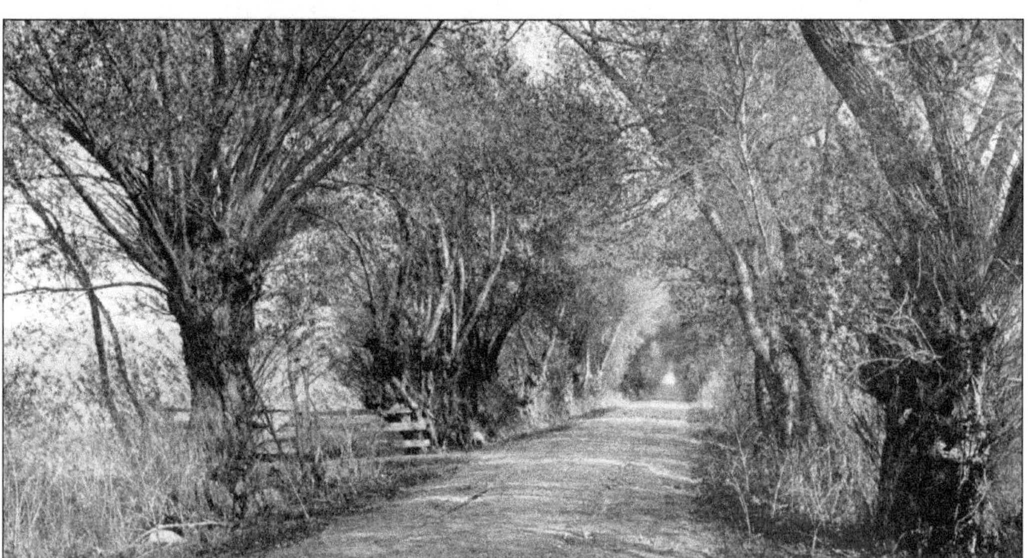

In 1803, the Cambridge and Concord Turnpike Corporation laid out a turnpike between Cambridge and Concord. The turnpike ran right through the center of what was to become the town of Belmont, along what is today Concord Avenue. The upper end of the road, between Mill Street and the Lexington town line, was known as the Willow Road and is shown in this *c.* 1890 picture.

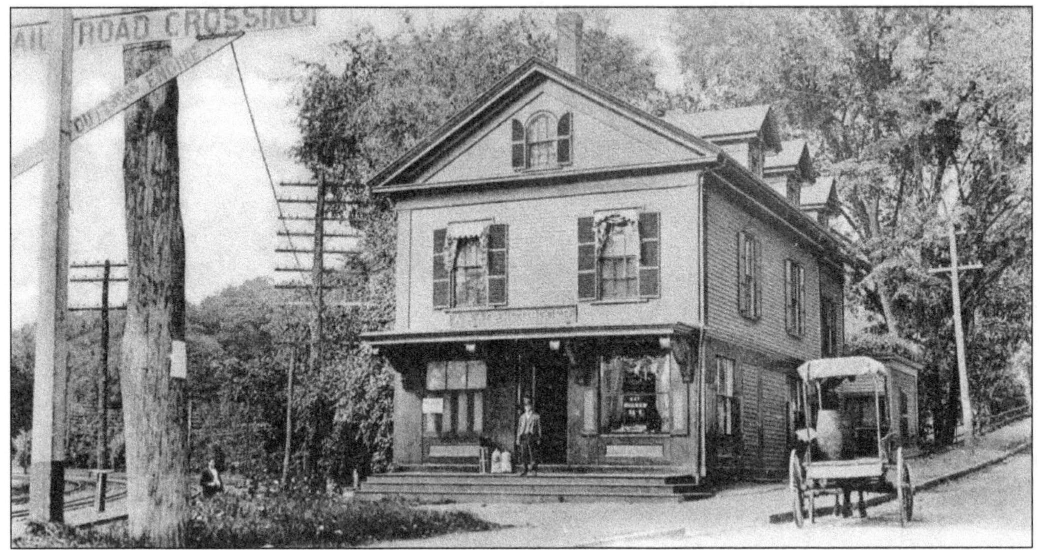

The A.A. Adams General Store was the first store in what is now Belmont Center. It also housed the first village post office. It was a popular gathering place for "the less busy gentlemen of the town" and was a flourishing grocery business, with a little bit of rum thrown in. The building was purchased by the town in 1931, torn down, and replaced with the present-day municipal light department.

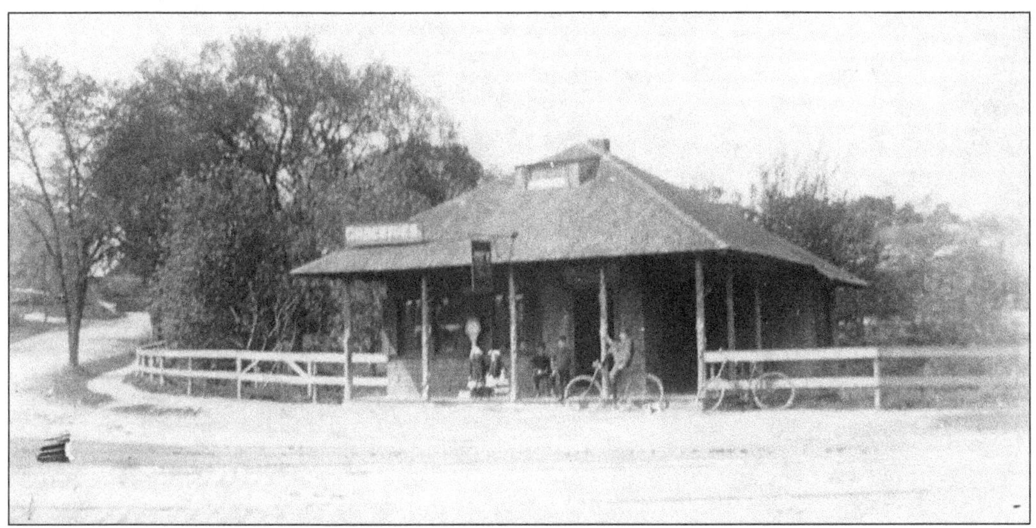

The Merrow Country Store, established in 1905, was the first store in what is now Cushing Square. Originally on the corner of Trapelo Road and Common Street, it was moved in 1914 some 200 feet up Common Street and converted into a five-room, one-family bungalow. In 1947, it was moved to 47 Creeley Road, remodeled, and enlarged. It is still used as a single-family dwelling.

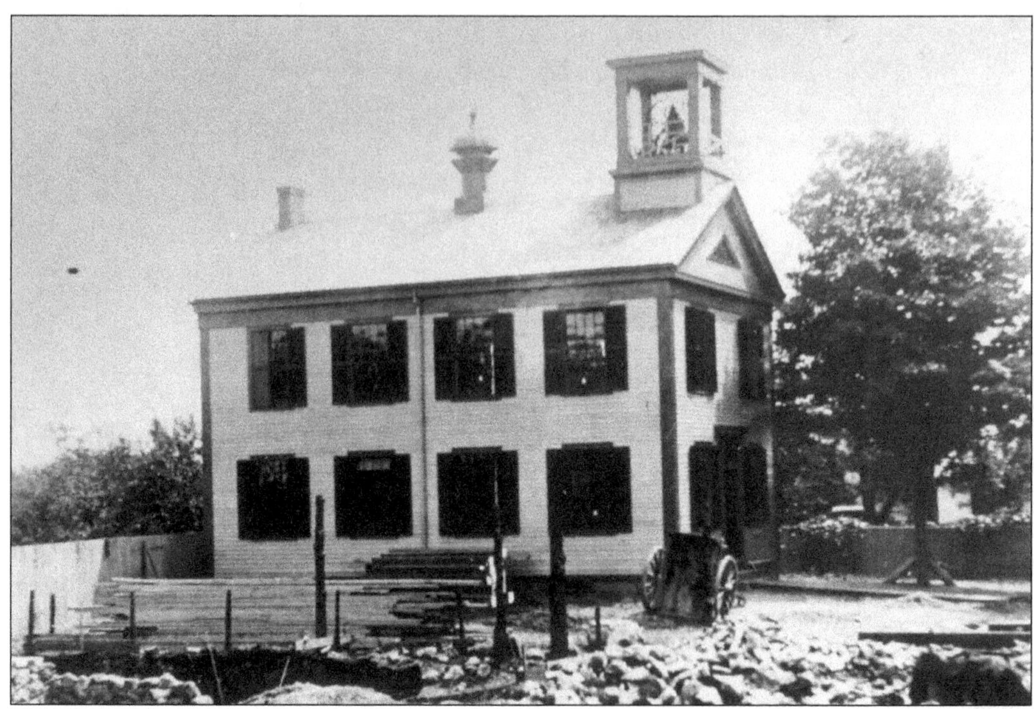

The Brighton Street School was built in 1842 by the town of West Cambridge and was transferred to Belmont in 1859 at its incorporation. It was used as an elementary and intermediate school. It was closed in 1921 and torn down in 1935.

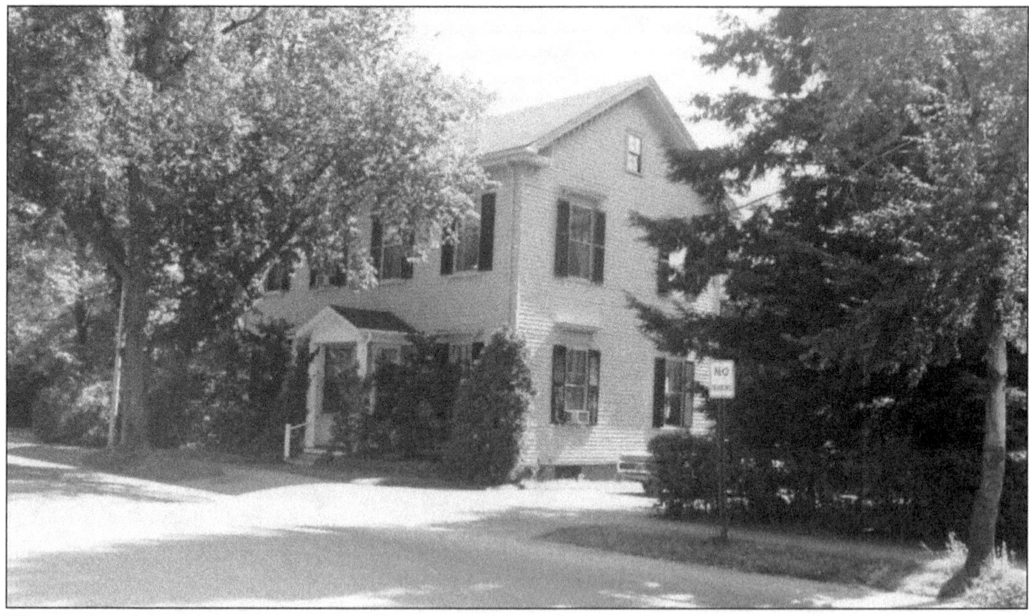

This school building was originally erected by the town of Watertown on the corner of Washington and Common Streets and was transferred to Belmont in 1859. In 1867, it was moved to School Street next to the original high school. It was closed and sold at auction in 1891 for $150, moved to the corner of Concord Avenue and Cottage Street, and converted into a general store. Today, it is a private residence.

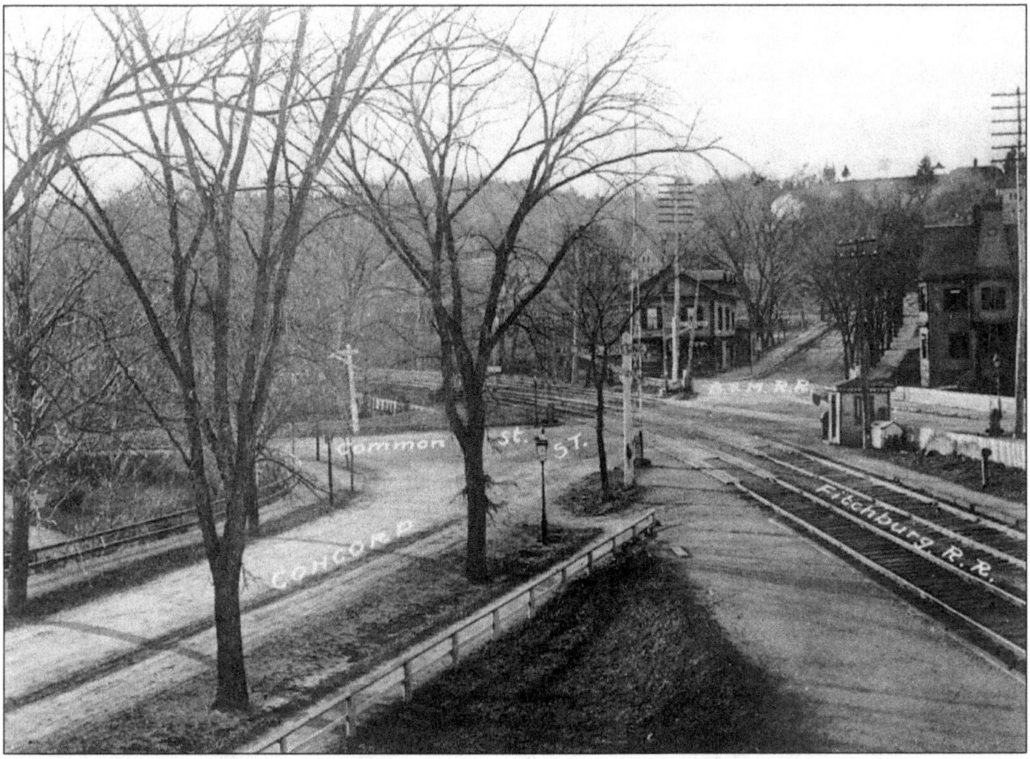

This *c.* 1900 picture shows Concord Avenue as it originally crossed Common Street and the Fitchburg Railroad tracks, all of which were at grade level prior to the construction of the present underpass. The tree belt later became the streetcar reservation, before it became the westbound lane of Concord Avenue.

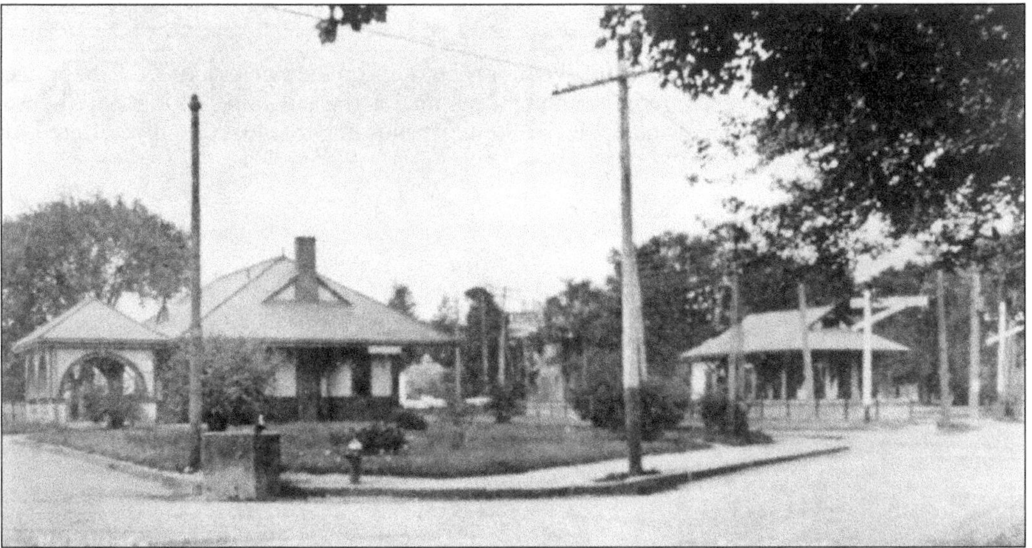

In 1892, the Fitchburg Railroad erected a large station on Church Street, complete with a porte cochere. The station was torn down in 1954 to make room for a parking lot. Also shown is the smaller Massachusetts Central station, which was torn down about that same time. (Courtesy of Dr. David Alper.)

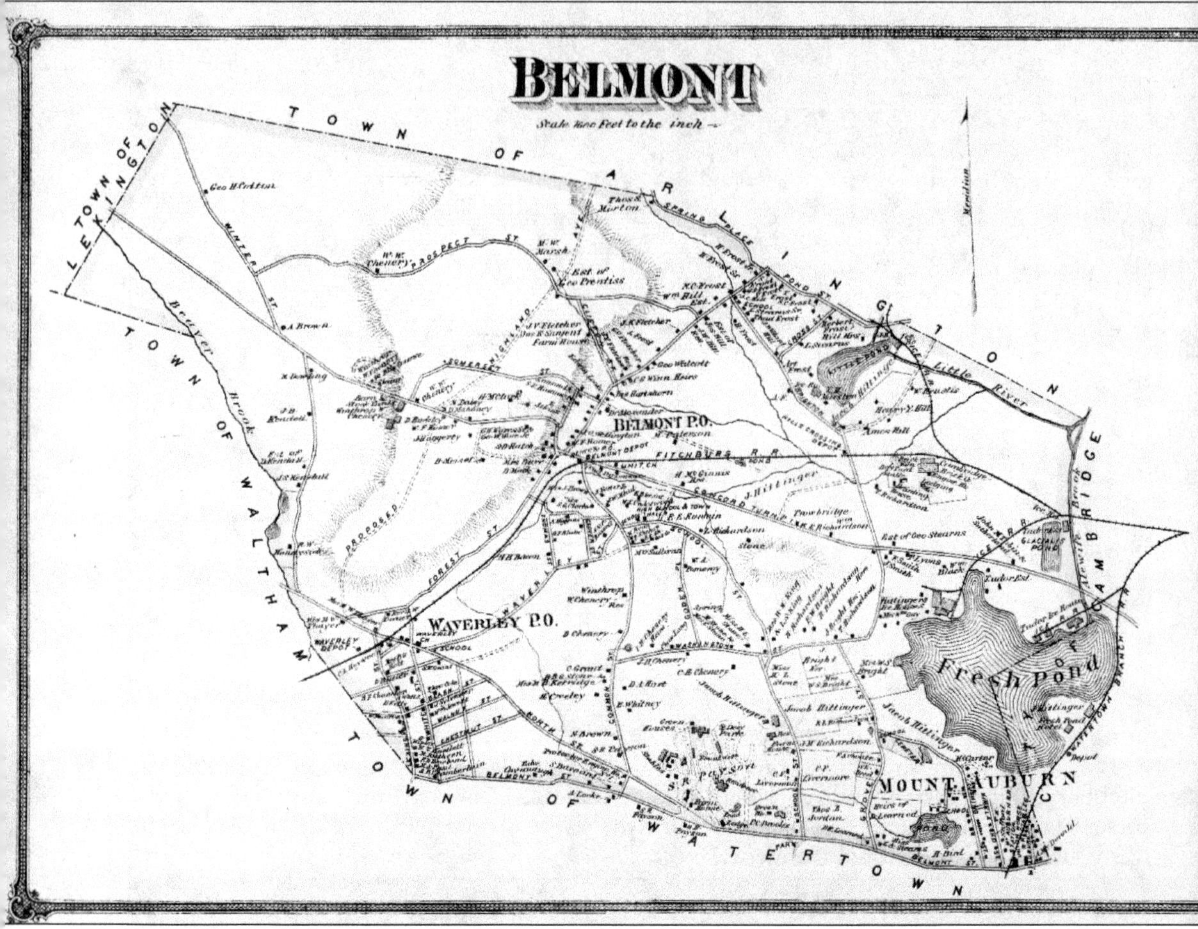

This map shows the original town of Belmont before the reannexation by Cambridge in 1880. A controversy over Belmont's issuing a permit for the erection of a slaughterhouse on Concord Avenue along the banks of Fresh Pond, threatening the water supply, resulted in the reannexation.

Two

Market Gardens and Country Estates

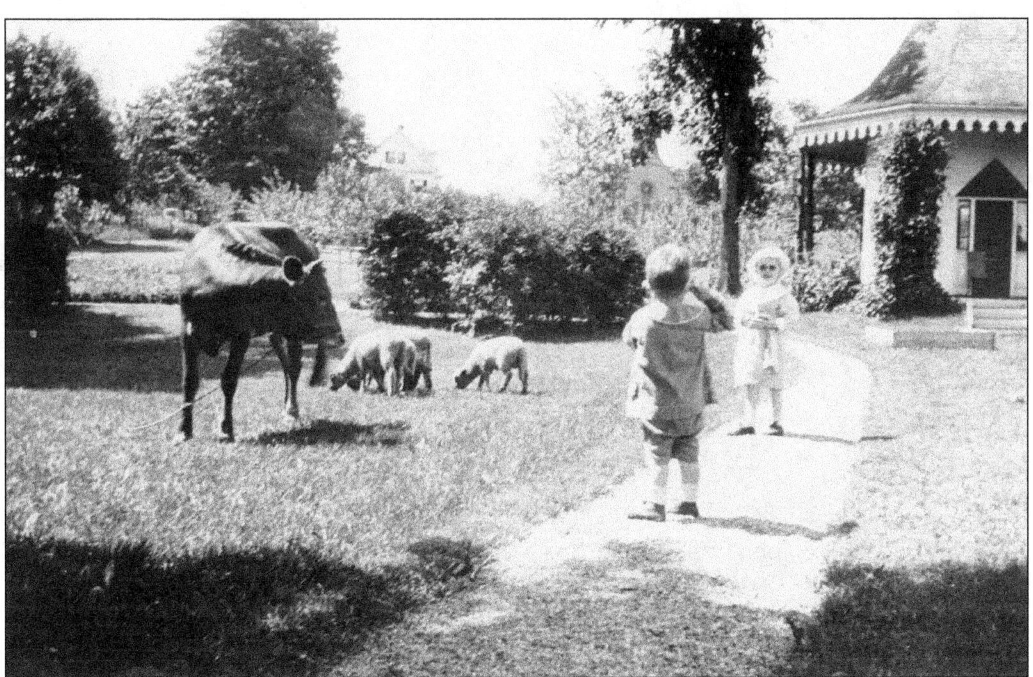

This view of the Underwood Estate, *c.* 1918, shows the former Wellington Hill Railroad Station. Built in the 1840s on Concord Avenue as a private school, the building was sold to the Fitchburg Railroad in 1852. When a new station was erected, the building was repurchased and moved onto the estate. Later, it was given to the Belmont Historical Society and moved to its present site on Common Street at Concord Avenue. (Courtesy of Helen Underwood.)

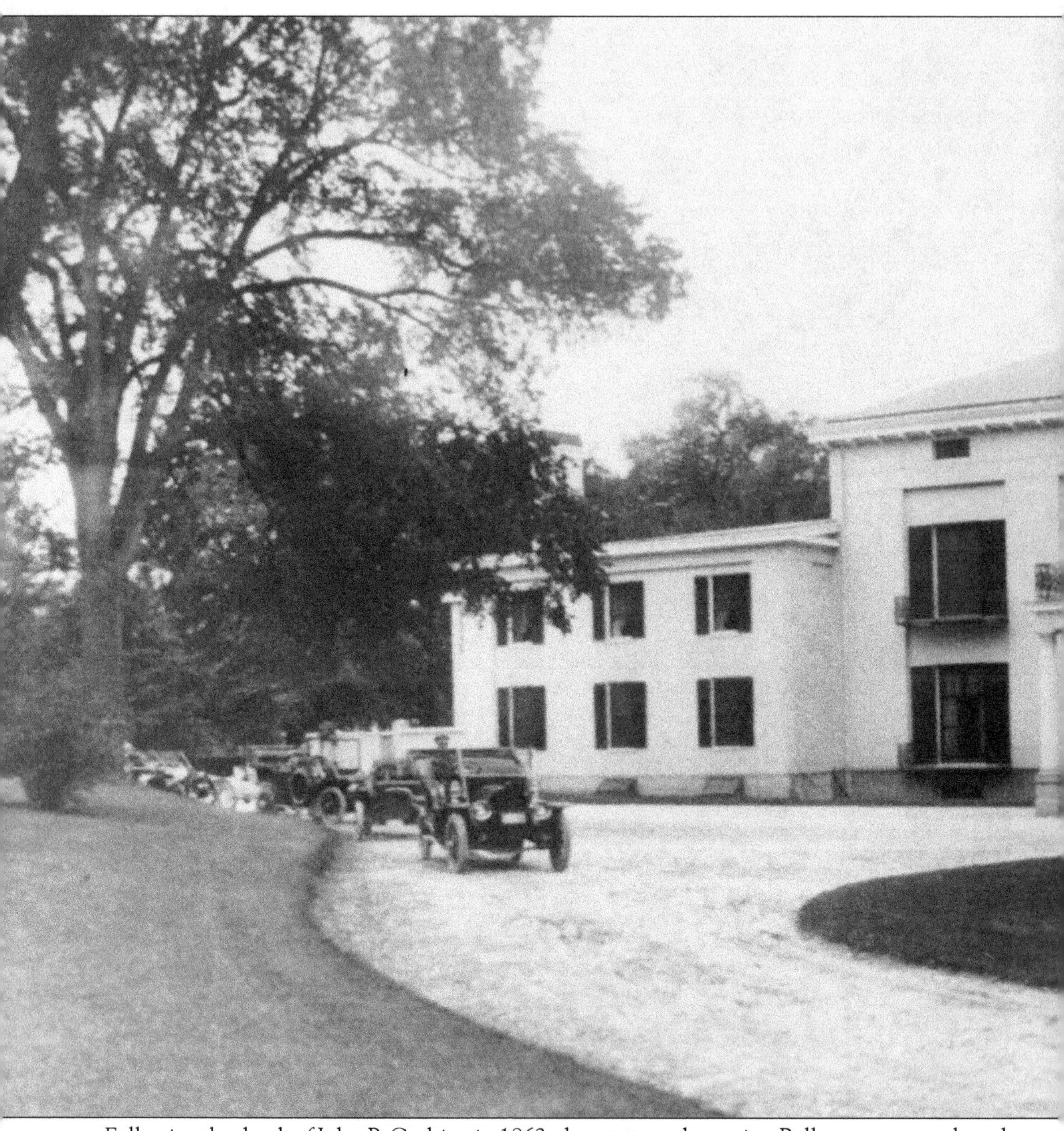

Following the death of John P. Cushing in 1862, the estate and mansion Bellmont was purchased by Samuel R. Payson. Payson laid out the property on a new scale of magnificence. Herds of

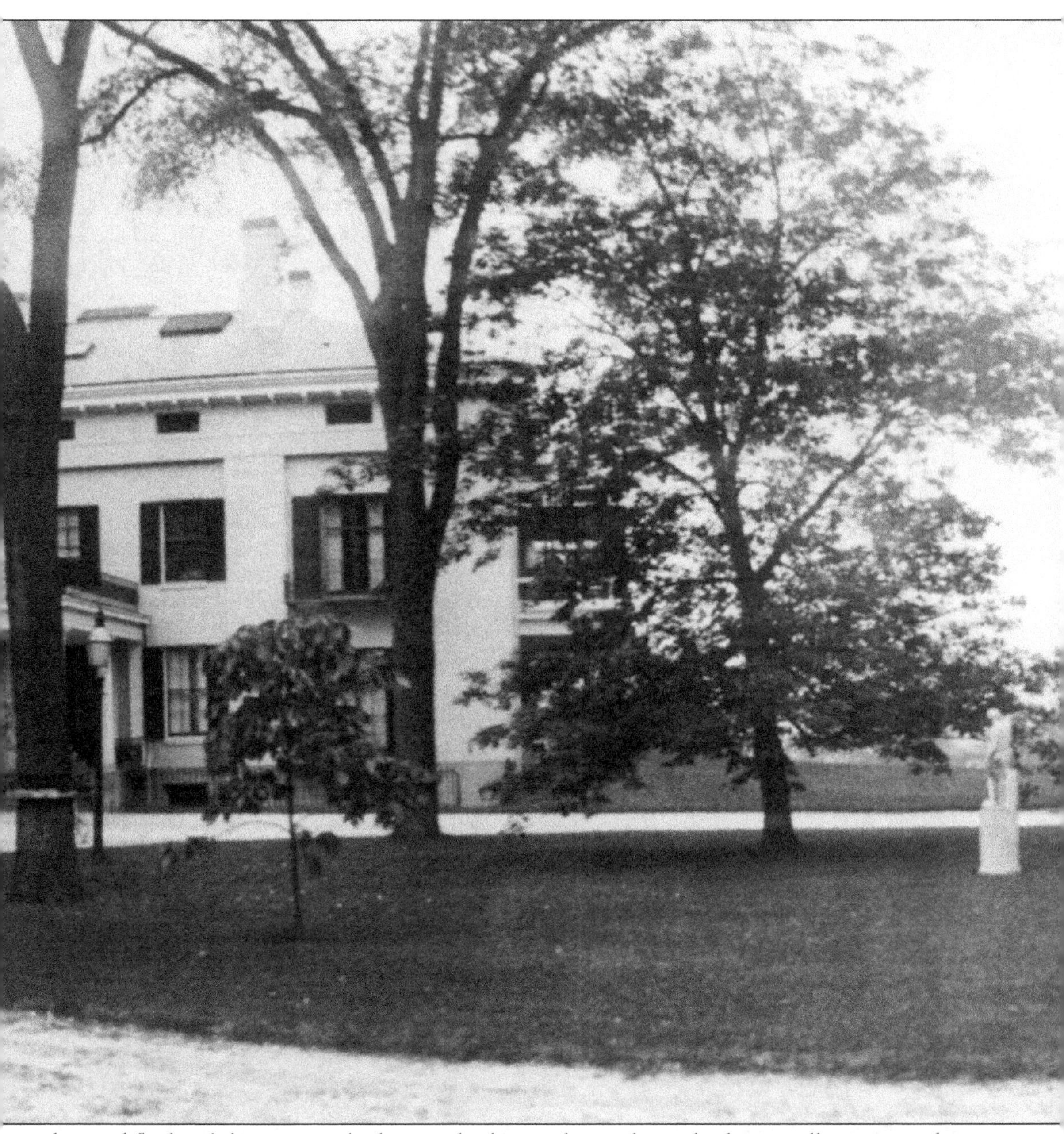

deer and flocks of pheasants and other rare birds, together with rare hothouse collections, made the grounds an even greater attraction.

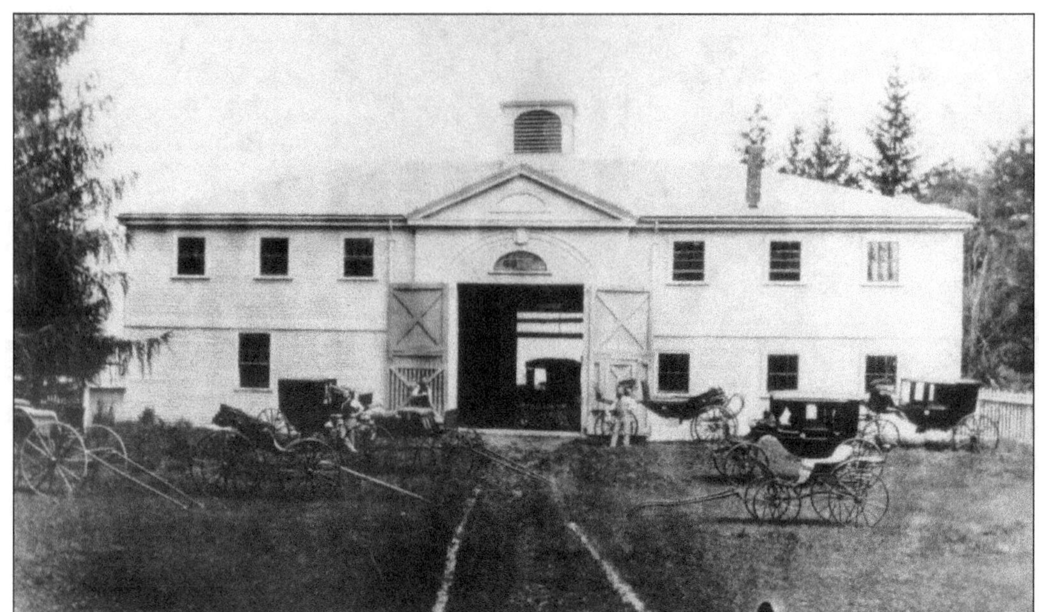

Among other buildings on the Cushing Estate was a magnificent center-entrance, two-story stable, which was always ready to take care of guests' carriages. In fact, Bellmont lacked nothing that either money or imagination could supply. In 1886, Samuel Payson sold the land around the mansion to the Payson Park Land Company and the house to Benjamin F. Harding, who used it as a boys' school.

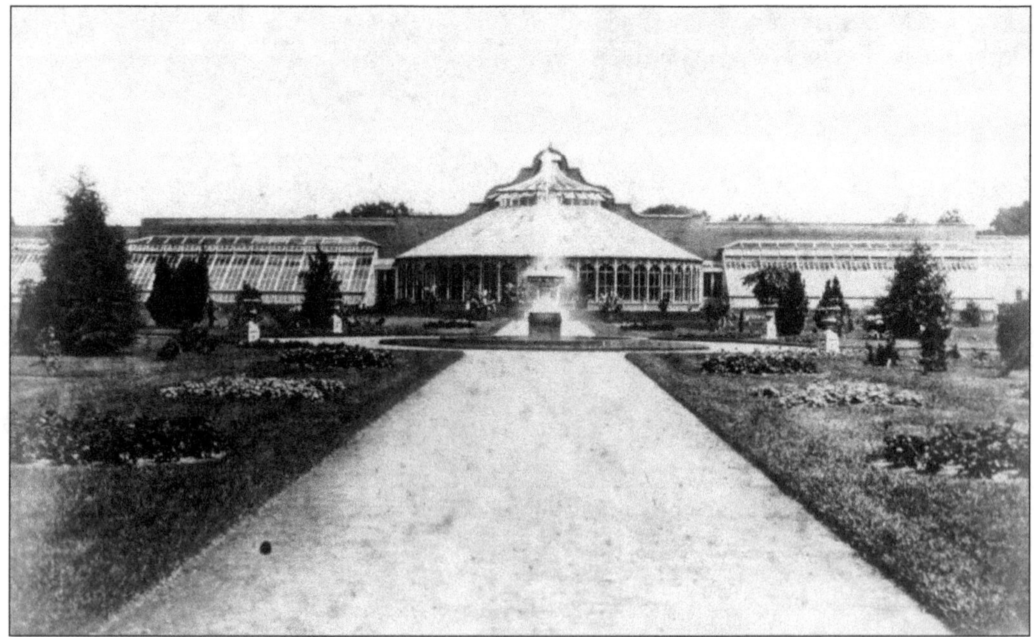

At the end of the garden on the Cushing Estate was a 60-foot-long conservatory and 14 greenhouses devoted to the cultivation of orchids, palms, azaleas, grapes, peaches, nectarines, figs, fruits, vegetables, and other plants. In 1903, Col. Everett C. Benton became the owner of Bellmont and lived there with his family until his death in 1925. The mansion was closed, badly damaged by fire, and torn down in 1929.

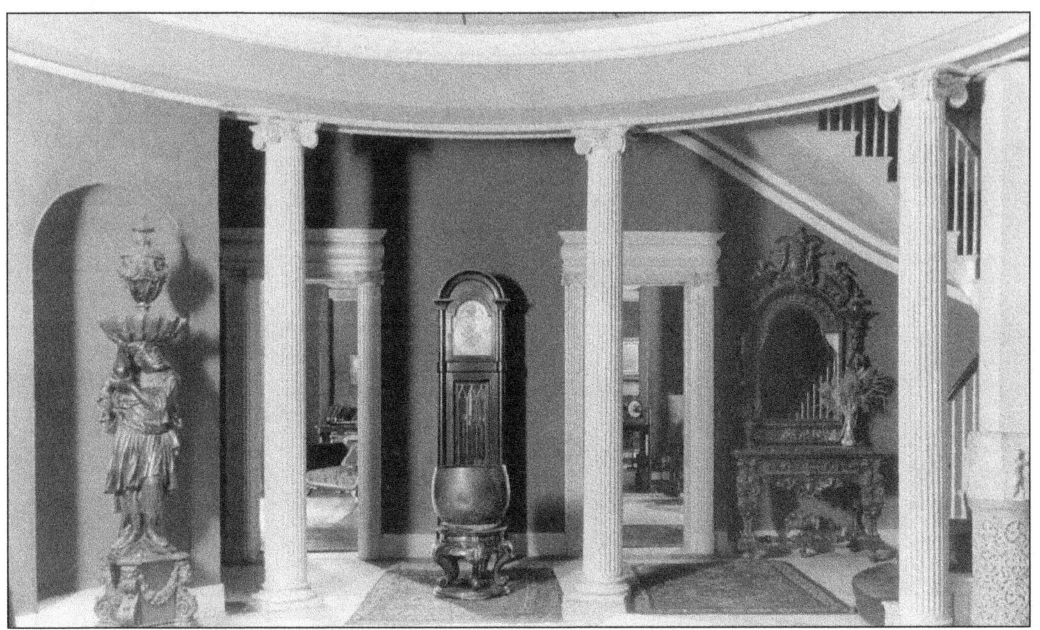

The Cushing house was designed by Asher Benjamin in the style, on the outside at least, of an English manor house. This interior view shows the foyer. All the materials, including the marbles and rare woods, were brought from Europe, Africa, and Asia. Many rooms were circular or oval and were finished in mahogany, Spanish cedar, oak, and ebony. The floors were ebony, and there were 50 fireplaces of Italian marble.

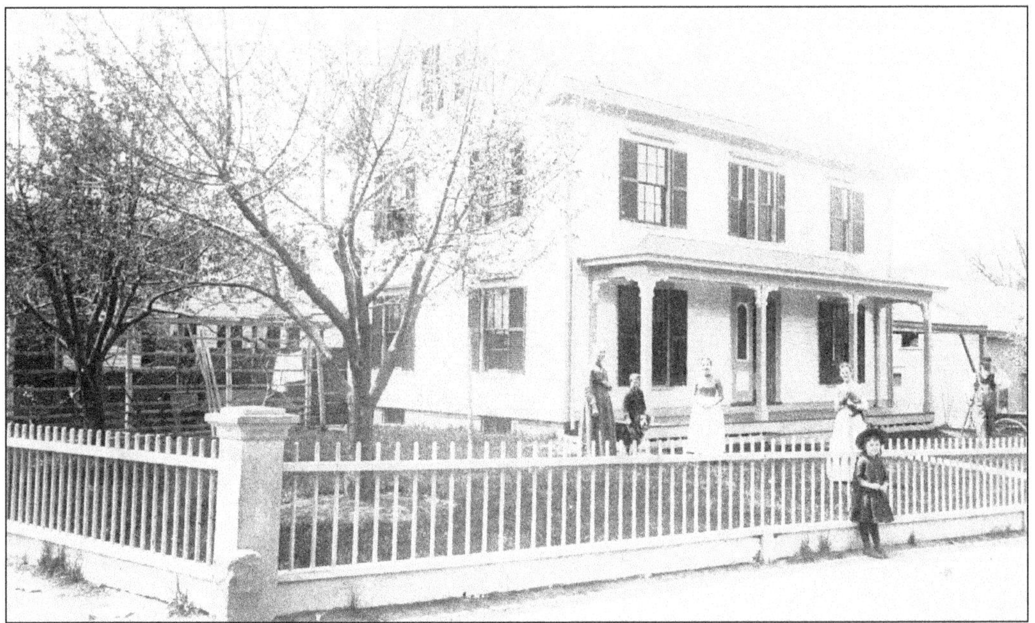

Lemuel Hatch came to what is now Belmont in 1856. As a carpenter and builder, he built this house at 86 Clark Street in 1863 and lived in it with his wife and seven children. He also worked on some of the finishing touches when the present town hall was built. Hatch was very active in town affairs. Upon his death in 1892, it was stated that "he was one of the best known and highly respected citizens."

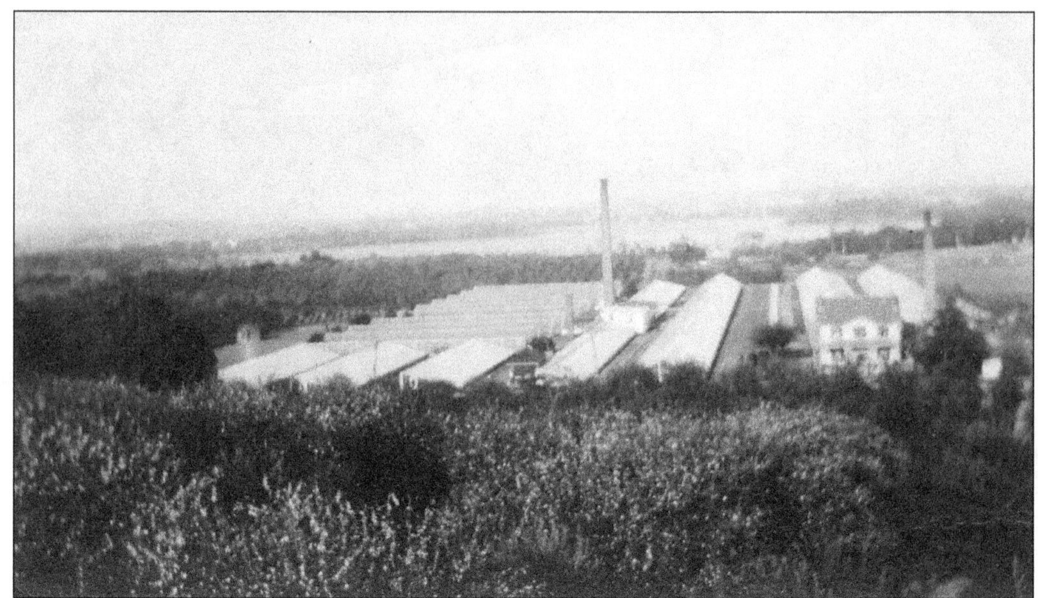

One of the first members of the Belmont Board of Selectmen was Jacob Hittinger, who was engaged in the ice business—cutting and shipping ice from Spy and Fresh ponds. In 1876, three of his sons developed the 40-acre market garden on the property. The upper section above School Street contained 12 acres of apple, pear, peach, and cherry trees. The lower section east of School Street contained 20 greenhouses.

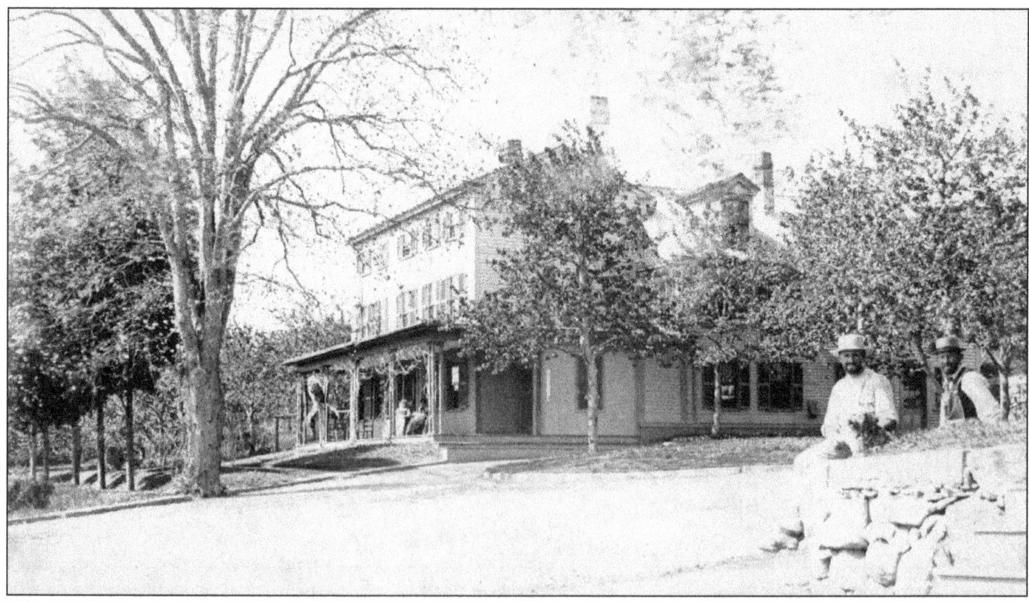

This is the homestead of Jacob Hittinger. In this house, Hittinger and his wife raised seven sons, three of whom followed their father's example and served the town as selectmen. The house, which stood between Lewis and Elizabeth Roads, was torn down in 1931, when the upper part of the farm was sold for house lots.

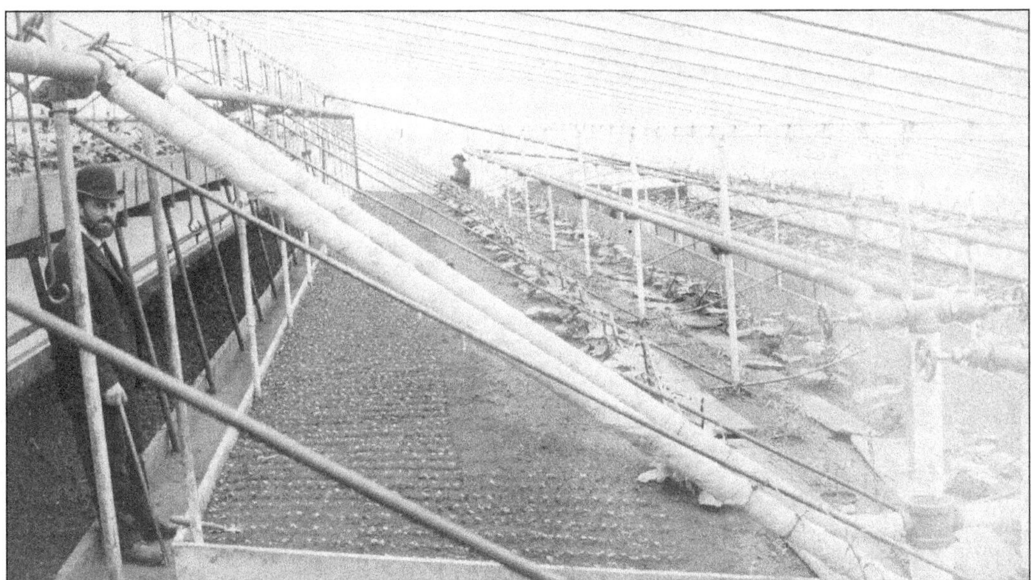

Richard Hittinger Sr., one of Jacob's seven sons, stands in one of the 20 greenhouses on the Hittinger farm. One greenhouse was 634 feet long—the largest in the country when built. The hurricane of 1938 blew down all of the greenhouses, thus ending the longtime market garden. Some 60,000 bushels of produce a year went to Quincy Market in Boston from the Hittinger farm.

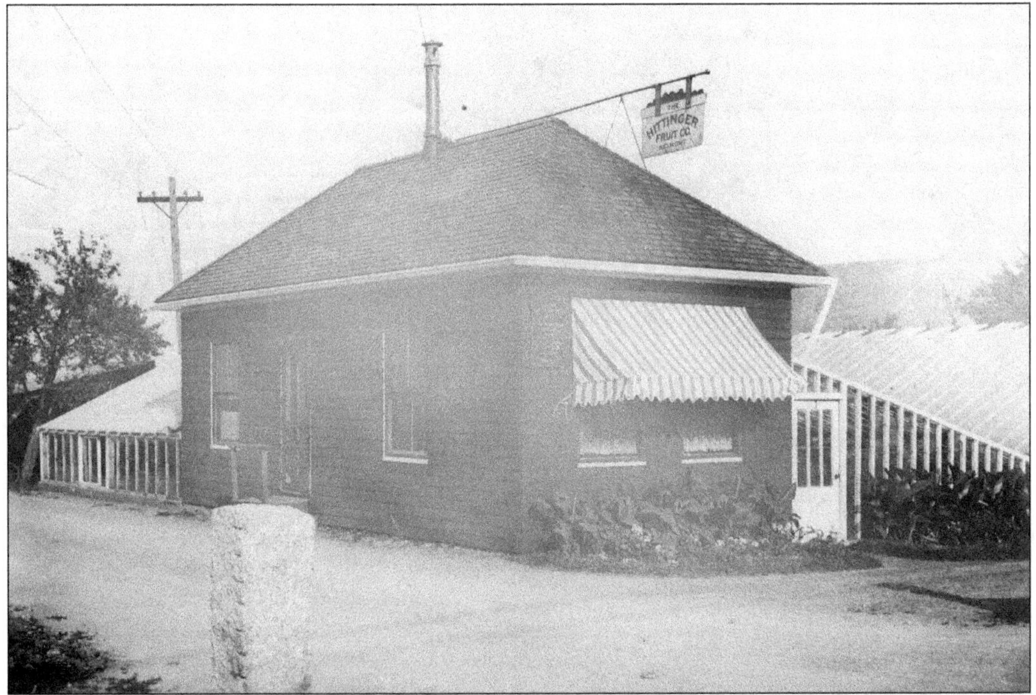

Along with the produce taken to the Boston markets, vegetables and fruits were sold to local residents from the Hittinger Farm office on School Street. The granite gatepost shown in the picture is still standing.

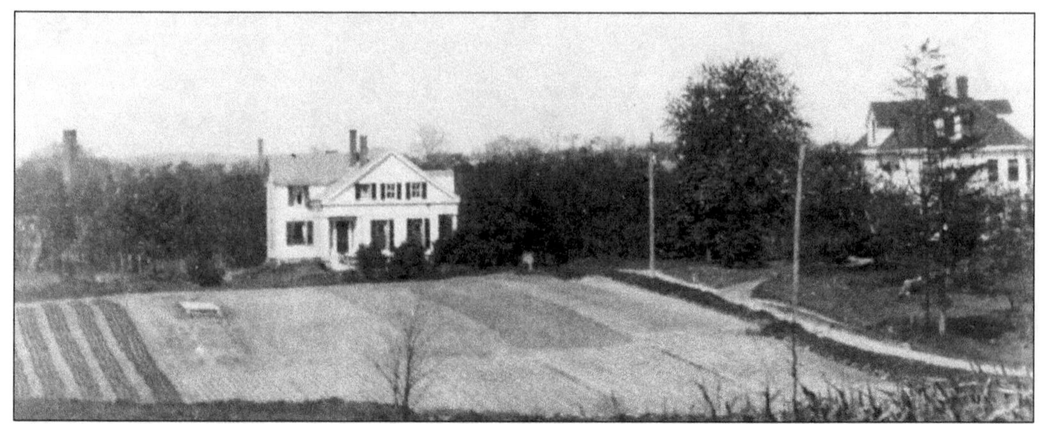

The Heustis farm predates the incorporation of Belmont. It was located on Hill Road between the Hill Estates and the Concord Turnpike. One of the largest pig farms in the area, it had some 1,200 pigs. The favorite was the short-nosed Yorkshire, which averaged over 150 pounds at the age of six months. The farm grew celery and strawberries, shipping 2,500 boxes a year, all of which were sent to Quincy Market in Boston.

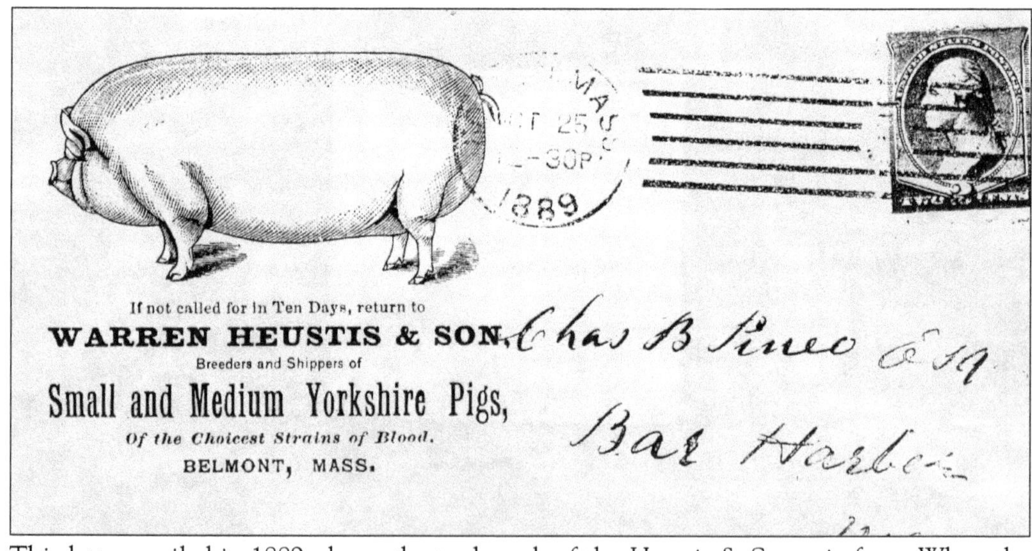

This letter, mailed in 1889, shows the trademark of the Heustis & Sons pig farm. When the family stopped raising pigs, they kept one named Snowball. Since the town had passed a bylaw prohibiting any new piggeries, Heustis kept that one pig to protect his nonconforming rights in case he decided to raise pigs again. The farm was in the Heustis family for more than 100 years and was sold in 1948.

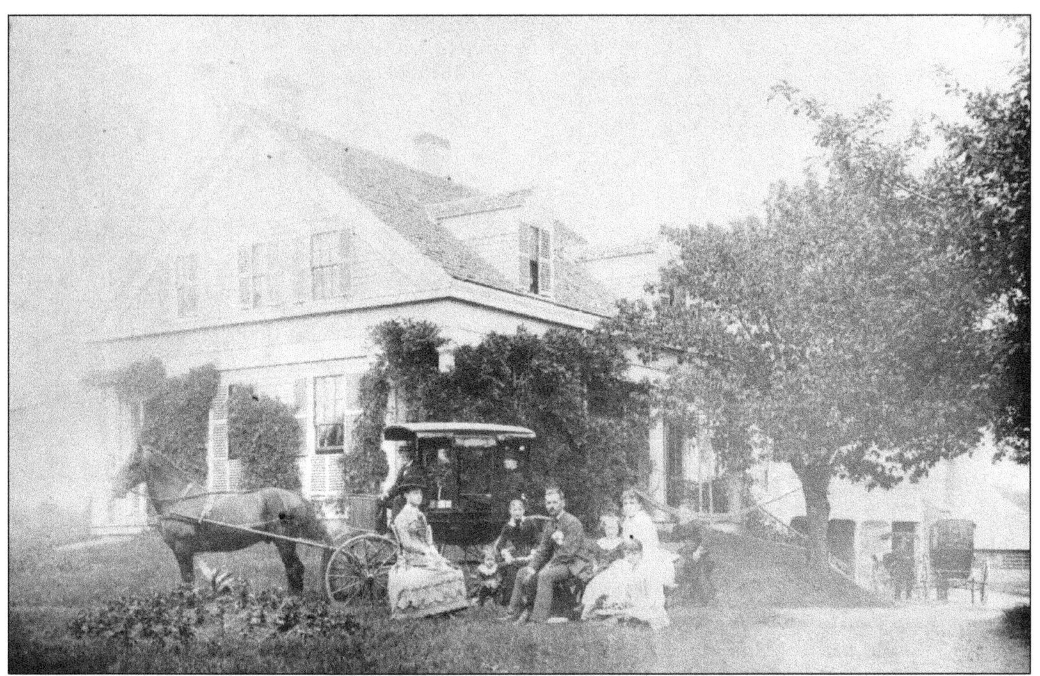

When the Heustis property was sold, the Heustis house was cut in two. Both sections of the house were moved to Lake Street, creating two single-family homes. When Route 2 was widened in 1967, both houses were taken by the state and torn down to make way for the present-day access ramps.

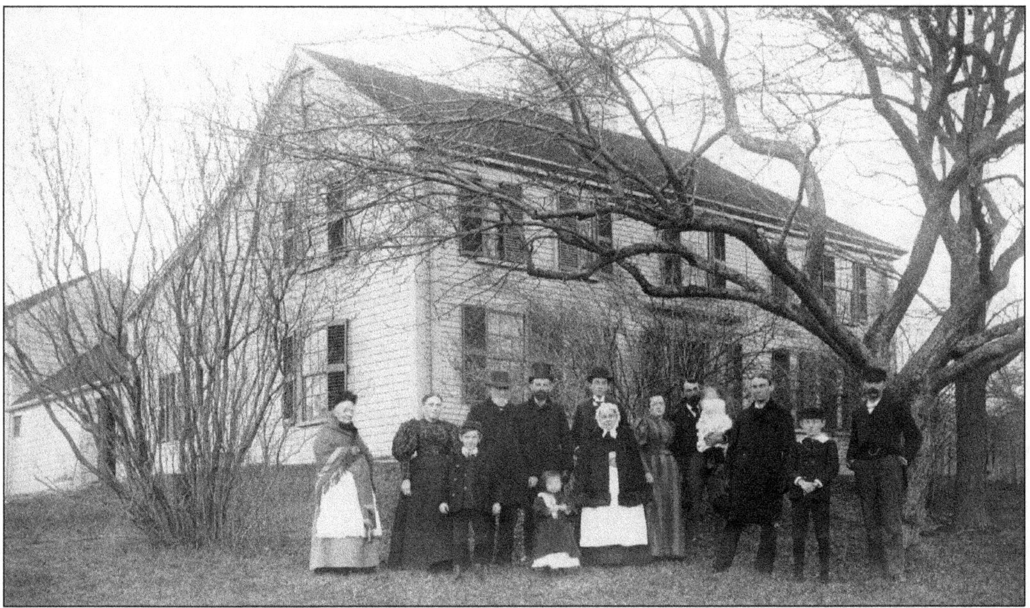

Captain Eaton, an English sea captain, built this house *c.* 1750 on Mill Street. In 1818, the house and farm were bought by Josiah Kendall and his brother David Kendall. The brothers divided the 120-acre farm, with Josiah getting the Eaton house. Josiah ran a sawmill and David ran a gristmill on Beaver Brook. Later, Josiah's son Josiah Shattuck Kendall inherited the property and ran a dairy and produce business.

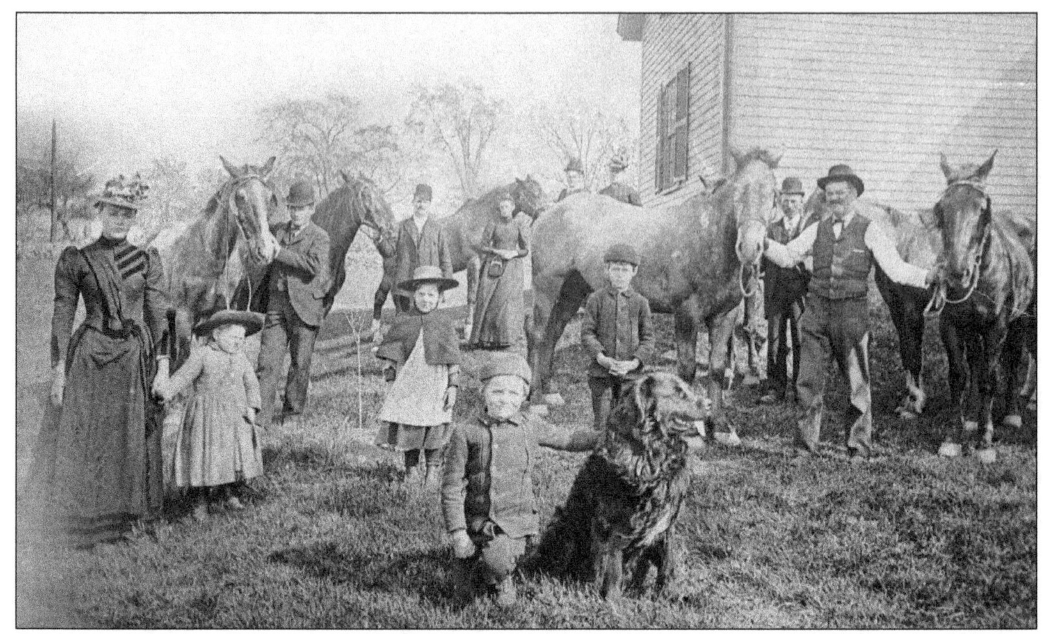

Charles Horace Slade came to Belmont in 1860 at the age of 18. After working on several farms, he purchased about 21 acres on Common Street in 1874 and began a market garden of his own. He and his wife eventually had 11 children. Slade died in 1912 and, in 1920, the old farm was cut up into 125 house lots. This *c.* 1888 picture shows the Slade family.

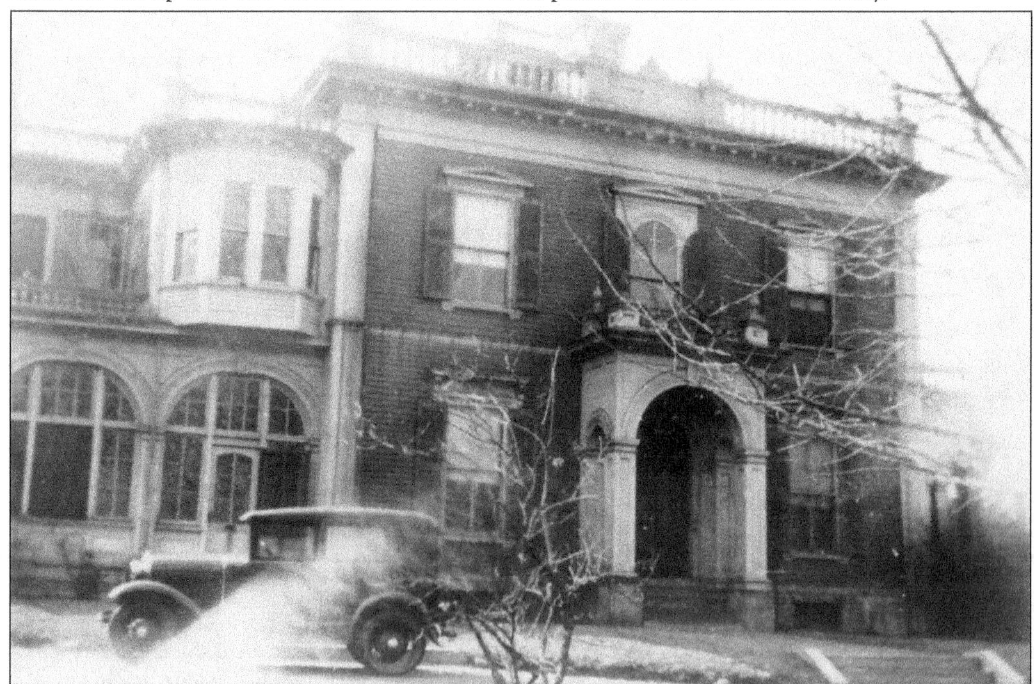

This house was built in 1869 on Clark Hill by George F. Blake, inventor of the Blake Steam Pump. In 1892, the house was sold to John Kilburn, a cotton manufacturer. In 1904, Kilburn was the fifth-largest taxpayer in town; his estate was assessed at $101,000. The mansion was purchased in 1927 by All Saints' Episcopal Church for a parish hall. It was torn down in 1934.

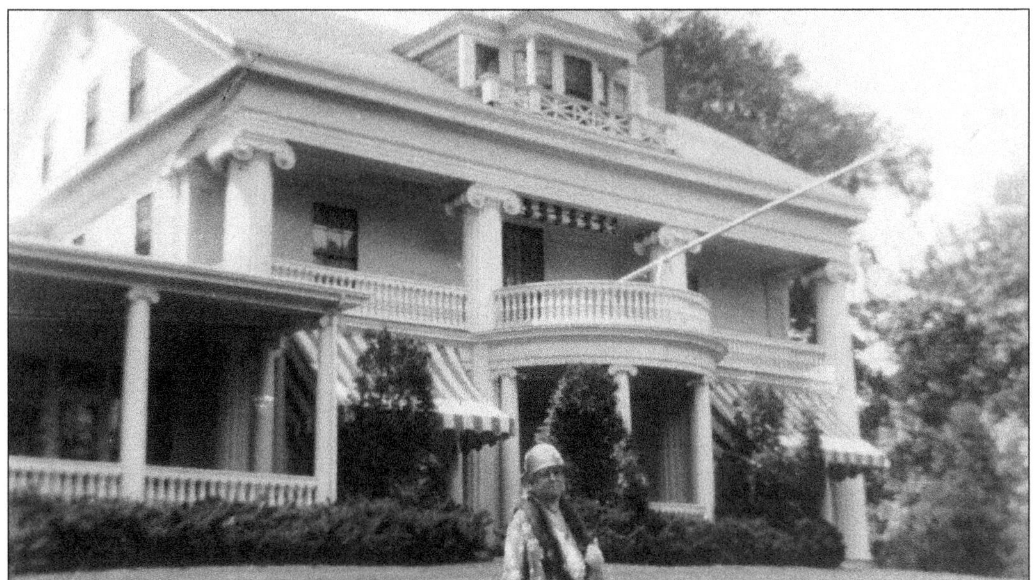

Built before 1859, this house on Common Street near Concord Avenue was owned by James Brown, the founder of Little, Brown and Company book publishers. Mrs. John Murray Brown was one of the last to leave the liner *Titanic* when it sank in 1912. John H. Kendall purchased the property in 1919. When the property was sold for house lots in 1931, the house was torn down.

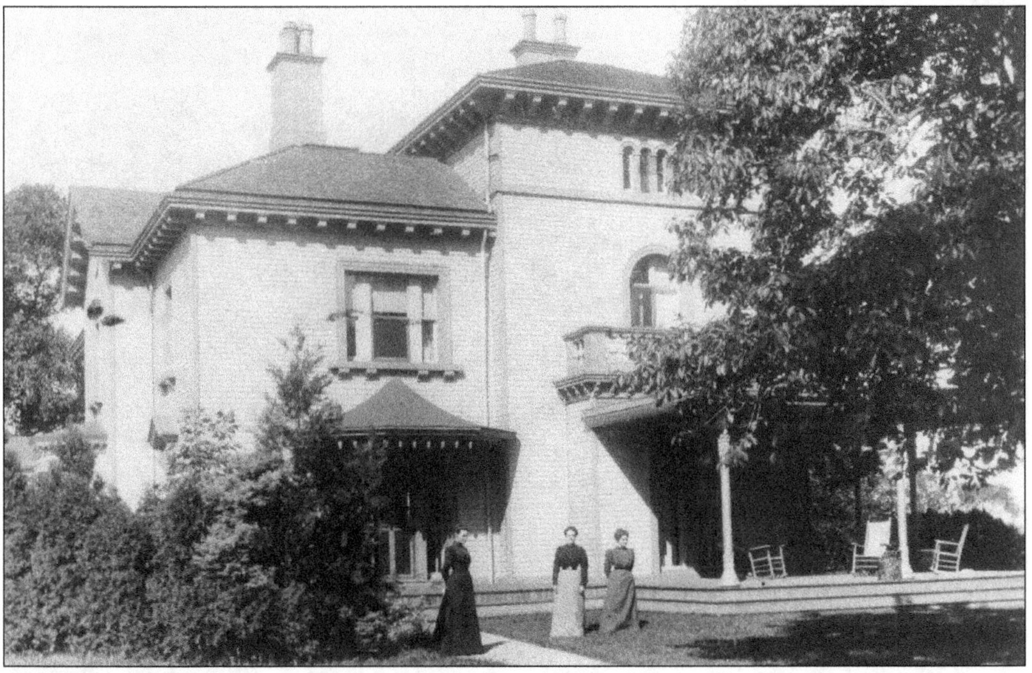

This house was built in 1864 on Belmont Street by Peter Chardon Brooks Jr. for a summer home and, in 1894, it was purchased by John Van Ness Stults. Stults, the first wholesale dealer in plumbing fixtures in Boston, rented several acres to local farmers. He had horses, cows, chickens, and pigs, and grew strawberries, raspberries, and grapes, along with cherry, pear, and peach trees. The house was torn down in 1924 when the estate was sold for house lots.

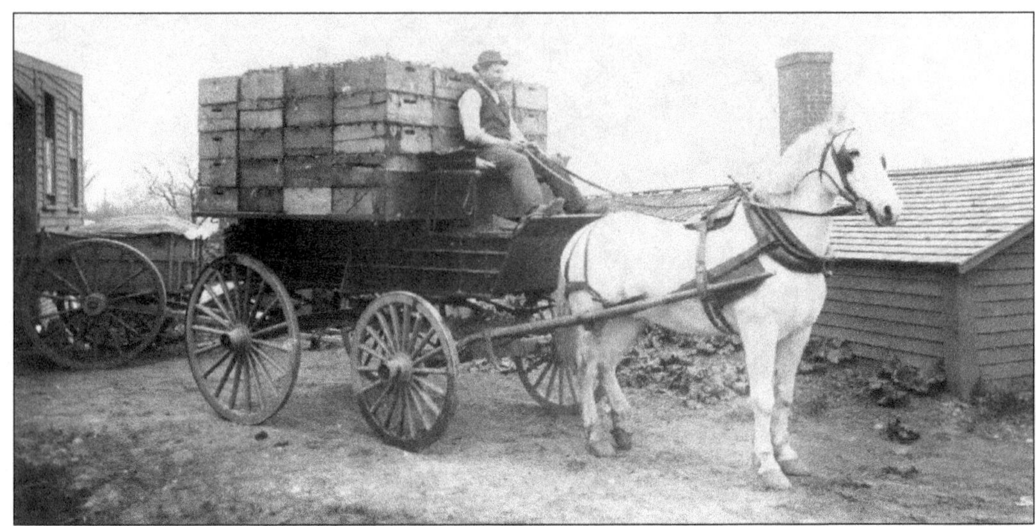

Another large market garden was the 25-acre Shaw farm, founded in 1874 by Herbert F. Shaw. There were 75,000 square feet of greenhouses, producing four crops of hothouse lettuce through the fall and winter. In the spring, cucumbers, celery, tomatoes, carrots, and beets were grown. Delivered in a wagon drawn by a horse named Charlie, all of the produce was sold at the Farmers Market at Faneuil Hall in Boston.

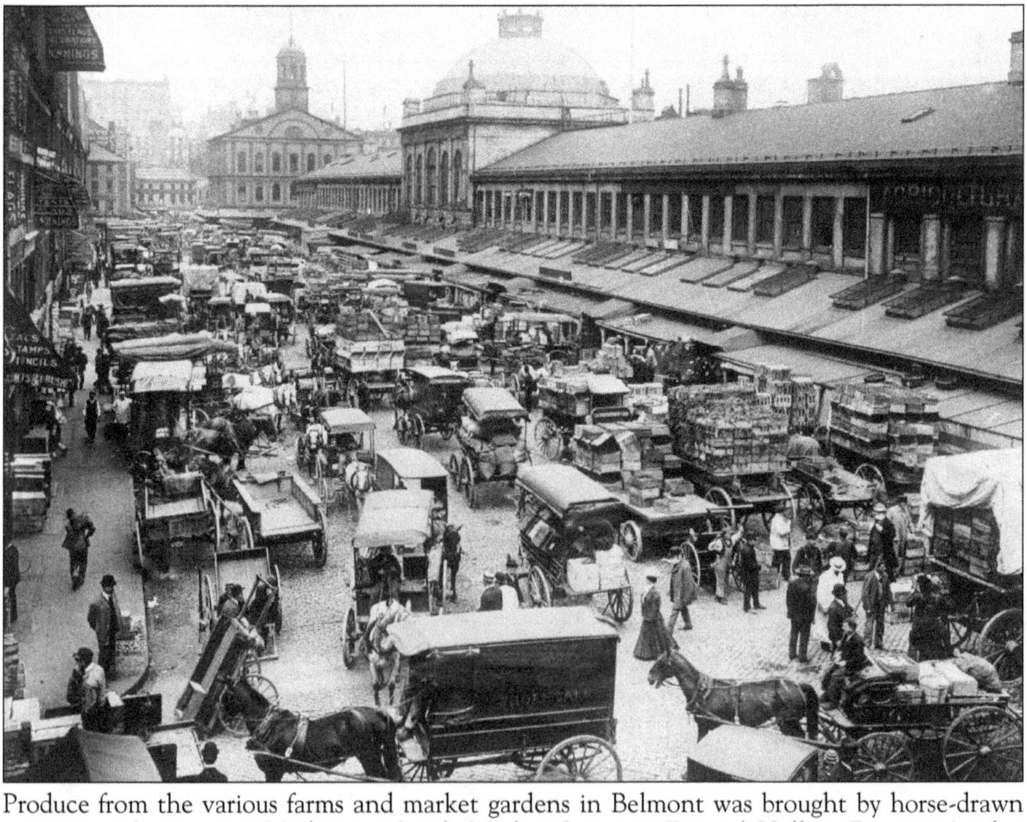

Produce from the various farms and market gardens in Belmont was brought by horse-drawn wagons to the Farmers Market on South Market Street at Faneuil Hall in Boston. As this picture shows, the Farmers Market certainly was a busy place.

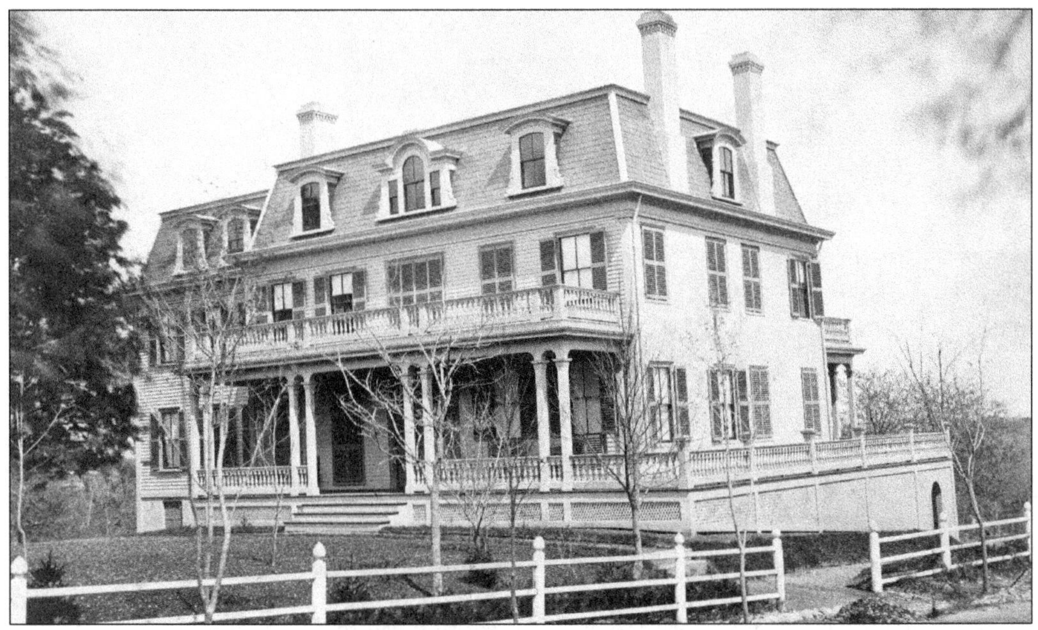

This home, built in 1825 of hand-hewn timbers, originally had 14 fireplaces. After the beginning of the 20th century, the house was leased and operated as the Belmont Inn. Purchased by the Plymouth Congregational Church in 1941, the house was moved next to the church for a parish hall. It was torn down in 1957 and replaced with the present church parish house.

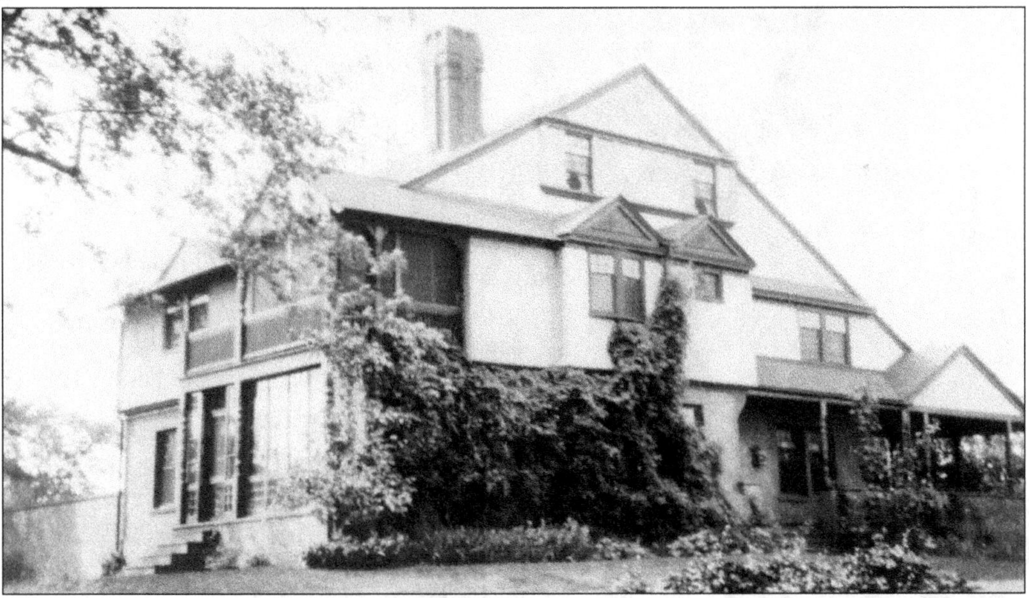

"Red Top" was the former home of William Dean Howells, the noted American literary critic, novelist, and editor of the *Atlantic Monthly* from 1871 to 1881. In this house, Howells entertained such American notables as Mark Twain and James Russell Lowell. Poet Henry Wadsworth Longfellow once came here to meet James Garfield shortly before Garfield was elected president. Howells wrote several of his better-known works here. In 1979, the house was declared a National Historic Landmark.

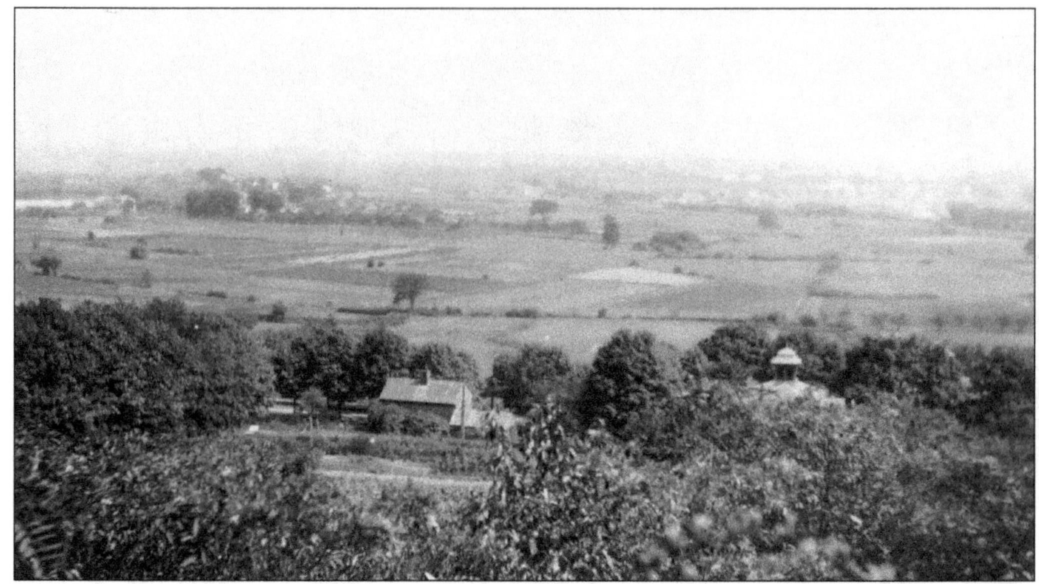

Roger Wellington became the first settler in what is now Belmont *c.* 1630. His farm remained in the Wellington family from early Colonial days until it was sold for house lots in 1925. The farm ran from Pleasant Street to the railroad at Brighton Street. This view from Belmont Hill, taken from behind the Capt. Stephen Frost house, shows the farm, which today is the Winn Brook section of Belmont.

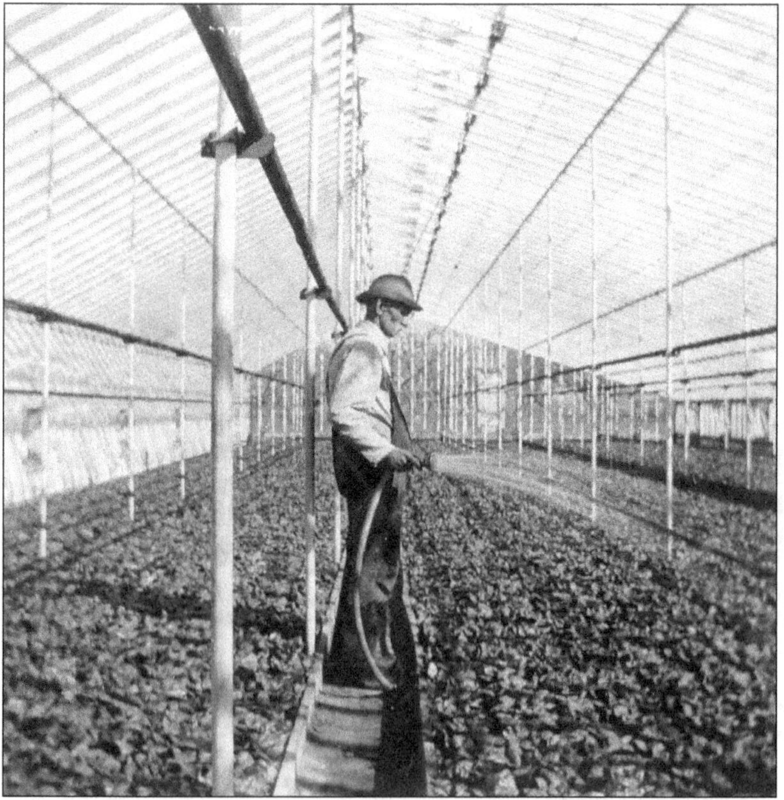

Through marriage, Charles Winn obtained part of the Wellington farm but, in 1909, the heirs of both families merged the two old farms, creating the Wellington Farm Company. This *c.* 1898 picture shows George Winn tendering his crops in the greenhouse, which was to the rear of present-day Belmont Center.

JOHN A. FINIGAN, Auctioneer and Sales Manager, Concord, Mass. Tel. 404-W

→AUCTION←

TO BE SOLD AT THE

Wellington Farm Company

BELMONT CENTER, MASS.

Saturday, Dec. 5, 1925

AT 9.30 O'CLOCK A. M.

The Biggest Auction of Its Kind

Ever Held in Belmont Center. Everything That You Need on a Farm

A collection of Farm equipment, consisting in part of Mowing Machine, Hay Rake and Tedder, Hay Wagons, Carts, Snow and Land Plows, Harrows, Cultivators, Rollers, Arlington Seed Sowers, Harnesses, 1000 Hotbed Sash, Hand Tools generally used about a farm; Ladders, Pots, Wagons, Planks and Boards, Celery Paper and Wires, Pipe and Fittings (Skinner System) of every description, and a variety of articles too numerous to mention.

Clearance Sale, without reserve or limit. Sale positive rain or shine.

TERMS CASH AT TIME OF SALE

LUNCH SERVED BY A CATERER

Huntley S. Turner, Printer, Ayer, Mass.

Wellington Farm was sold in 1925 for house lots and the farm equipment was auctioned off. The poster advertises the event as "the biggest auction of its kind," with a collection of both common and unusual articles "too numerous to mention."

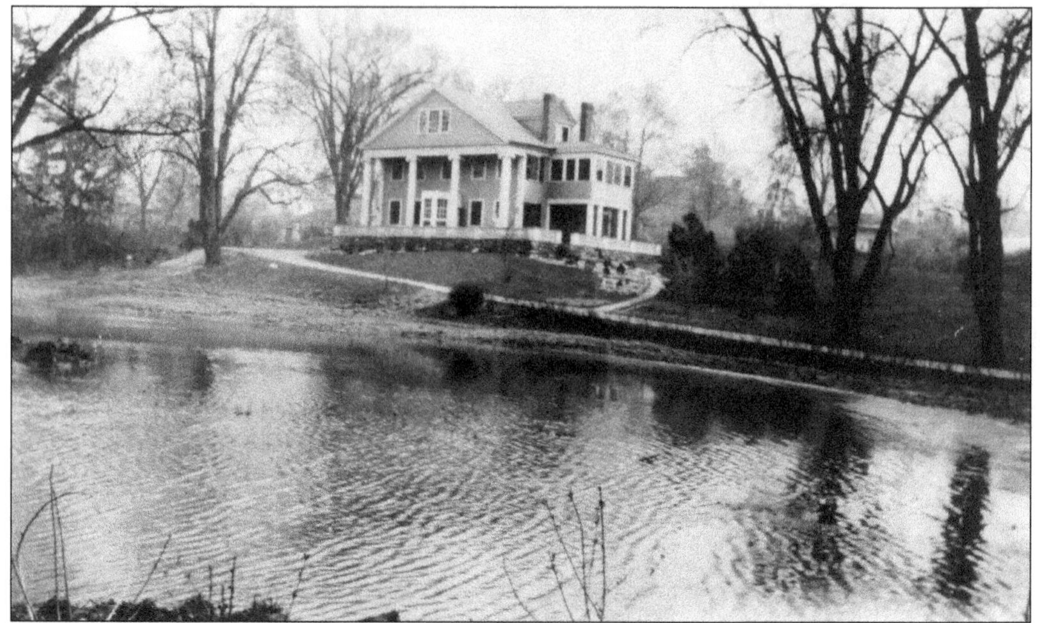

Built by Samuel O. Mead in 1836 for his wife, Maria Wellington, this house and the adjoining estate have been family owned and occupied ever since. The pond in the foreground was formed by damming Wellington Brook, thus creating a private skating rink on the Underwood Estate. Today, with the brook diverted, the Belmont Memorial Library on Concord Avenue sits on the site of the pond.

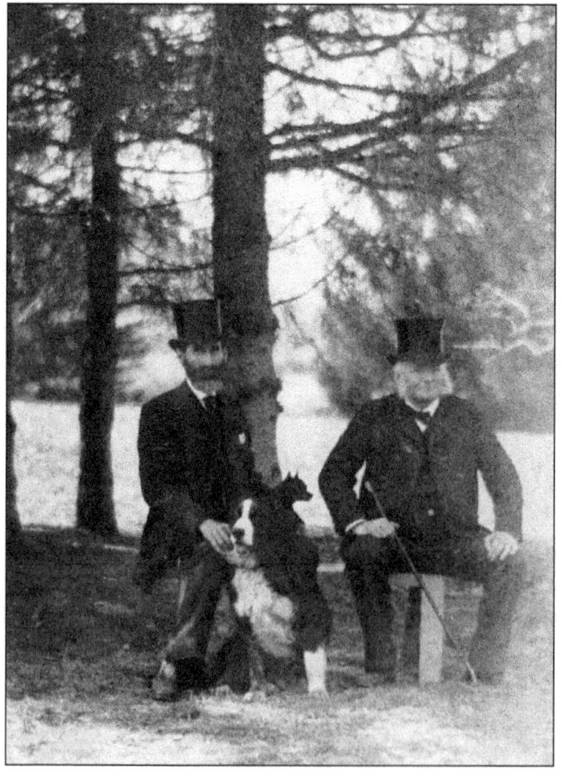

Thomas Brown and William J. Underwood are shown relaxing on the Underwood Estate. Underwood was the son of William Underwood, founder of the Underwood Company. He was the first chairman of the trustees of the Belmont Public Library, served as an assessor and as water commissioner, and was a member of the Belmont School Committee. He died in 1897, and his ashes were buried around a large tree on the estate. His descendants still live on this historic property.

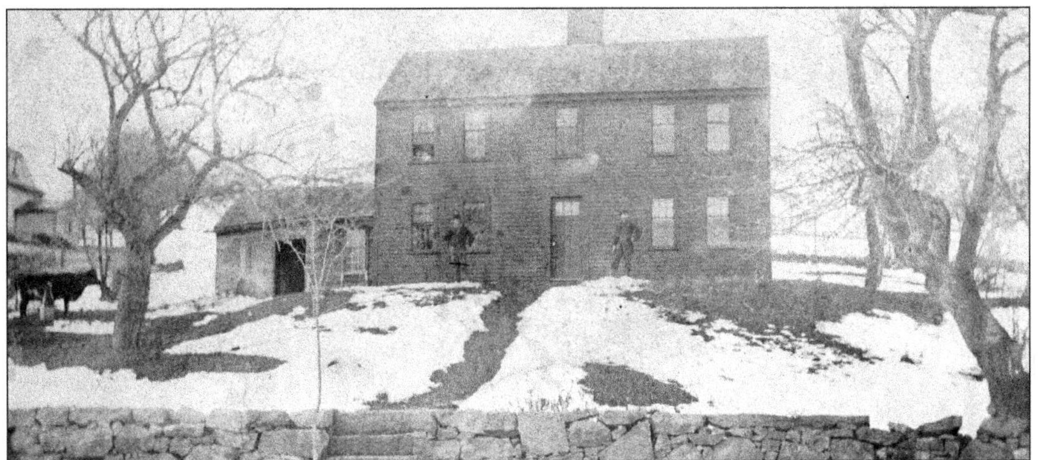

This picture, taken in 1895, shows the Capt. Stephen Frost house at 467 Pleasant Street, built *c.* 1763. On April 19, 1775, Ens. Stephen Frost, on his way to join his company of Lexington minutemen, came across the "old men of Menotomy" in line across the roadway in Arlington. He assumed command and succeeded in capturing an enemy supply train. This house remained in the Frost family until 1993.

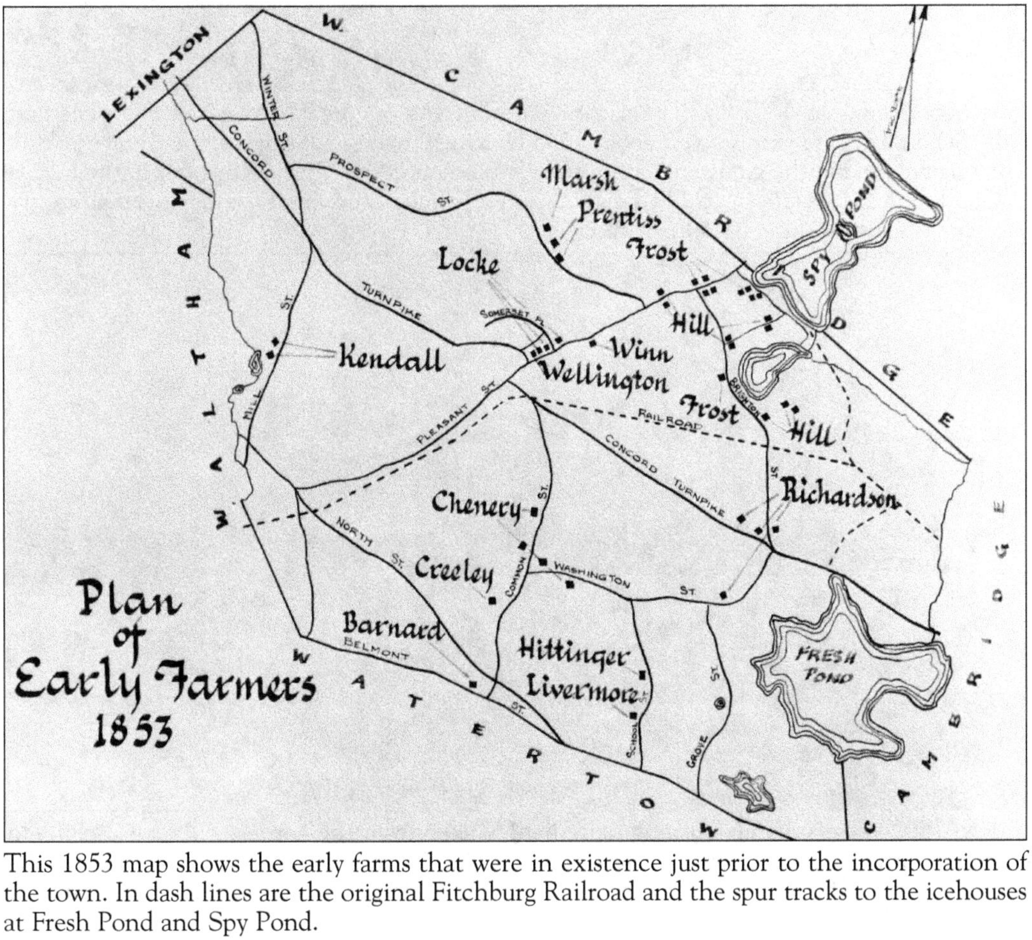

This 1853 map shows the early farms that were in existence just prior to the incorporation of the town. In dash lines are the original Fitchburg Railroad and the spur tracks to the icehouses at Fresh Pond and Spy Pond.

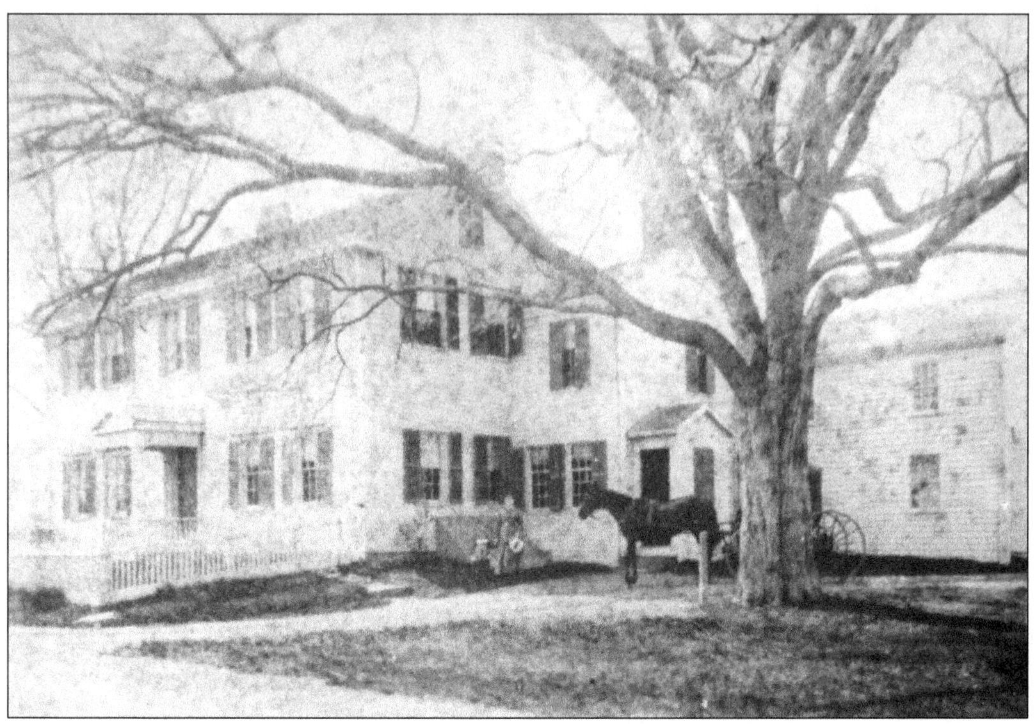

This house, built in 1807 for Thomas Richardson, sits on the last piece of the once-vast Hill-Richardson land grant, given about 1633 by King Charles I of England to Abraham Hill. The original land in the grant ran along Alewife Brook and the Mystic River out to the harbor in Charlestown. It is still owned by heirs of the Hill-Richardson family, and the remaining 11 acres are the last working farm in Belmont.

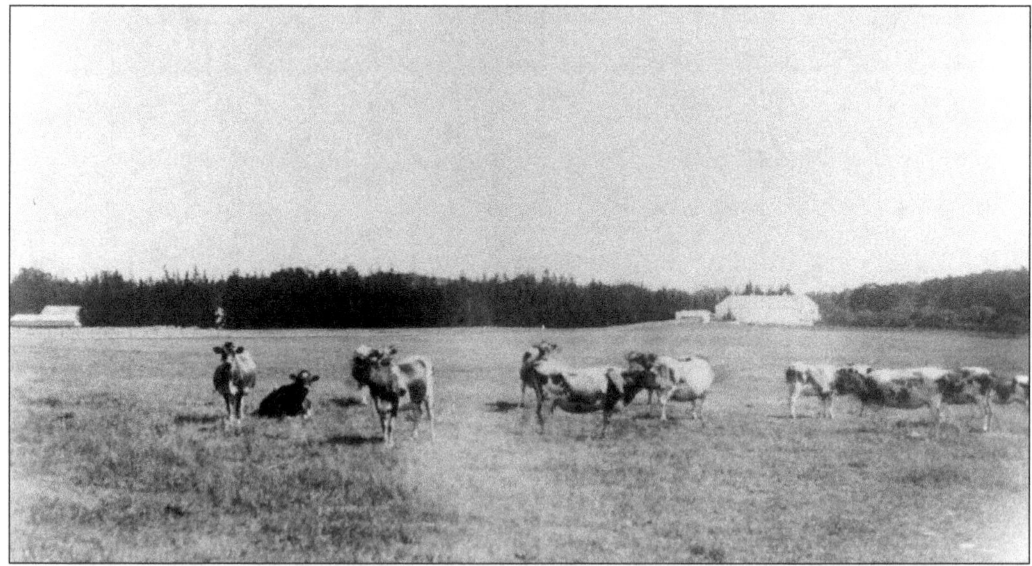

This *c.* 1860 view is of the Cushing dairy herd. Taken from the corner of Payson Road and Common Street, it looks over present-day Cushing Square toward Belmont Street. The farmhouse in the background was moved to 23 Oak Avenue where, as a private residence, it still exists today.

Three

Getting Around

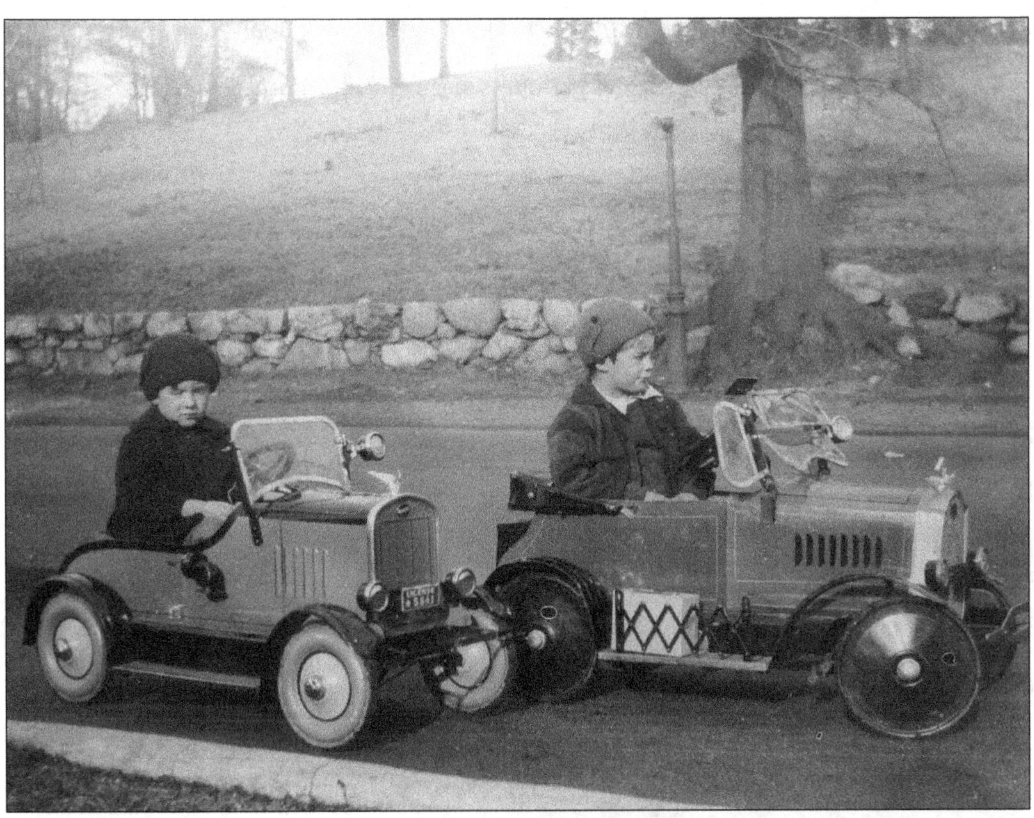

Four-year-old Robert Marsh, in his Willys Overland, and five-year-old Edwin Marsh, in his Packard Touring Car, ride along Trapelo Road near Waverley Oaks in 1930. This section of Trapelo Road was still a two-lane, undivided road and the speed limit 5 mph. Later, both boys served in World War II; Edwin Marsh Jr., a second lieutenant in the U.S. Army Air Corps, died in action in the South Pacific.

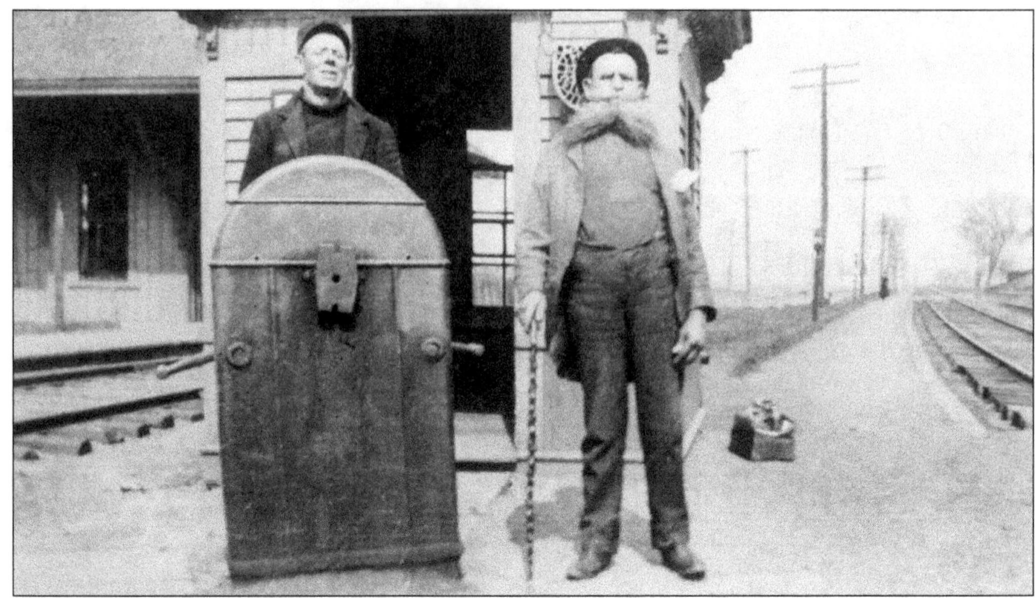

At Belmont center, sometime in the 1880s, crossing tender Tom Collins, left, stands with an unidentified passenger as they await the train to Boston. One can only wonder if the man has a brush in his bag to clean the train soot out of his magnificent beard and mustache.

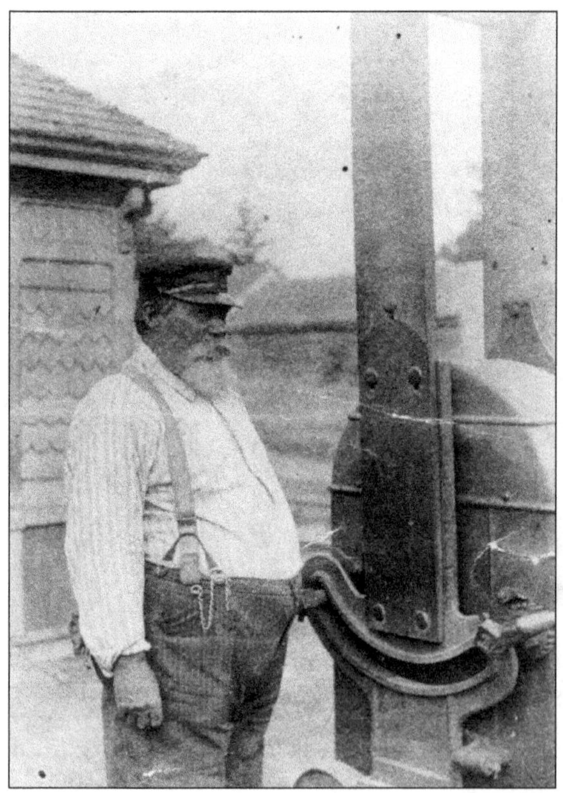

Maurice Welsh, crossing tender, mans his post in Waverley Square in the 1880s. Note the chain to his pocket watch, an important tool of the trade. Behind him is the gatehouse. (Courtesy of Barbara White.)

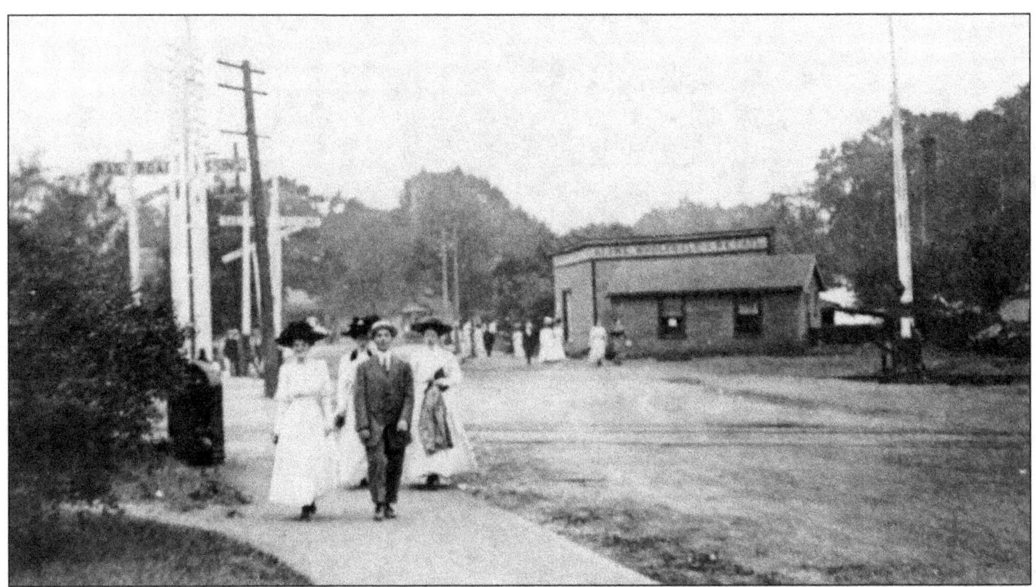

Dressed in their Sunday finest, this group leads the way across the tracks to the First Congregational Church of Waverly *c.* 1890. The building in the background is the Charles McGinnis Coal Company.

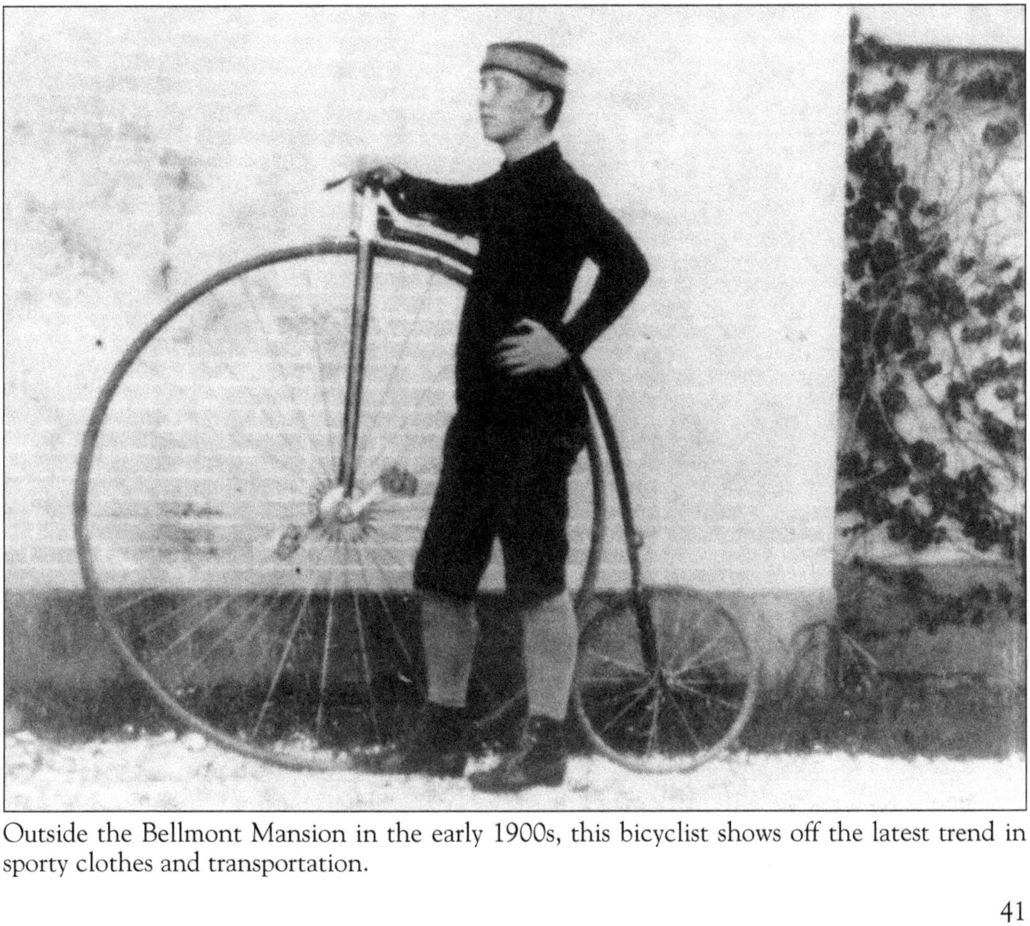

Outside the Bellmont Mansion in the early 1900s, this bicyclist shows off the latest trend in sporty clothes and transportation.

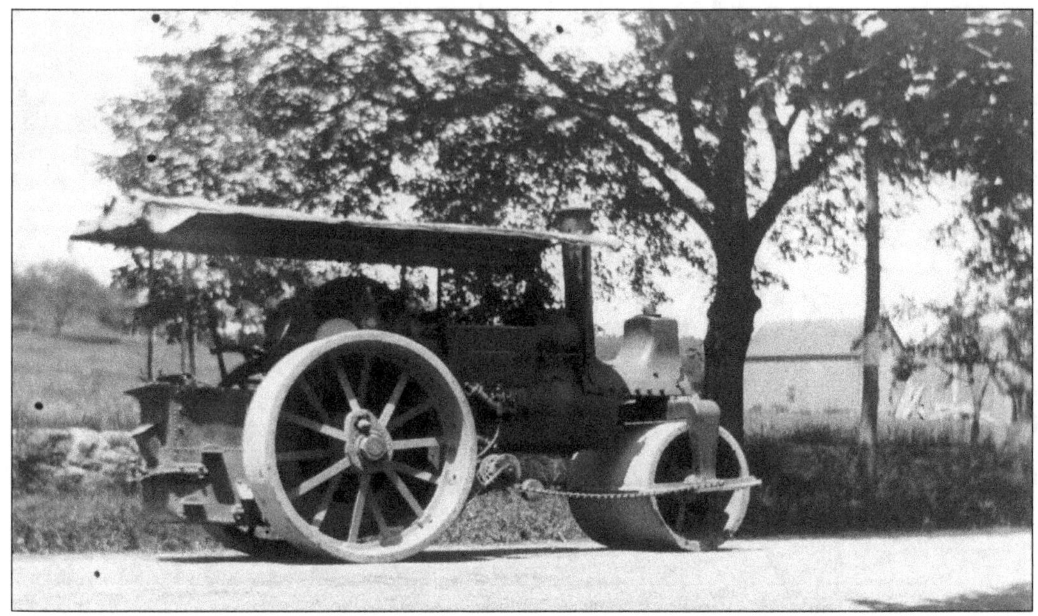

Getting around would have been much more difficult without the constant use of the town's steamroller. The laborers used the equipment and worked diligently to smooth out the gravel roads, including this stretch along Pleasant Street.

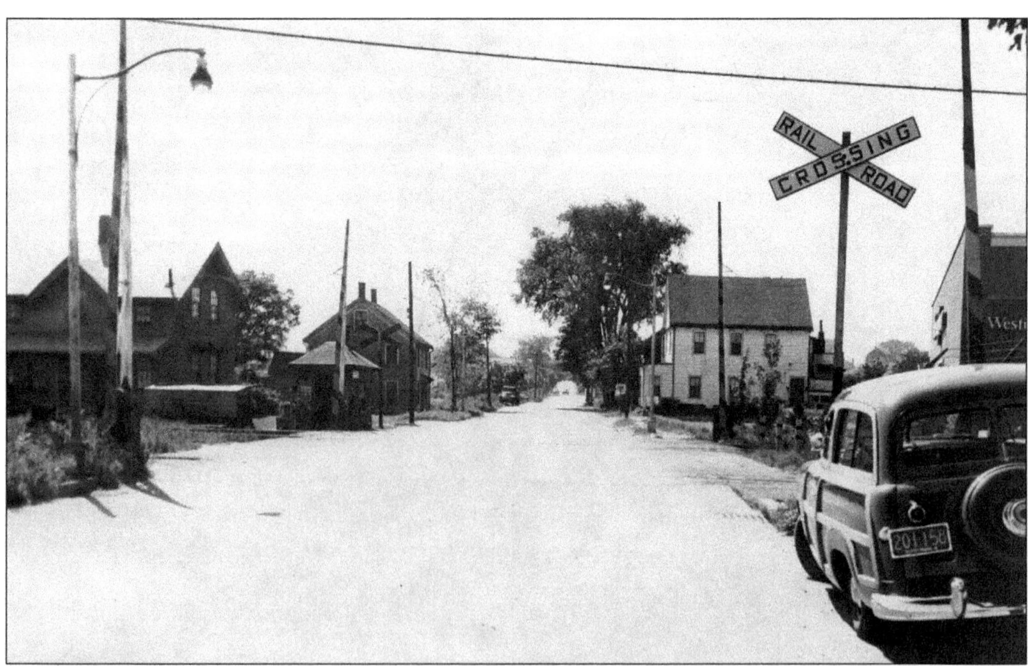

This photograph shows a 1952 view of Hill's Crossing, looking south up Brighton Street to Concord Avenue. A rural atmosphere still existed, the railroad station was still there, and little commercial development could be seen.

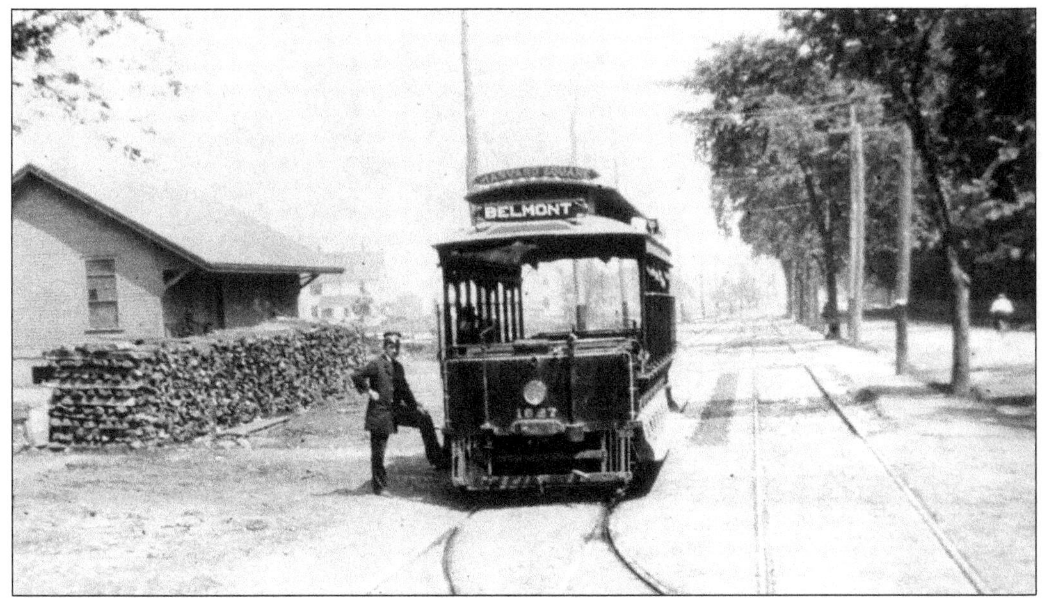

An early trolley car stands ready to make the trip to Park Street in Boston. Passengers endured the ride down Concord Avenue to Bright Road, to Grove Street, to Belmont Street into Harvard Square. Then the trolley route traversed Massachusetts Avenue across the Charles River to Boylston Street, along Tremont Street, to Park Street. All this in 45 minutes and for a 5¢ fare.

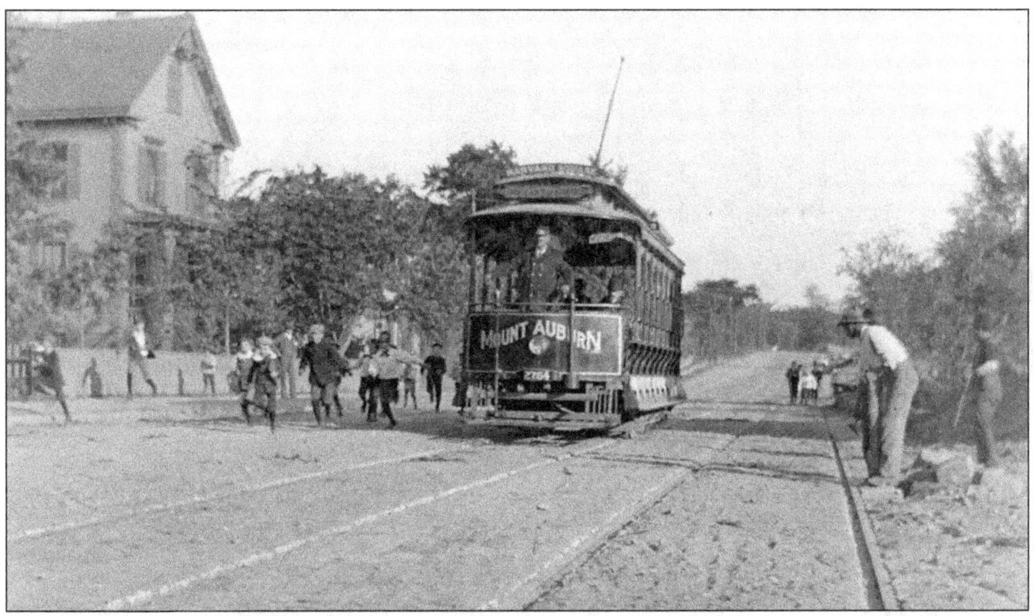

The first car on the Waverley branch of the Boston Elevated Railway made this trial trip in September 1898. This photograph was taken opposite the residence of A.B. Shedd, which still stands near the Waverley Branch of the Belmont Public Library.

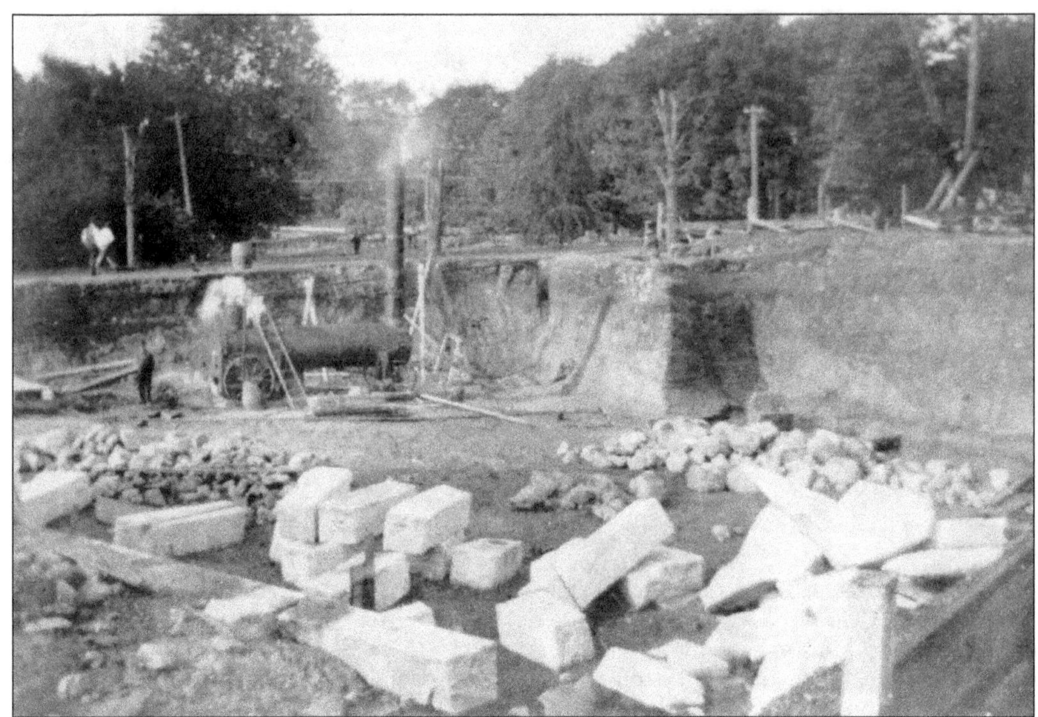

The Belmont Center Railroad Bridge is shown under early construction in 1906. This view is looking from Belmont Center past the construction site and up Common Street. Starting from Hill's Crossing, the grade had to be gradually raised some 7 feet at the bridge. The road under the bridge had to be excavated some 14 feet down from the original level.

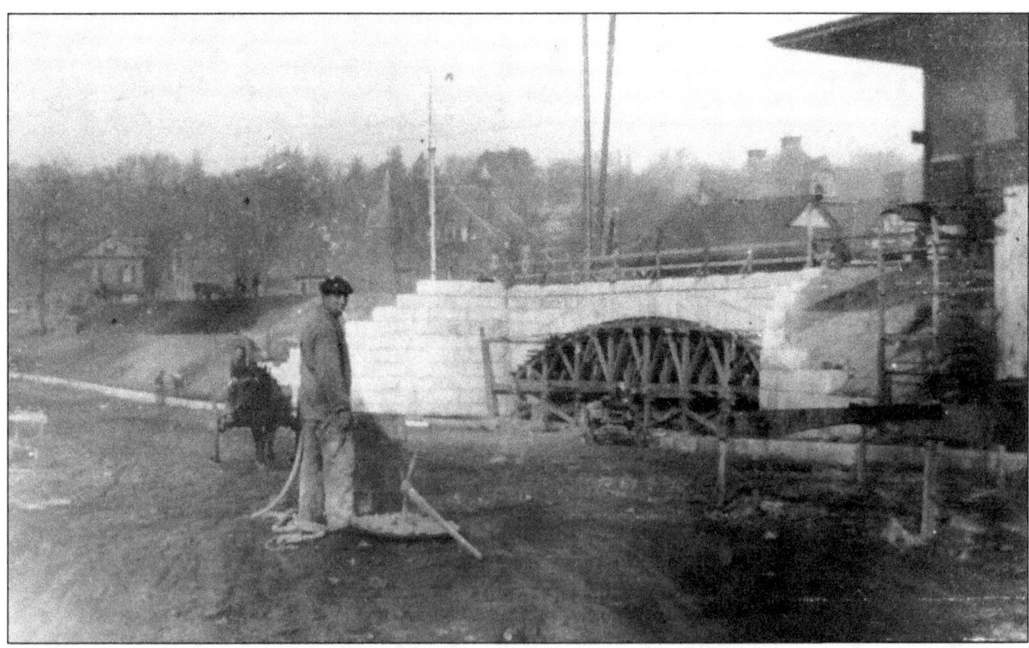

In 1907, the Belmont Center Railroad Bridge was nearing completion. On the right, is the corner of the two-story Fitchburg Depot.

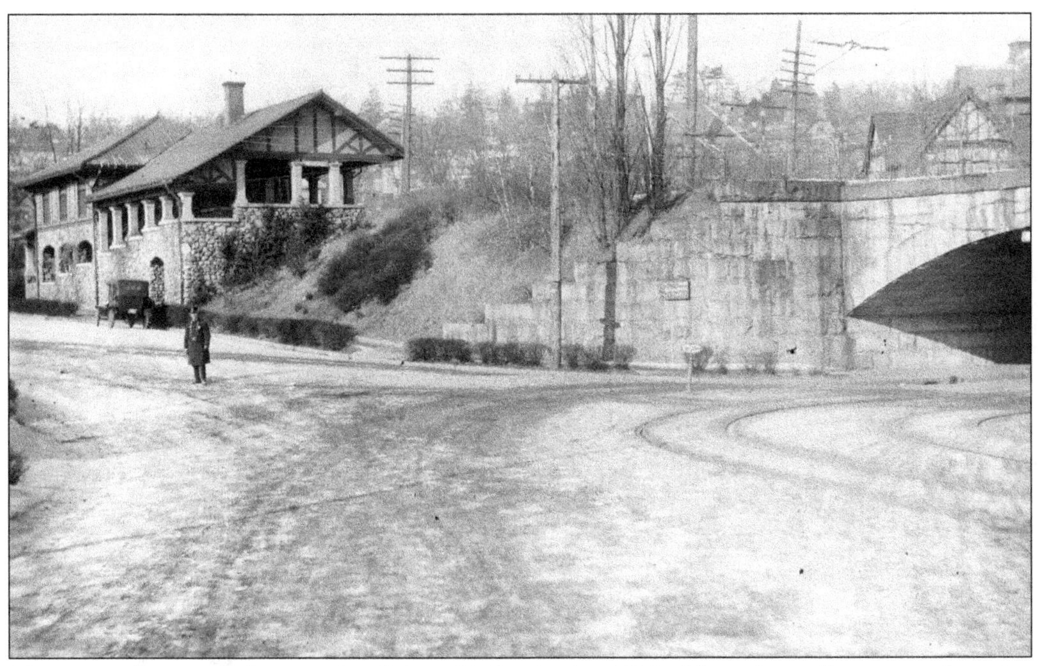

This view shows rush hour at the Center Bridge in the 1920s. Note the trolley car tracks going under the bridge and the original Boston and Maine Railroad Station with its arcades still open.

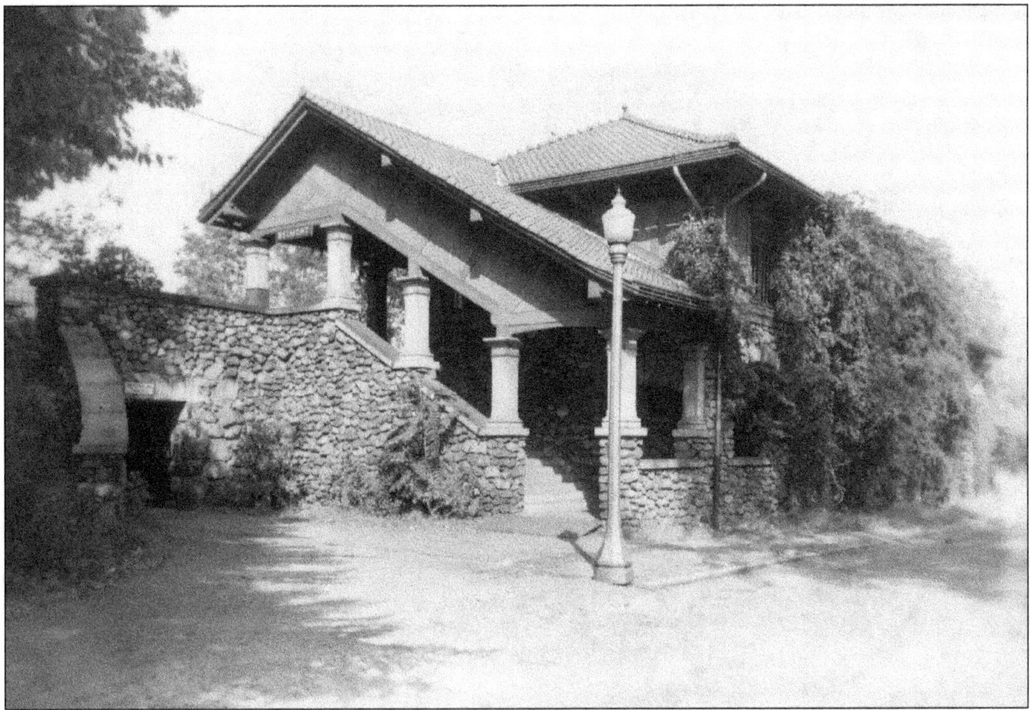

This photograph shows the new Belmont Center Railroad Station. Constructed after the bridge was completed, the station was made of 365 tons of fieldstones, dug and hauled from Belmont Hill by farmer David L. Thomas. Thomas claimed the bragging rights to that achievement for the remainder of his life. Notice the roof with its unusual Spanish tiles.

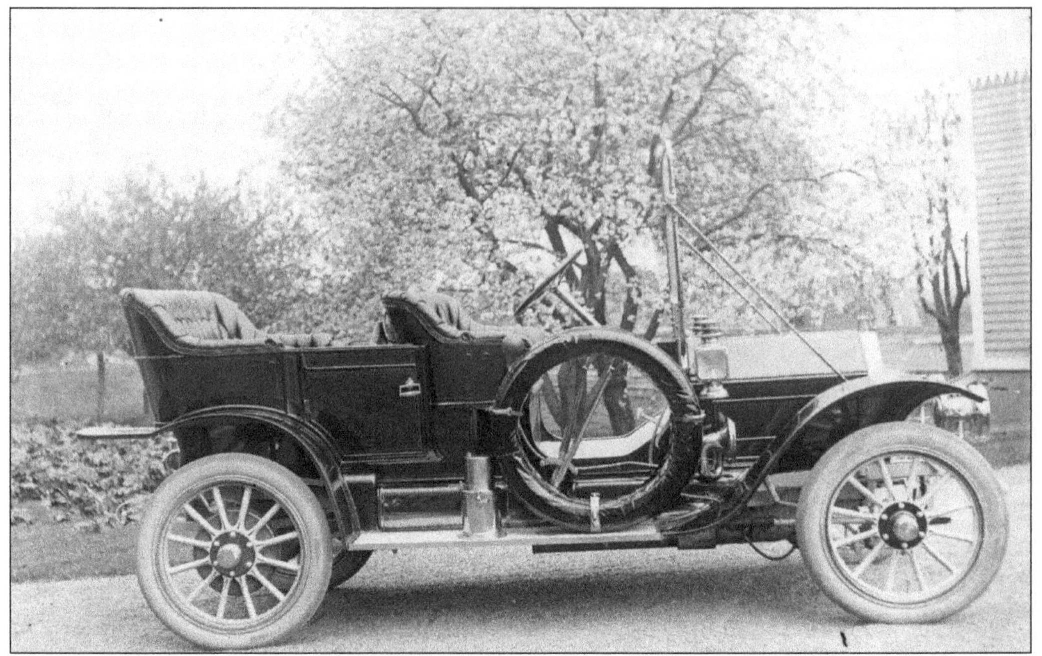

This 1910 Buick is parked outside of the Abraham Hill House. Motor transportation had taken on a new prominence with the advent of grand automobiles such as this one, and soon it completely replaced the horse and carriage.

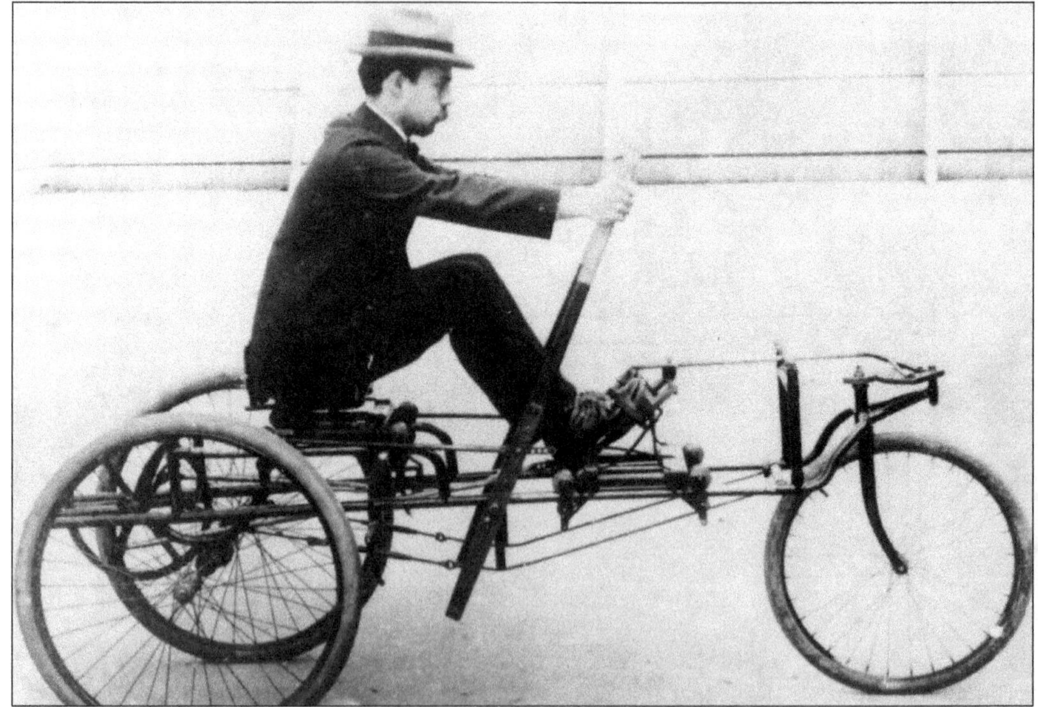

Clarence B. Van Wyck, a Belmont resident and secretary of the department of physical education at Harvard University in Cambridge, was easily recognized by his unusual transportation.

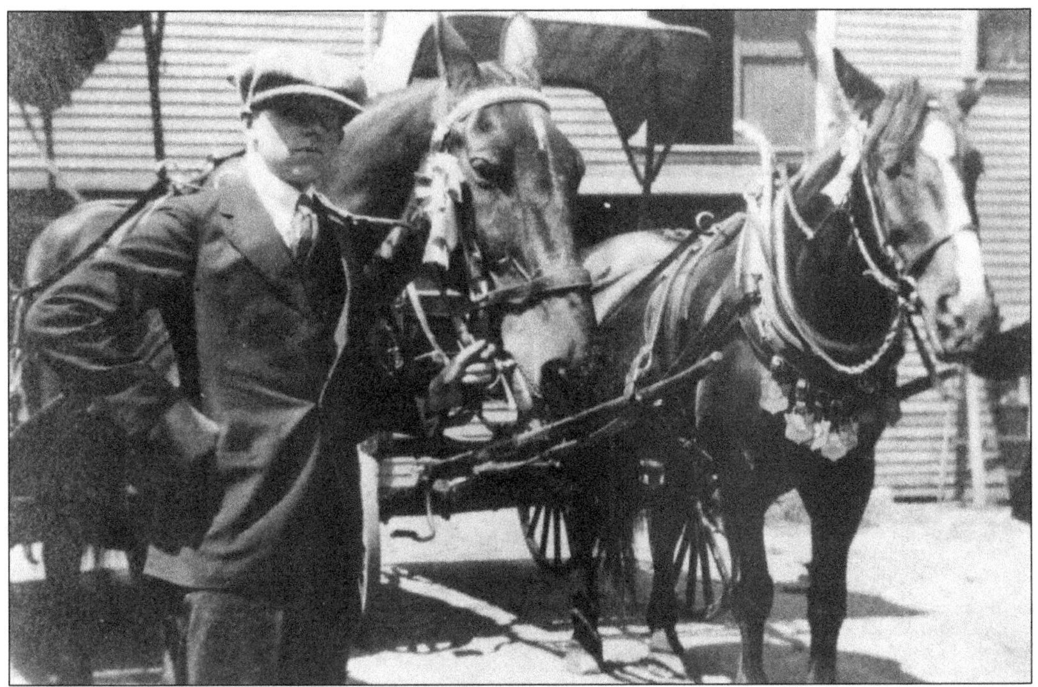

This photograph shows a driver and a prized team of horses from the Taylor Express Company, located at 52 Waverley Street. Teams carried the winter supply of groceries and staples, including sugar and flour in barrels, from local stores to kitchens and pantries in the area. These early Belmont delivery wagons never missed a chance to be in the numerous parades that were held in town.

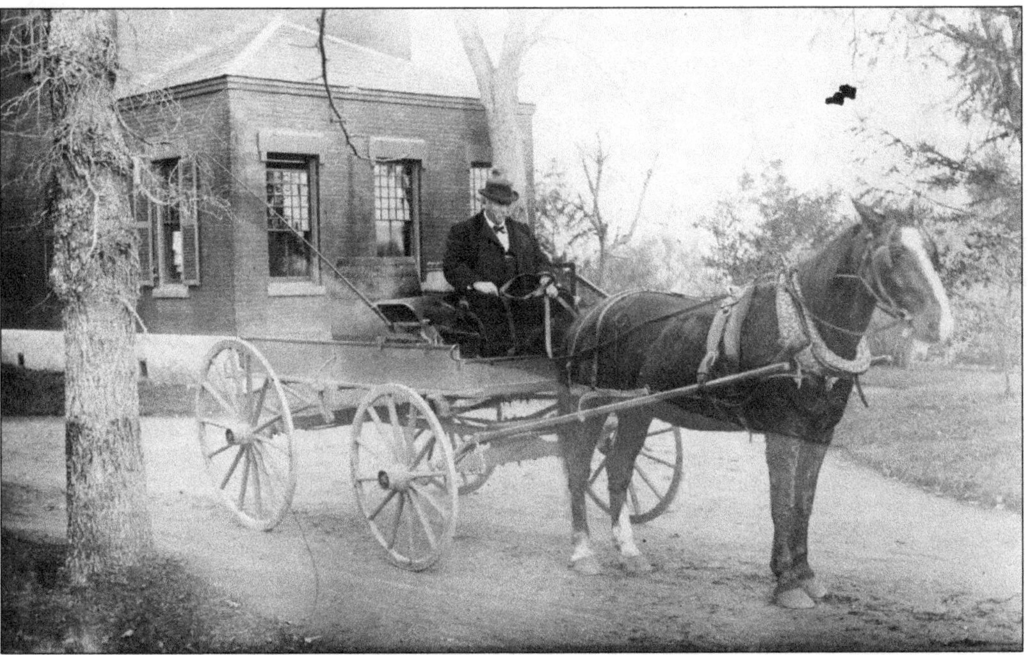

Mr. Simonds hauls a large keg on the property of Elisha and Katherine Atkins, at 580 Concord Avenue. This typical means of getting around was used to transport a variety of goods.

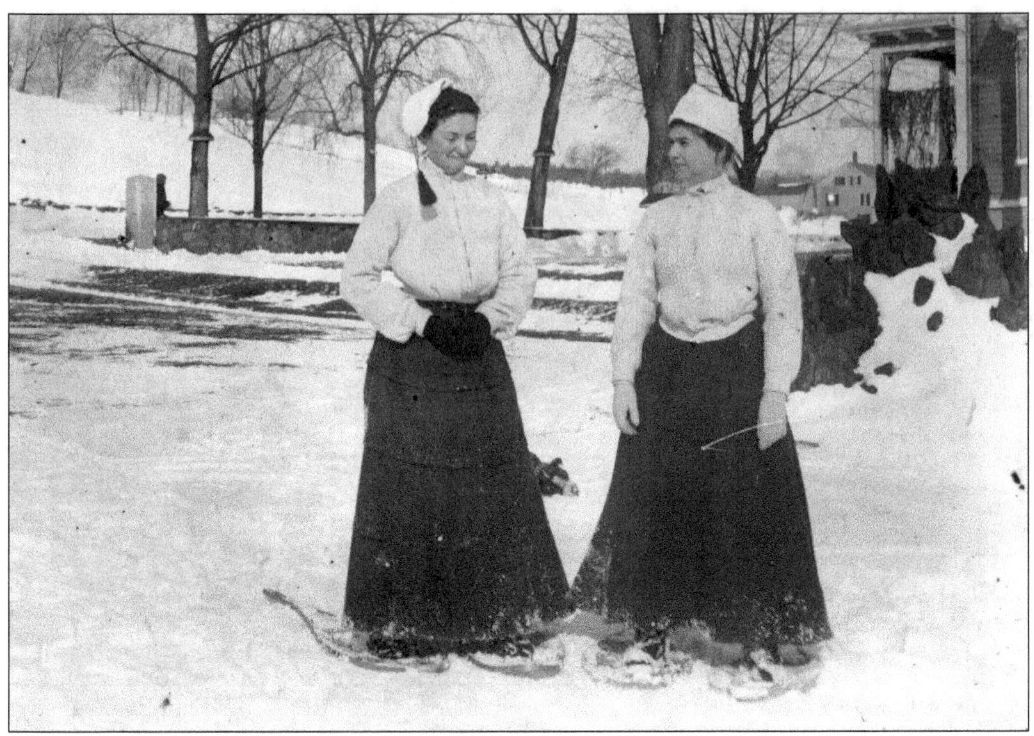

Two young women on Pleasant Street practice getting around on snowshoes. The snow, however, does not seem to be much of an obstacle to the fun.

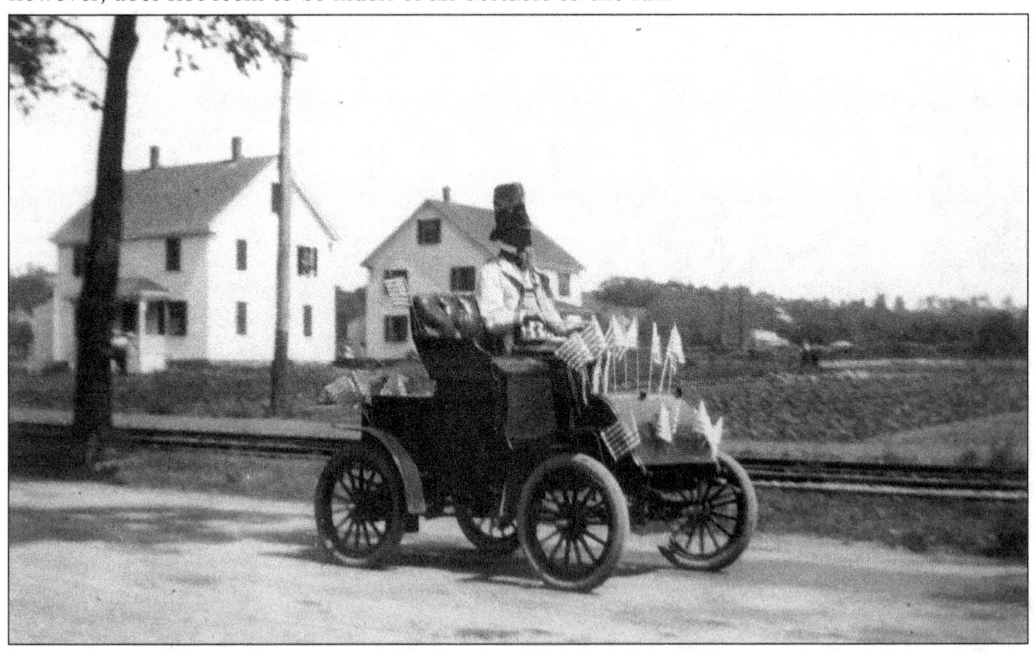

A handsome George P. Armstrong, school superintendent of Belmont, is shown enjoying his participation in the 1907 Belmont Park celebration. Belmont Park consisted of the neighborhoods of Myrtle, Goden, and Oak Streets along with contiguous sections of School and Orchard Streets.

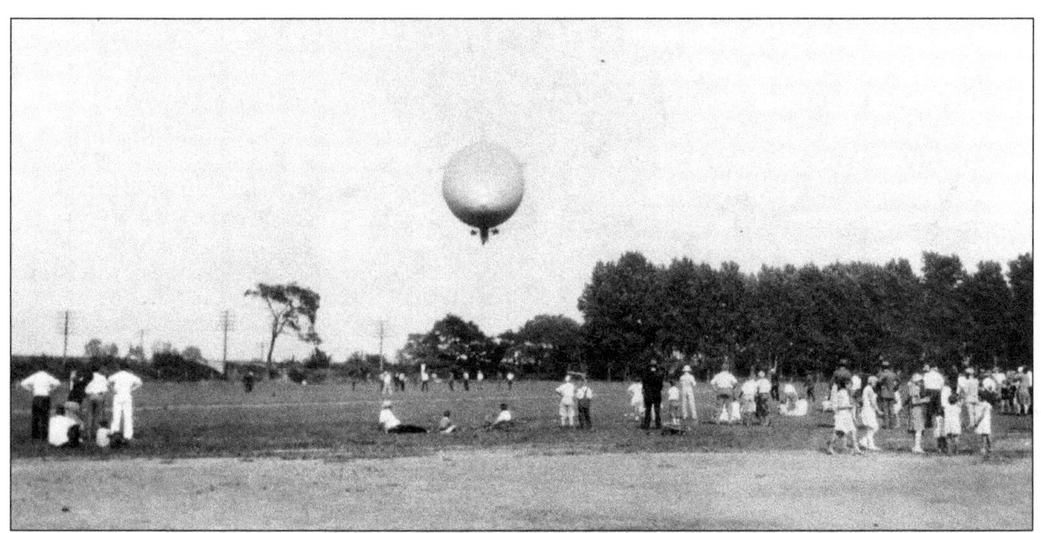

The Goodyear dirigible *Mayflower* is shown here landing on the Concord Avenue playground in 1930. It is not clear from the photograph if anyone was invited to go for a ride.

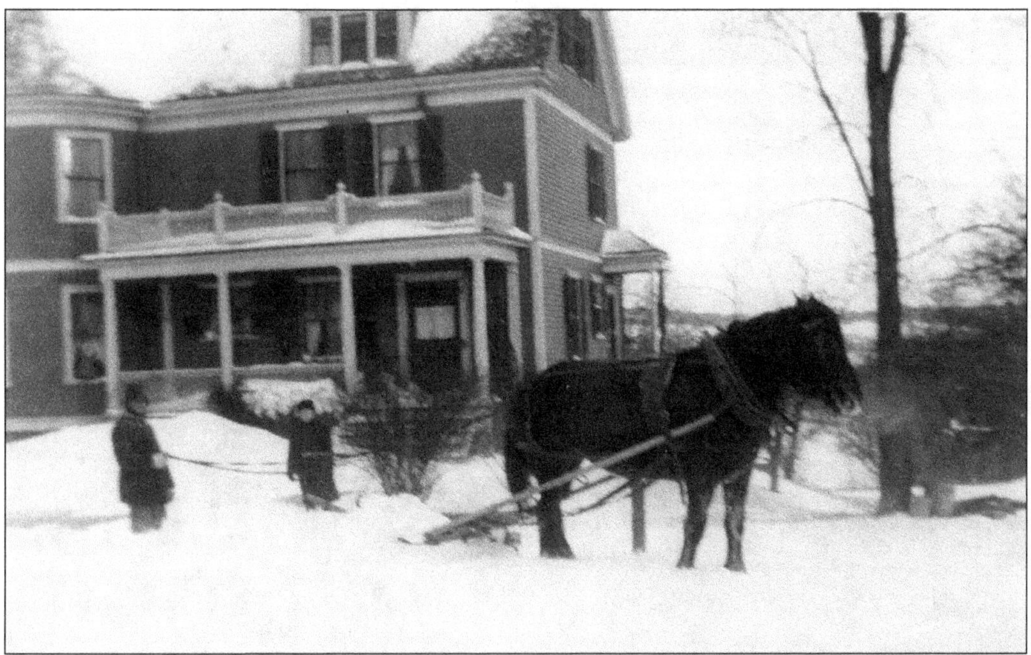

In this 1904 photograph, Mr. Birch and his young son clear the snow from the sidewalk along Fairmont Street with the help of a horse-drawn plow. The snow drifts were no match for horsepower.

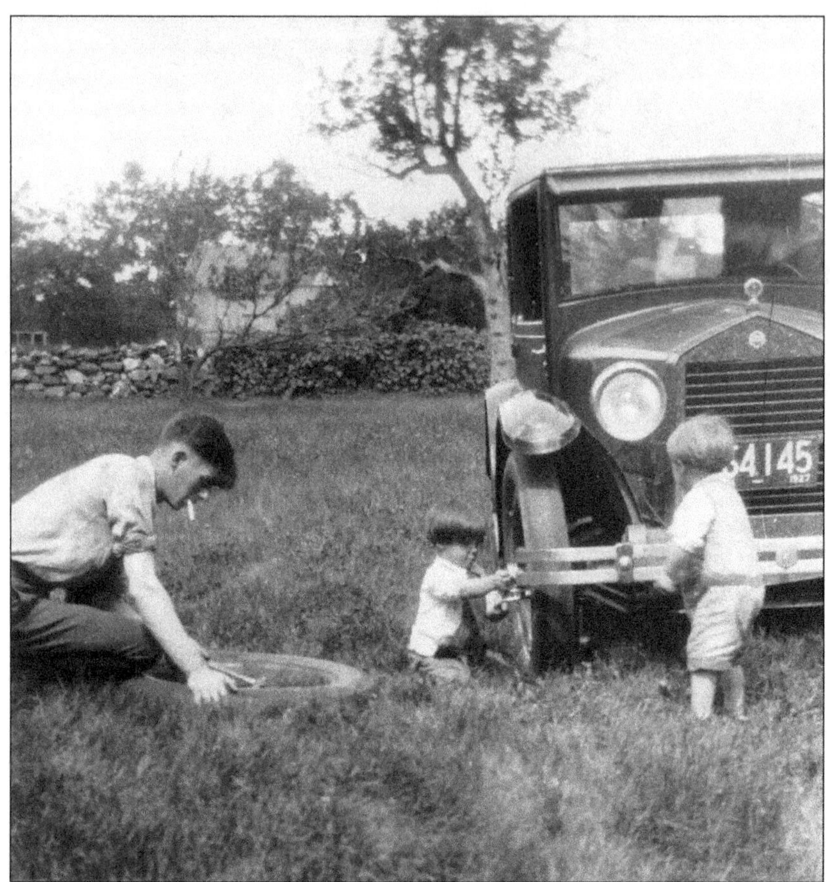

A typical road scene in 1927 shows a father fixing a flat tire. The two young sons are learning the basics of auto ownership.

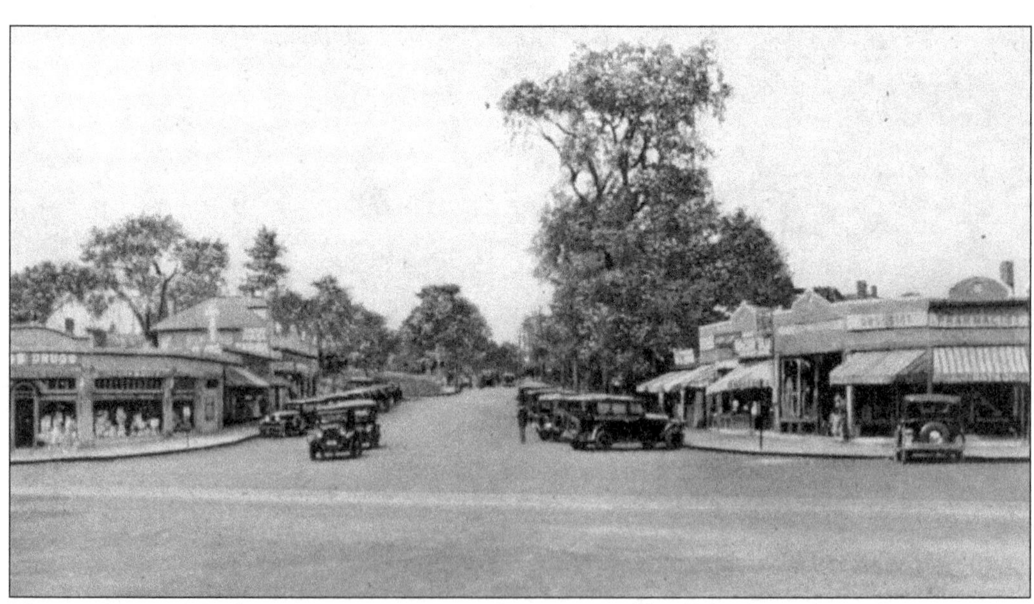

This is a view of Cushing Square *c.* 1930—when you could still find a parking place.

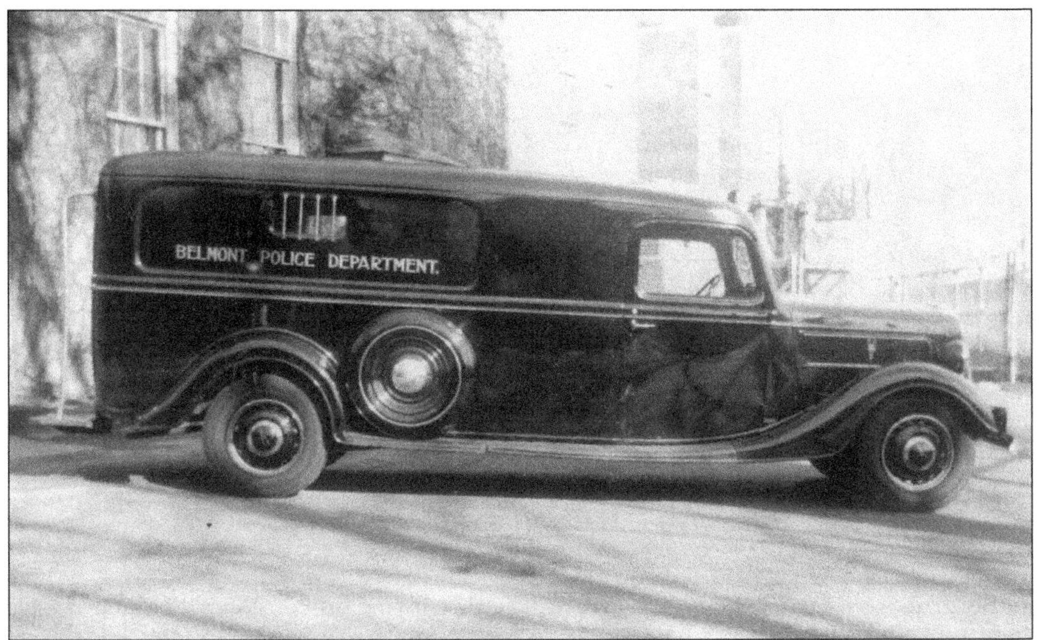

Getting around in this police wagon usually meant you were up to no good.

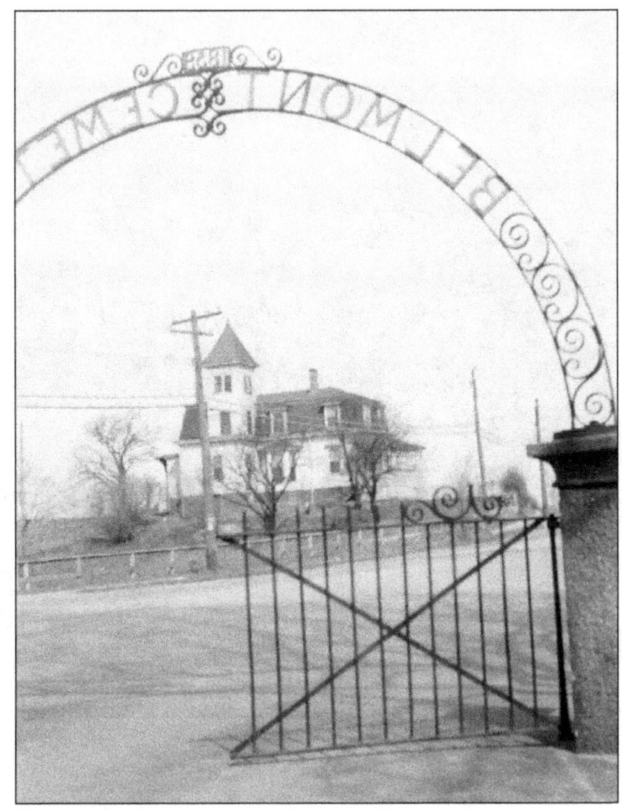
Even houses got around in earlier Belmont. This one, first owned by Reubin Richardson, had to be moved when the town laid out the Grove Street Playground. The house is now on the corner of Grosvenor Road and Grove Street. The front steps of the house were left behind and may still be seen along the wall on Grove Street.

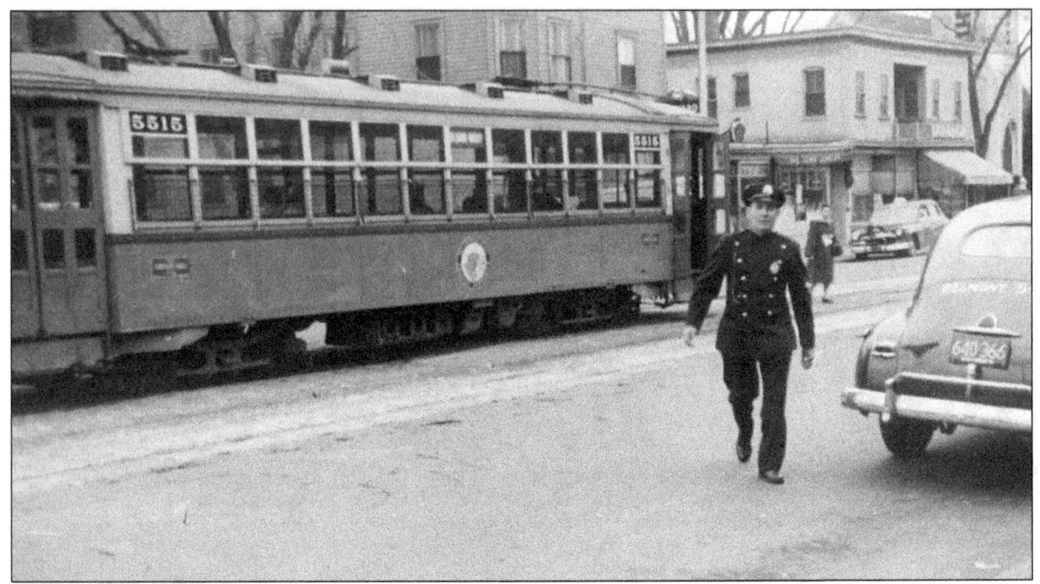

In the 1950s, police officer Ed Murphy was still getting around his beat the old-fashioned way, on foot. Behind Murphy is one of the streetcars destined to be replaced by the trackless trolleys of today.

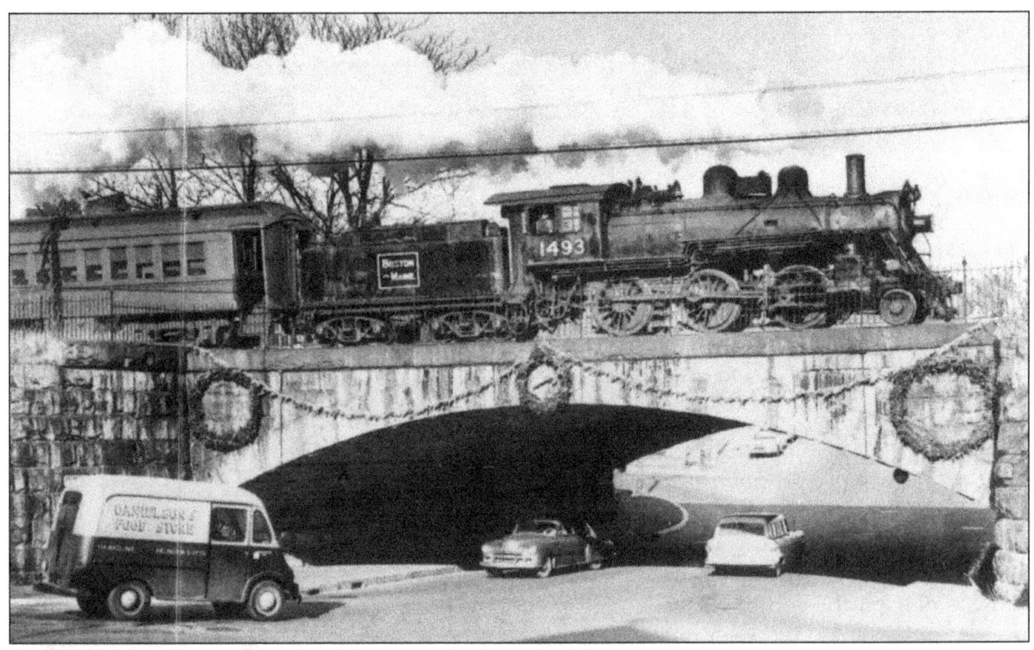

One of the last steam locomotives to cross the Belmont Center Bridge signifies the end of an era in the 1950s. Note the bridge is appropriately adorned with wreaths and garland for the occasion.

Four

A Community Prospers

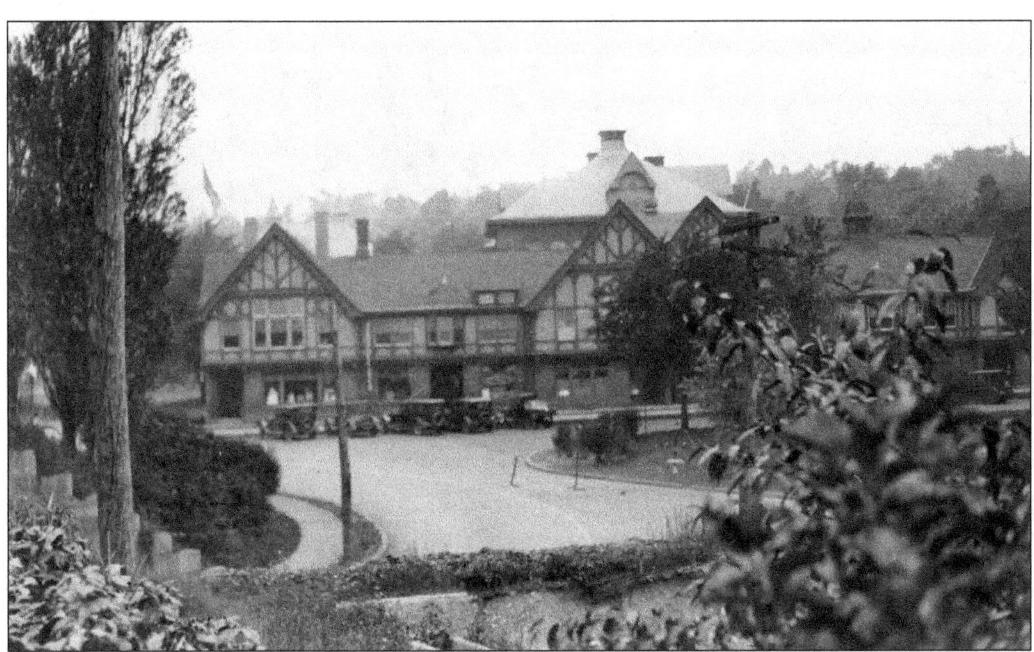

The Tudor block, built in 1897, was known as the most beautiful building in Belmont. It served as the town's first community center, with a meeting hall on the second floor and a billiard room and bowling alley in the basement. Referred to over the years as the Block of Shops, the Old Masonic Block, and the Olive Block, its tenants included the post office and first telephone exchange, to name a few.

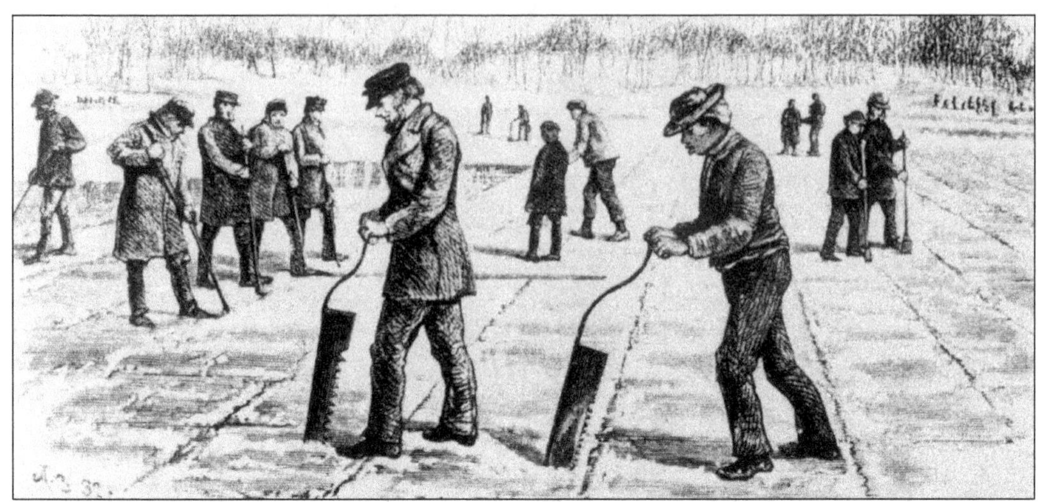

Gangs of men cut ice on Fresh Pond, then part of Belmont, where Frederick Tudor, nicknamed "the Ice King of New England," organized the Fresh Pond Ice Company. In an 1806 voyage, his was the very first shipment of ice to a port outside the United States. Fresh Pond Ice, known as black ice, was a trademark in all world markets for its clear, brittle characteristics.

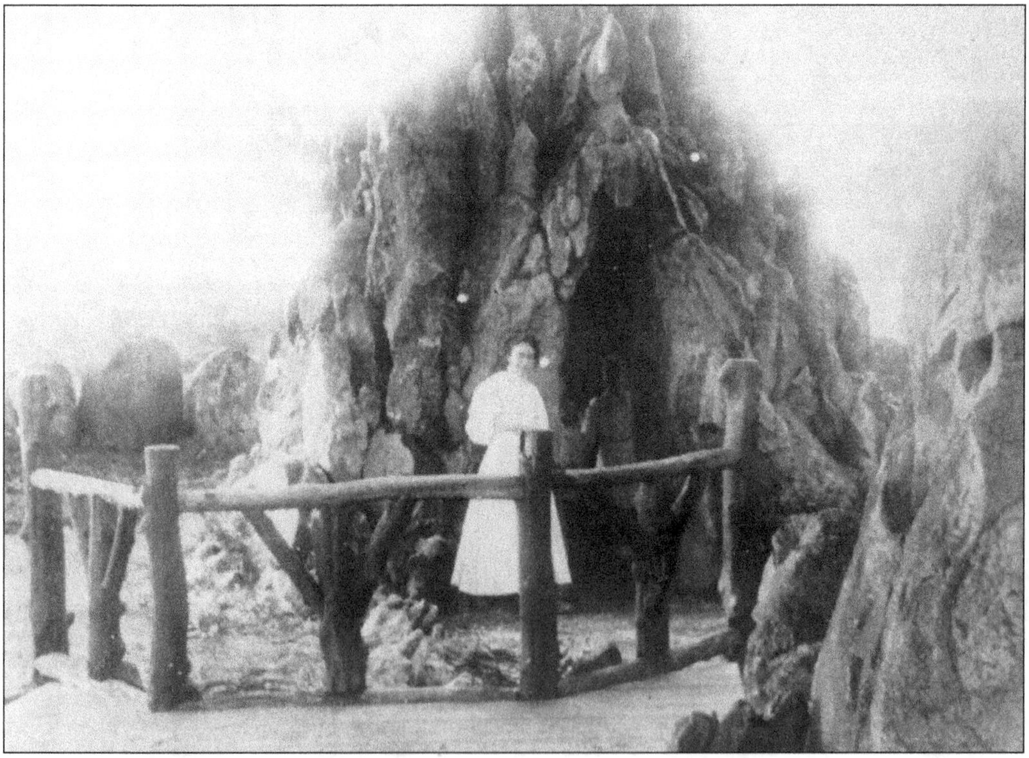

The Belmont Springs Water Company is the oldest continuous business in Belmont, incorporated in 1876. The natural springs were said to be discovered by early settlers who followed a Native American footpath. A popular Sunday outing in the 1800s was a carriage ride to drink from the grotto. During World War II, the company supplied 10,000 gallons of water a week to be canned for use in lifeboats on naval vessels.

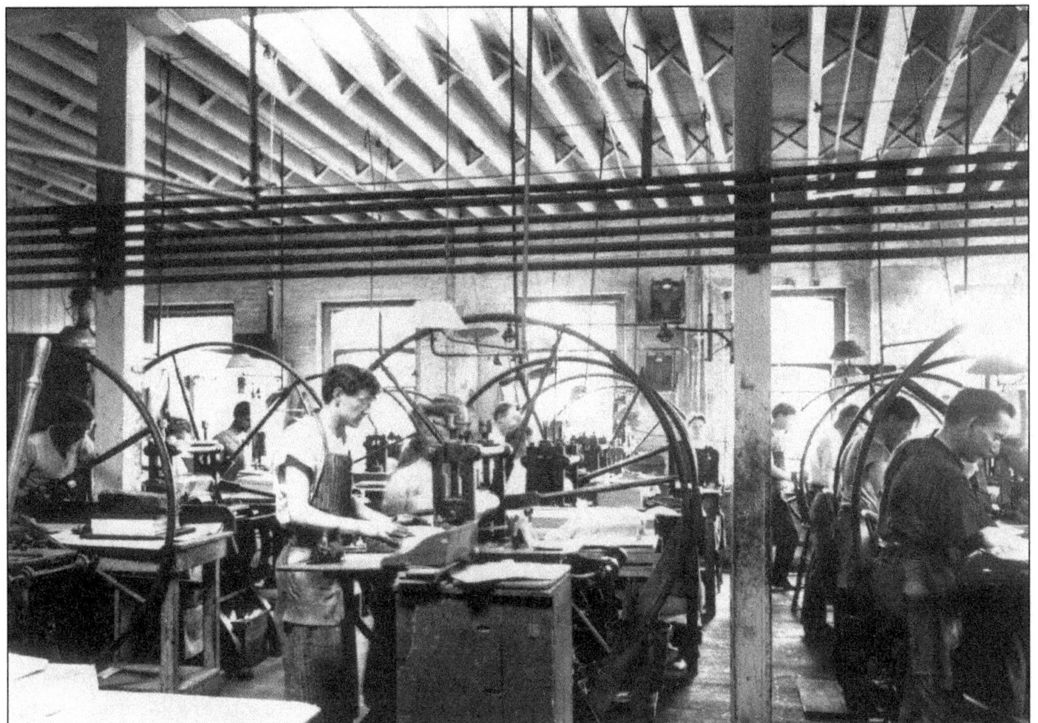

Mr. Elson came to Belmont about 1898 and, in a large brick building on Locust Street, he began the Elson Art Publishing Company. The business became known throughout the country for its reproduction works of art. Its main business was the printing of educational maps. Almost every school had an Elson map hanging over the blackboard. Records show that in 1907, the business supplied 744 schools in 45 states.

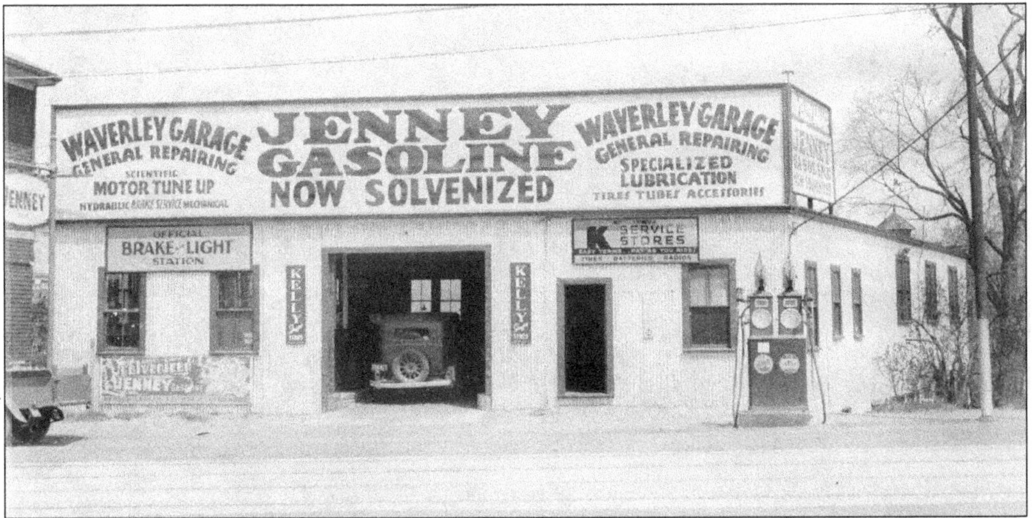

Mr. Jenney, a descendant of the family that owned the Jenney Oil Company, lived on Brighton Street and built the first Jenney Gasoline Station in town. Founded in 1812, "America's oldest oil company" was the first to sell motor gasoline in New England. Jenney became well known for its petroleum products and gas stations, which numbered as many as 600 from Maine to Rhode Island.

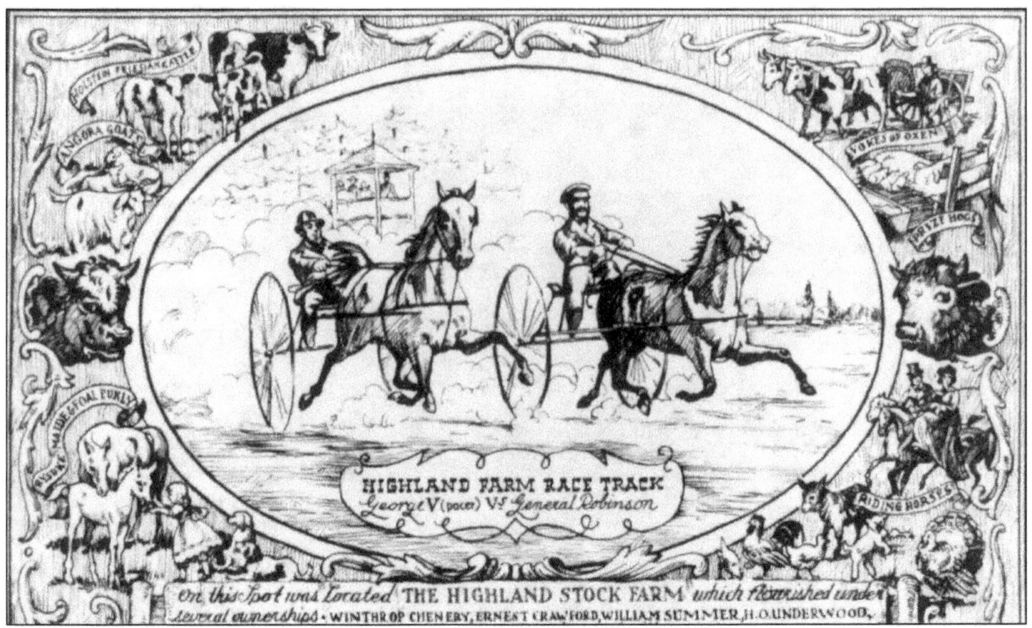

Winthrop W. Chenery, state representative and successful businessman, owned for pleasure both a farm and a racetrack on top of Belmont Hill. Chenery purchased the Dutch breed of cattle and continued the import of this milk-producing Holstein breed into the United States. The Highland Farm Racetrack was said to draw Sunday afternoon crowds of 3,000 spectators to view the sulkies race on the half-mile of fast track.

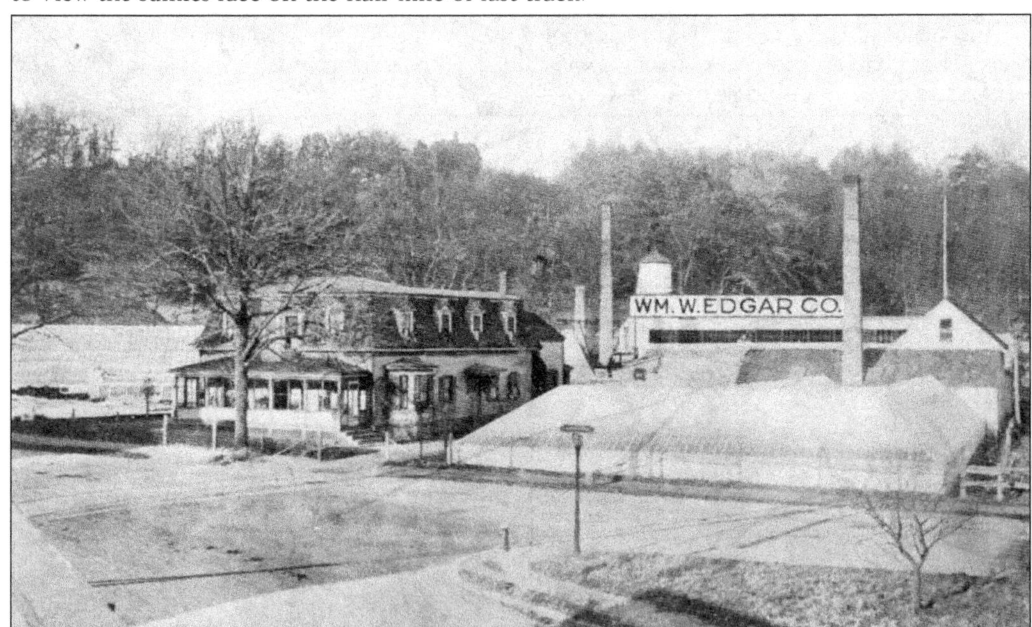

William W. Edgar established his company in 1884 along Trapelo Road. In a town of market gardeners, the business grew and soon included nine greenhouses with 30,000 feet under glass. Edgars Florist remained a local landmark, producing prize flowers and unusual plants. The family business was sold in 1948, following the death of Mrs. Edgar, who had helped run the company since her husband's passing 41 years earlier. (Courtesy of John Garrity.)

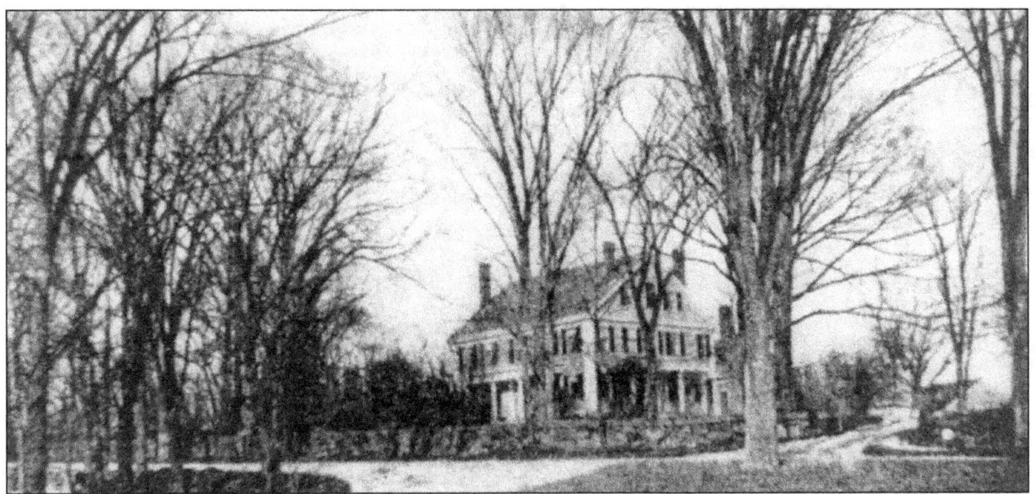

The Elm Hill Country Club, located on the corner of Washington Street and School Street, was managed by H.O. Davis. This property was earlier the home of the Stone family and was later rumored to be a speakeasy. This rare photograph represents one of the many landmarks included in Belmont Historical Society's "Lost Belmont" collection. (Courtesy of John Garrity.)

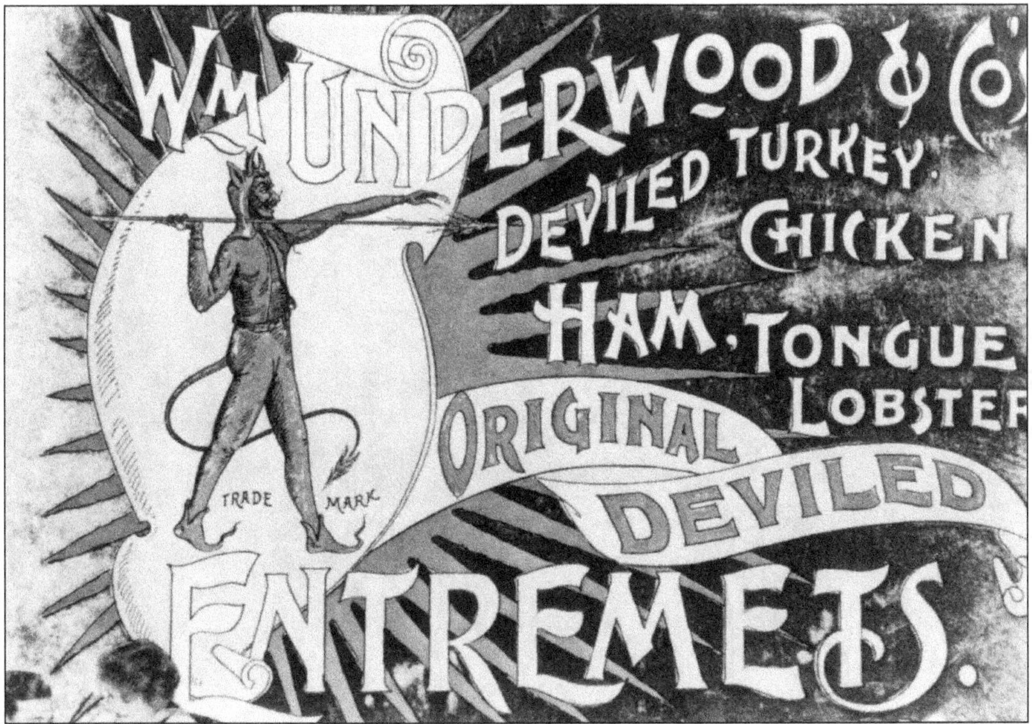

The Underwood Company, established in 1825 as a condiment manufacturer, began business preserving foods such as mustards and berries. The largest growth to the family enterprise was during the Civil War, when the company supplied the Union Army with canned goods. It was at this time that deviled ham was added to the list. Again, during the Spanish American War, the U.S. government supplied troops with Underwood products. The Underwoods made their home in Belmont at their estate on Common Street.

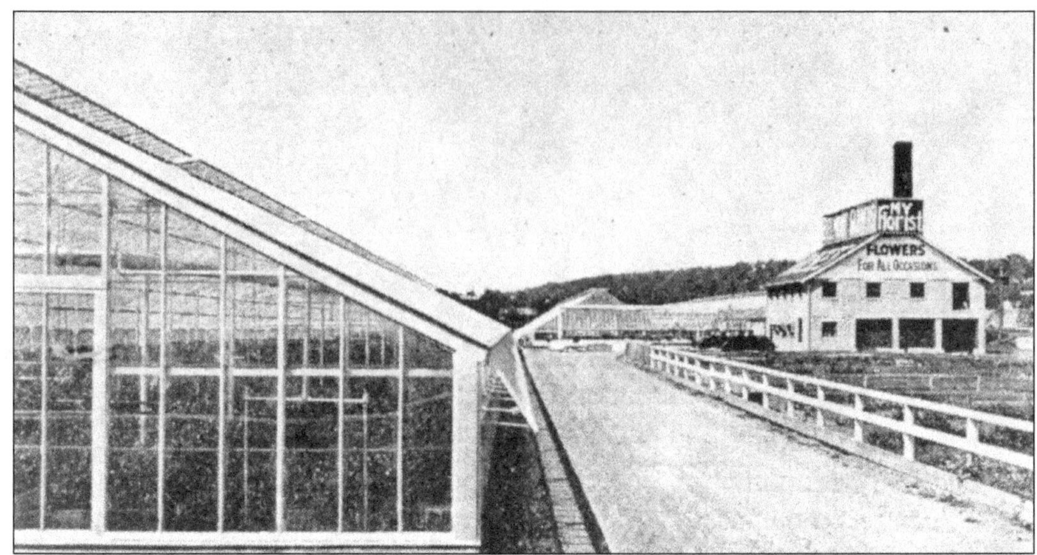

Belmont Gardens was founded by Walter E. Lenk in 1921 in greenhouses along Brighton Street. Lenk succeeded in developing an exceptionally large and hardy breed of gardenias, for which he applied and received one of the first patents issued for plants. The Belmont gardenia was shipped worldwide and, during peak seasons, the Lenks supplied 8,000 of the beautiful flowers per day. In 1954, the business was sold for residential development.

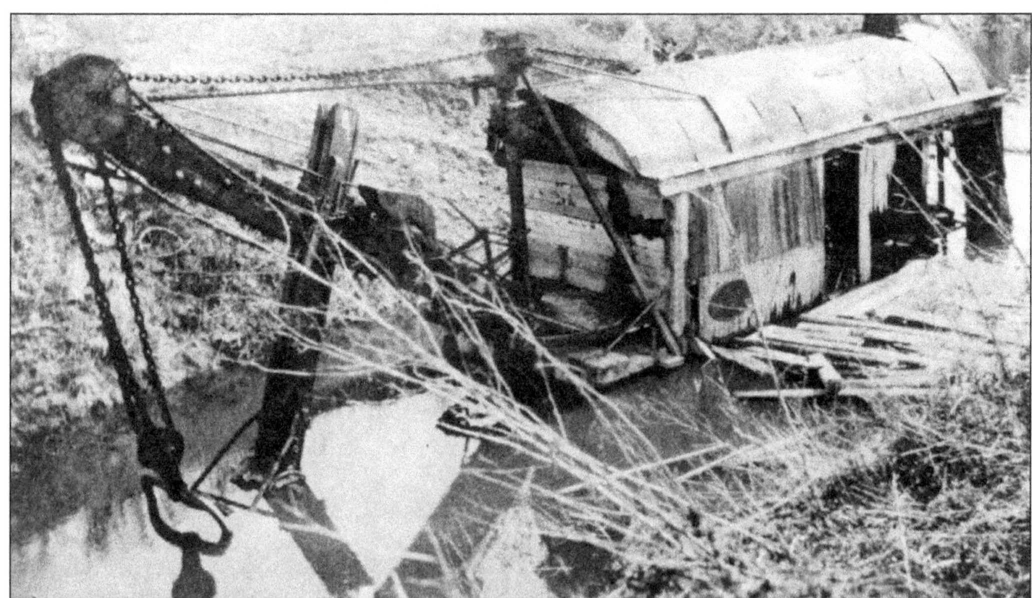

In 1888, the Parry brothers bought 21 acres of land on Concord Avenue and Underwood Street for their brick manufacturing business. A 1900 merger with the New England Brick Company increased production to 300,000 bricks a week at the Belmont yard. The clay was considered the very best in this part of New England. When the supply ran out in 1926, the yard was abandoned, leaving behind this Marion steam shovel.

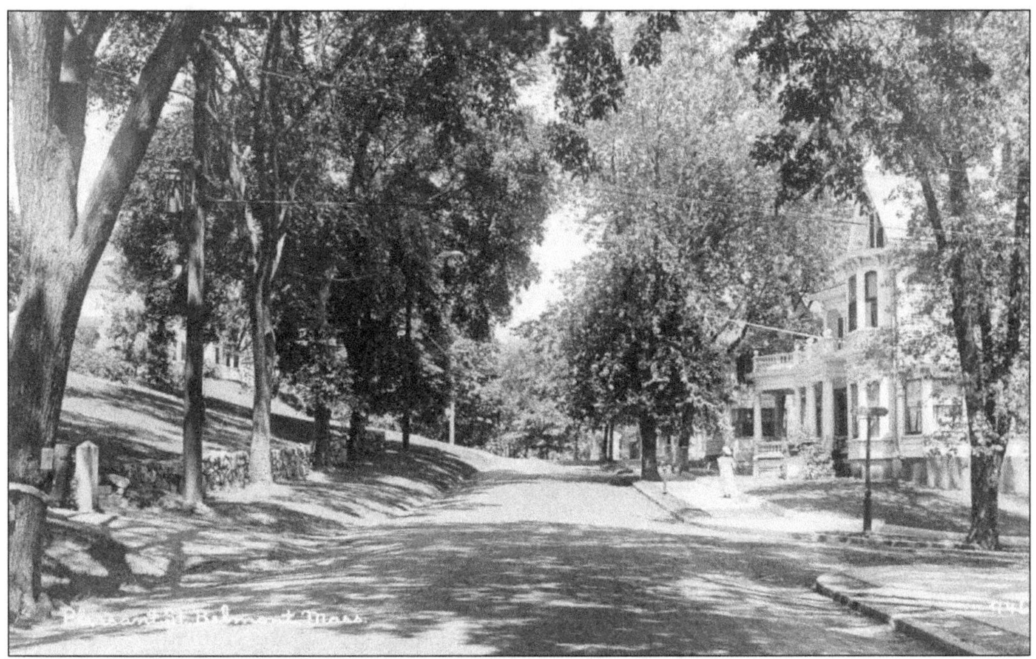

This picturesque view of Pleasant Street reminds us of the scenic beauty that makes Belmont a desirable bedroom community. Large tracks of farmland were developed to accommodate different styles of architecture of both the 18th and 19th centuries, adding to Belmont's reputation as "the Town of Homes." Pleasant Street, earlier known as Kings Way, remains a well-traveled route between Waltham and West Cambridge (Arlington).

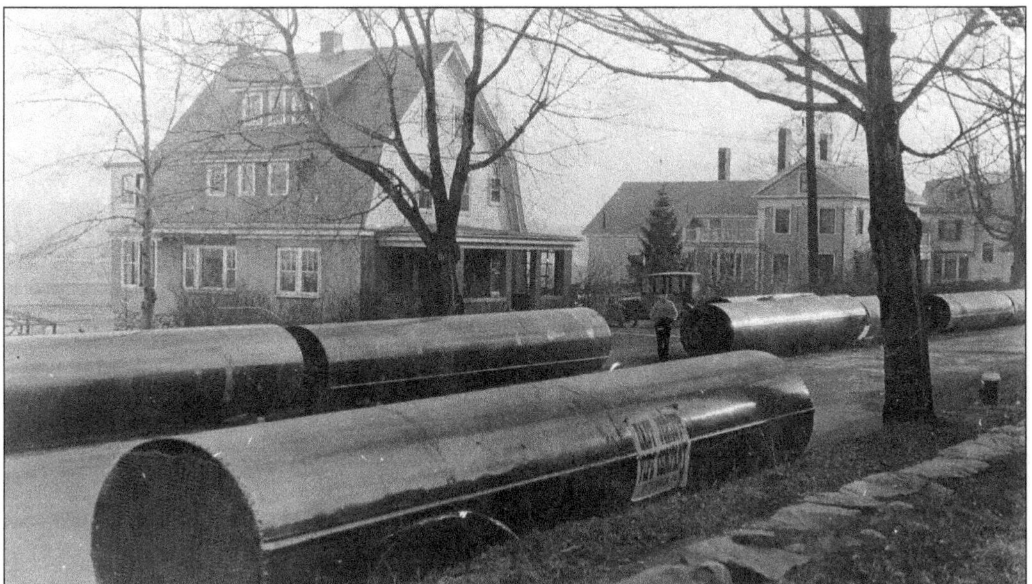

In 1887, the Belmont town meeting voted "to construct a system of water works" and, by 1889, approximately 9.5 miles of pipes were laid. At first, town water was supplied by the private enterprise Watertown Water Supply Company; since 1898, Belmont has received all of its supply from the Metropolitan District Commission. This photograph, taken in 1925, shows the laying of large water pipes in front of 480 Pleasant Street.

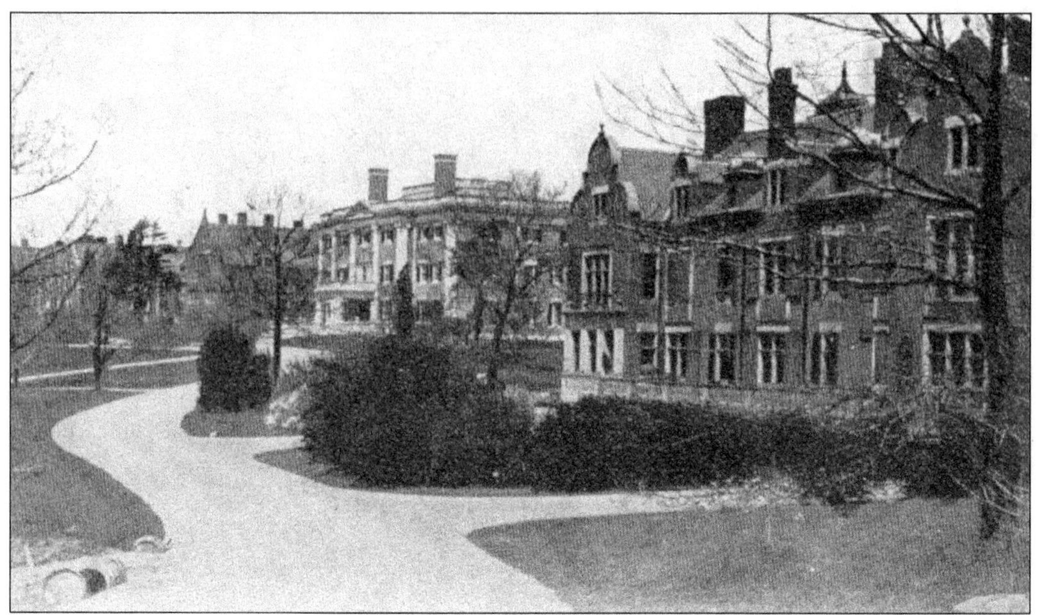

McLean Hospital history began in 1811, when the state legislature granted a charter to Massachusetts General Hospital. The first asylum opened in Charlestown in 1816. It was not until 1875 that the hospital purchased 114 acres from the Waverley Land Company and another 126 acres from private landowners, making it the largest real estate holder in Belmont. Landscaping of the 240-acre grounds was based on a design by Frederick Law Olmstead. (Courtesy of John Garrity.)

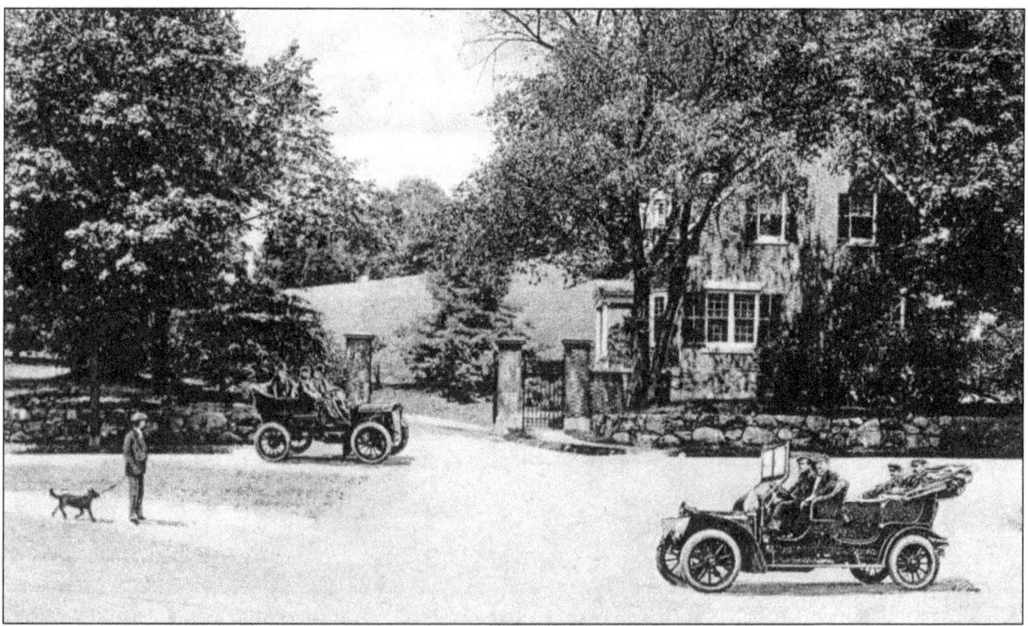

In 1882, McLean Hospital opened the first school of nursing to be organized in a psychiatric hospital and later became the first mental institution to introduce women nurses in male wards. The daily operations of the hospital were accomplished on site, and the facility was self-supporting in food, water, heat, and electricity until World War II. (Courtesy of John Garrity.)

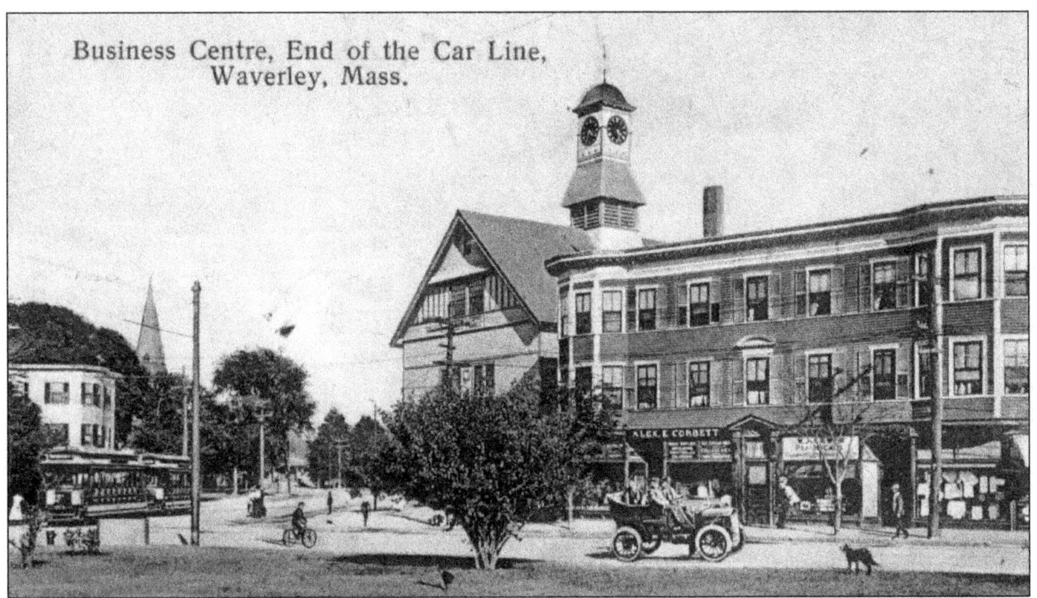

Waverley was laid out in the mid-1850s by the Waverley Company of Watertown, after the Fitchburg Railroad extended its tracks in 1843, making the agricultural community accessible. Waverley Hall, built in 1882 on the corner of Trapelo Road and Church Street, was the center of activities for the village. The building housed Hose Company No. 1, the first A & P, and the first movie theatre. It was torn down in 1922.

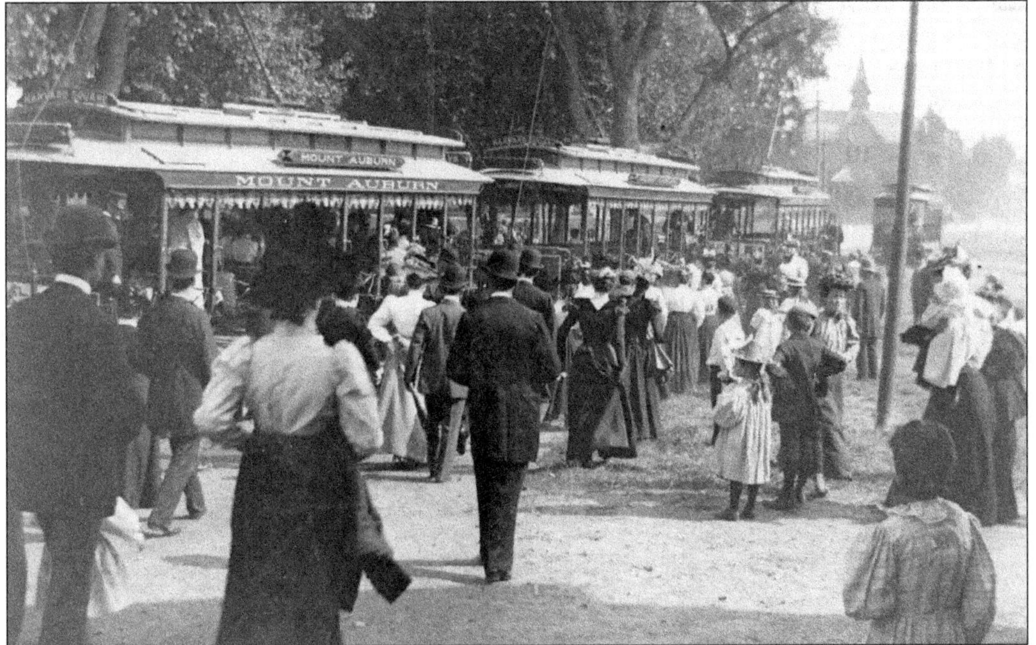

A crowd gathers for the inaugural trip on the new electric railway from Waverley Square to Mount Auburn on October 1, 1898. The *Belmont Bulletin* reported, "Waverley has taken an immense stride in importance and is now heard of as far east as Boston and none knows how far her fame may reach in the other points of the compass." The tracks were used until 1958, when the MTA converted to trackless trolleys.

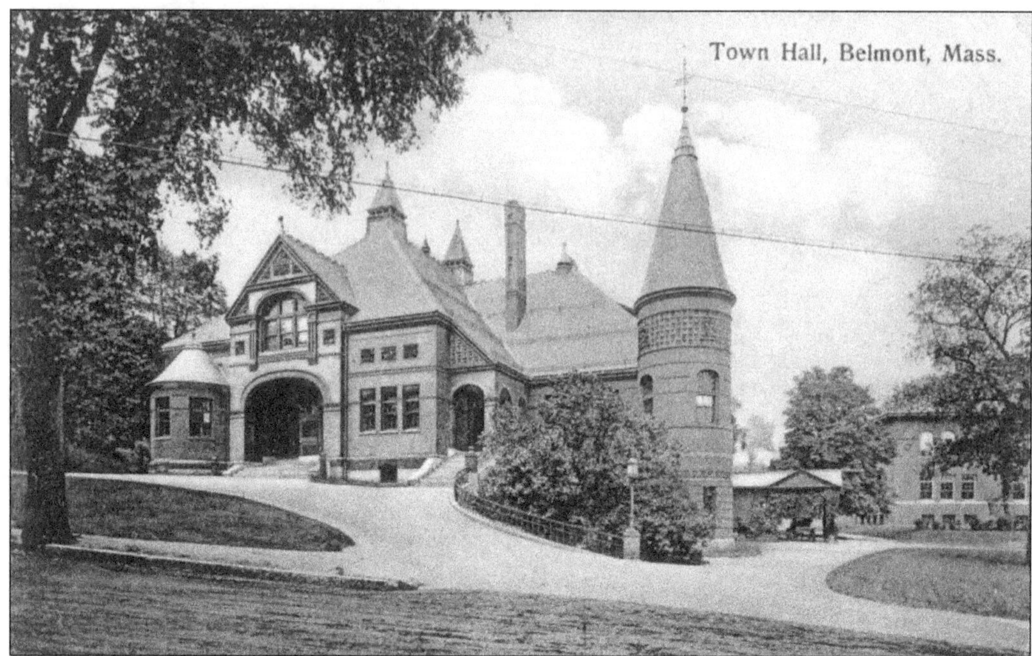

In 1881, the town hall was erected near the site of the former Wellington homestead and tavern. Hartwell and Richardson were the architects for the Queen Anne-style building, which contained an auditorium, rooms for the selectman and school committee members, a library, the fire department's chemical engine and hose carriage, and later two jail cells. The dedication was held on June 22, 1882, with an opening prayer, congratulatory speeches, and an evening concert.

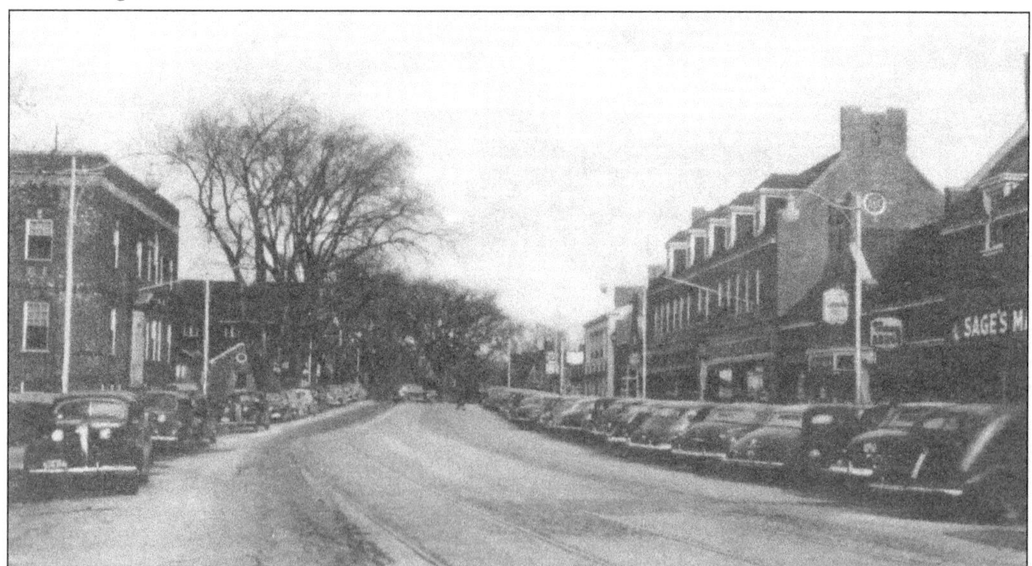

This familiar view of Leonard Street is captured on this 1930s postcard showing Belmont's business center. Note the angled parking of cars along the street and some of the merchants' bygone signs, both popular at the time. The lands, now known as Belmont Center, were previously part of the Wellington family's large farm, running from Pleasant Street to Brighton Street. The property was sold for development in 1925.

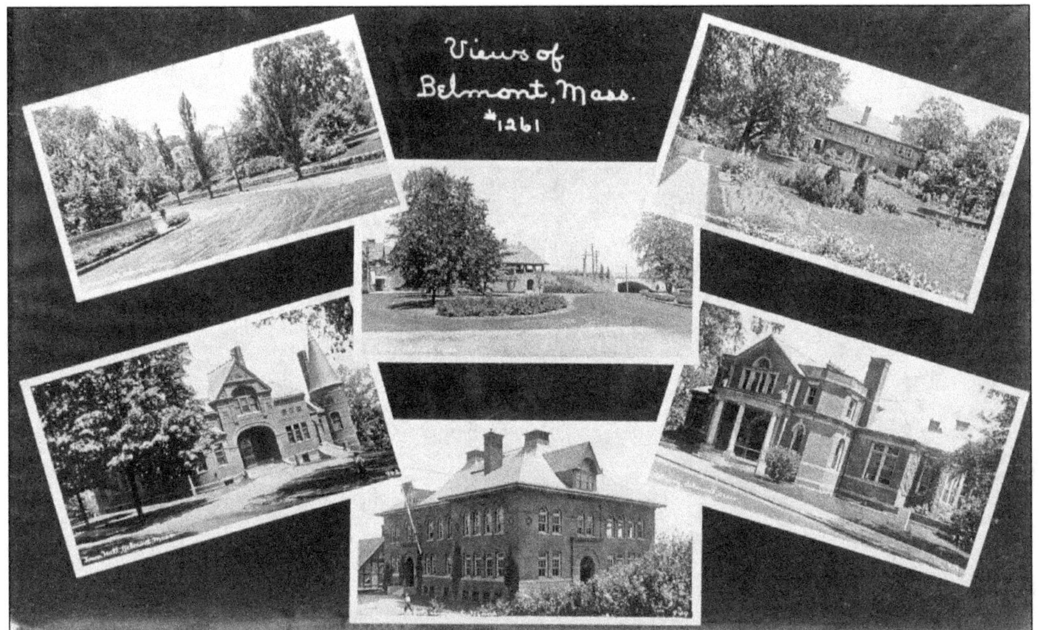

Scenes from around town adorn this c. 1910 postcard and depict the theme of this chapter. Pictured here are views of Common Street, the town hall, the Fitchburg Railroad Station, the Homer School, the Loring Underwood Estate, and the Underwood Library. (Courtesy of John Garrity.)

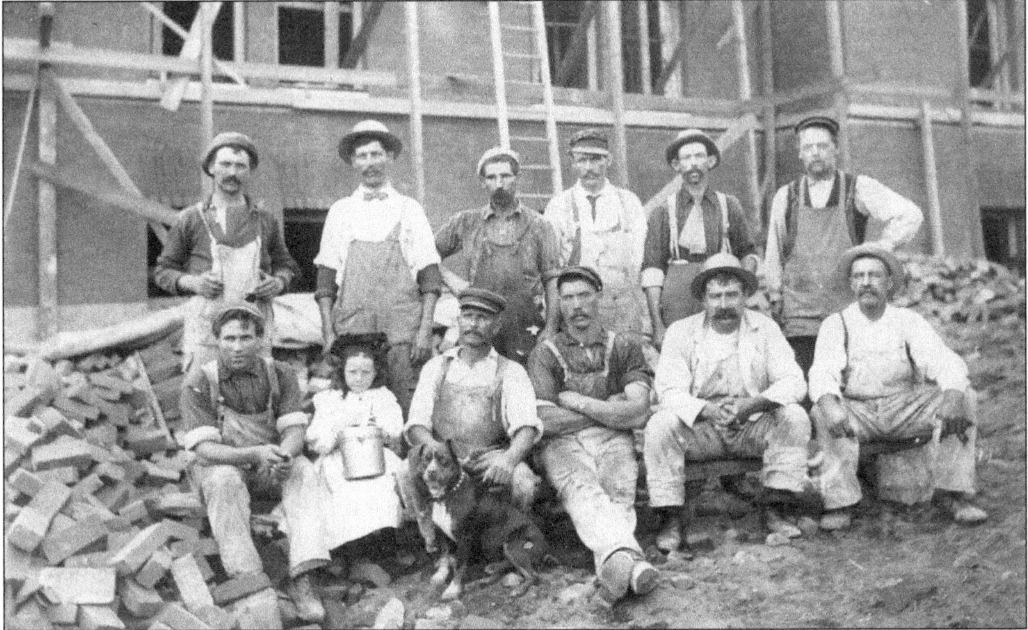

Tired workmen pose on a water break provided by little Susan Calabro during construction of the new high school in 1897. The brick building replaced the original two-story wooden structure on School Street and housed 84 students in grades six through nine. Five seniors were awarded diplomas, becoming the first graduating class in 1899, when enrollment included grades five through 13. The school was renamed the Homer School in 1917.

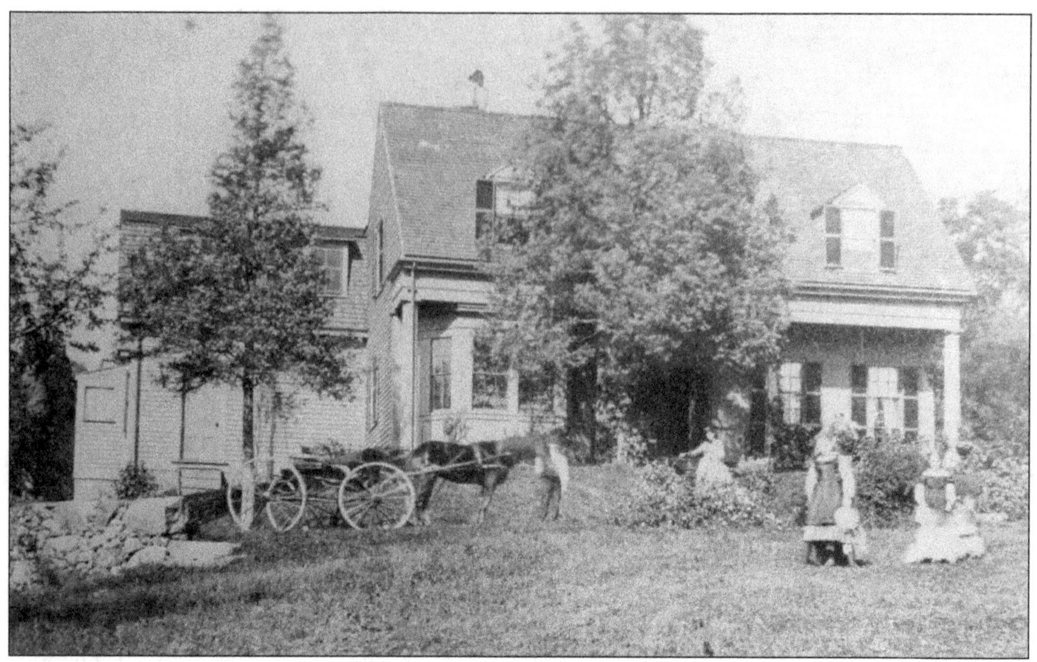

An 1875 map of Belmont shows the house on Mill Street that was owned by R.W. Handyside and his wife, Jeannie Kendall. Built in the 1830s, the house and property changed hands several times. It was finally sold in1893 by William Howard, who cut ice from the two millponds for his Howard Ice Company, as part of the land acquisition for Beaver Brook Reservation.

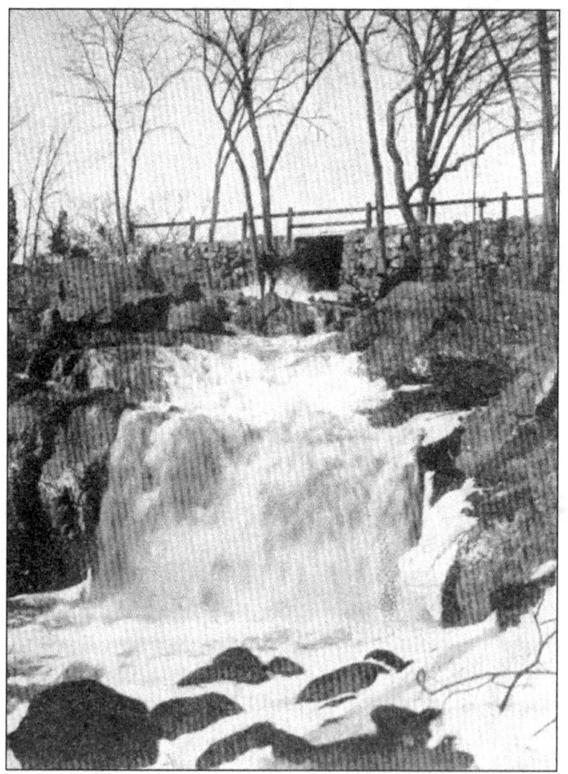

Beaver Brook was named in 1631 when Gov. John Winthrop and his men went up the Charles River about 8 miles above Watertown. They named the first brook on the north side Beaver Brook because of the beaver dams. The waterpower generated by the falls was harnessed to run numerous businesses, including a gristmill and sawmill. The brook is part of the Metropolitan Park System formed in 1893.

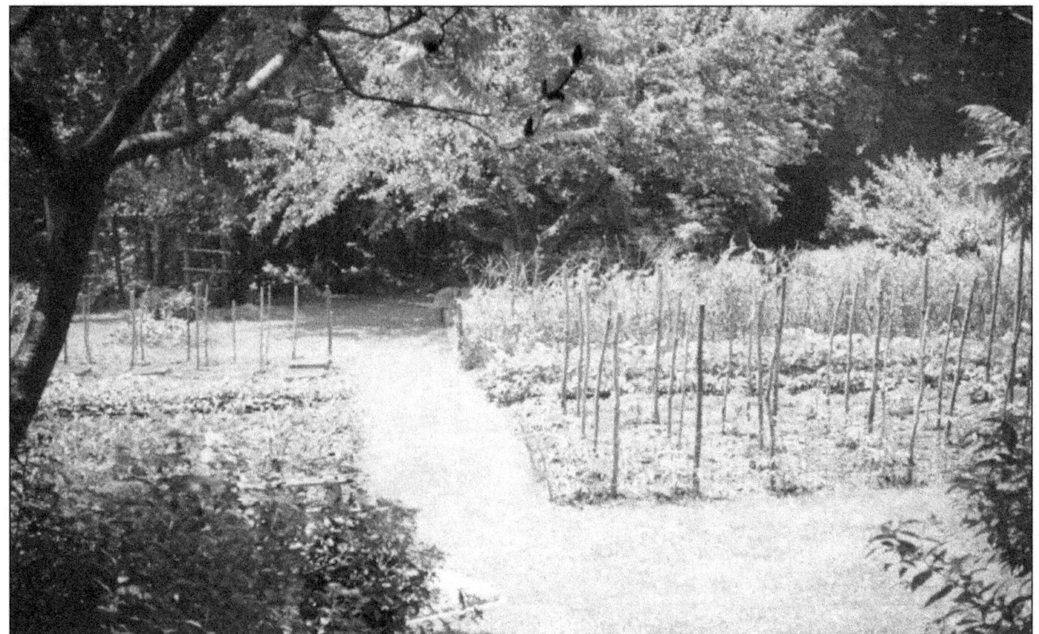

This 1943 photograph shows one of the plots of land where local residents maintained small gardens to raise vegetables. These community gardens were especially common during the war years and supplied fresh vegetables, which were in great demand. Several locations around town, such as this area off Fletcher Road, were familiar sites.

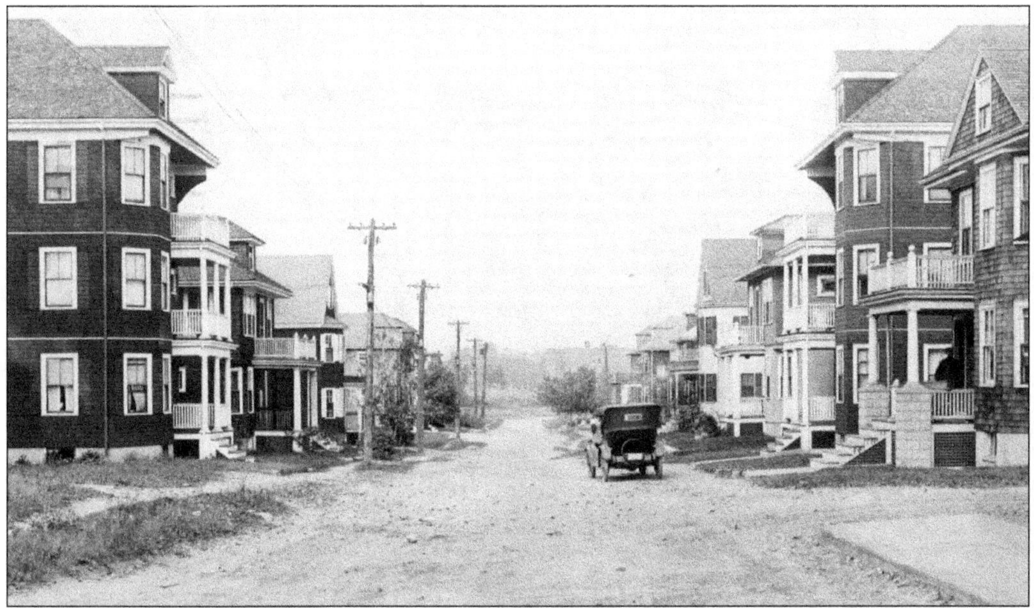

The Tenement House Act of 1912 was successful in discouraging the building of three-family houses, such as these on Davis Road, by requiring fireproofing in the construction, which was cost prohibitive. Belmont was the first town in Massachusetts to adopt the act and, in 1922, formed a town planning board "to exercise foresight in furthering the responsible development of Belmont." More comprehensive zoning regulations were added in 1925. (Courtesy of John Garrity.)

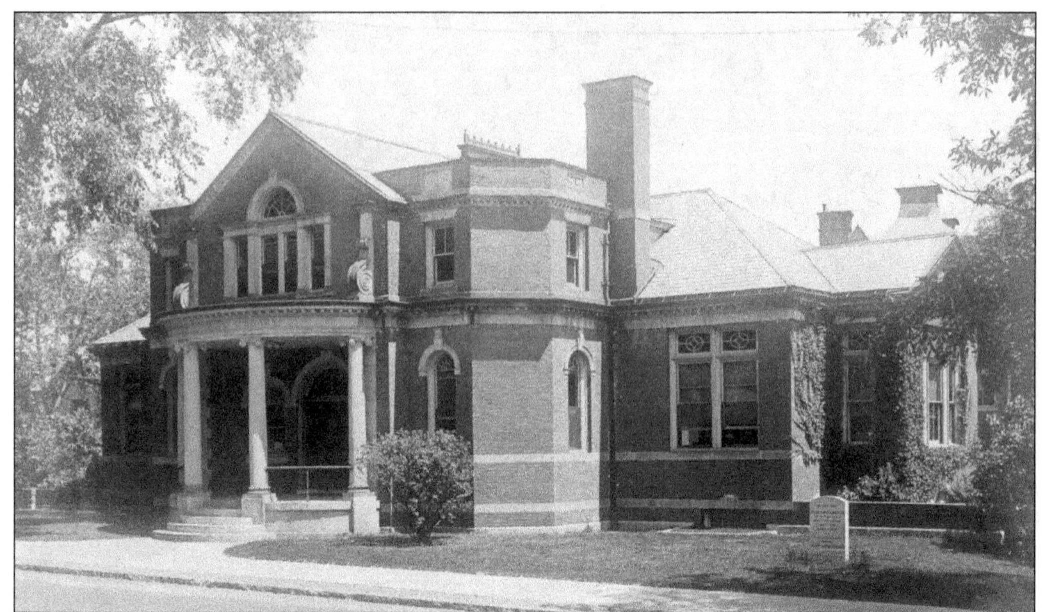

The Underwood Library was given as a gift to the town of Belmont by Henry O. Underwood in memory of his parents William and Esther Crafts Underwood. It was constructed on the site of early settler Roger Wellington's homestead, which dates from 1636. Later, Jeduthan Wellington, a descendant of Roger Wellington, built a home on the site and lived there with his large family until 1897.

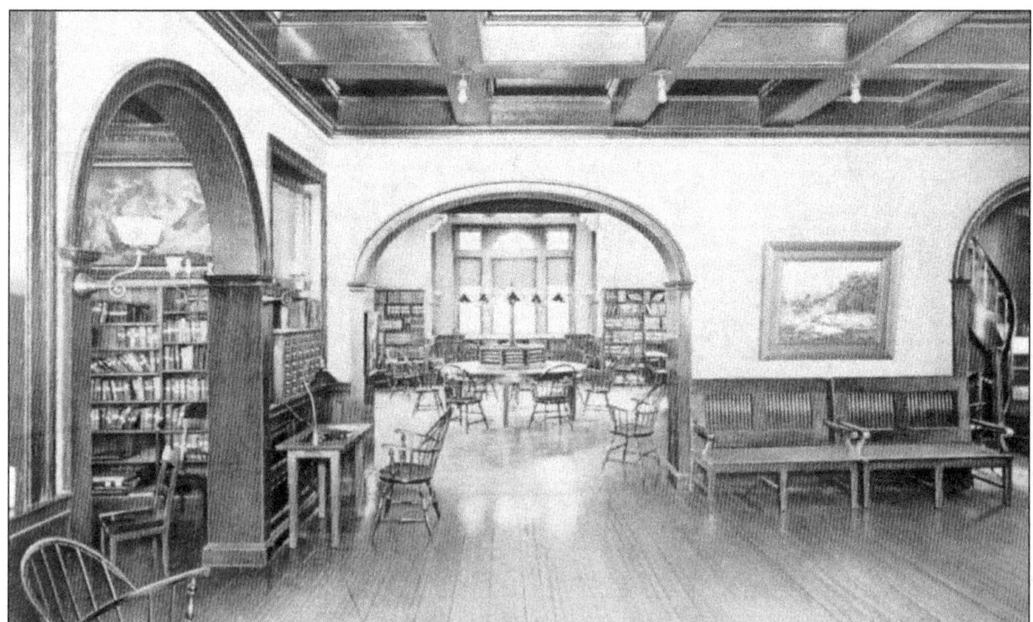

The library building of Colonial-style brick architecture was the very latest in design, with a capacity to house 50,000 volumes. The basement contained a room for bicycles and a room for smoking, which could be monitored by the librarian through a series of mirrors. In 1902, the library moved to this new location from the room in the town hall that it had occupied since 1882.

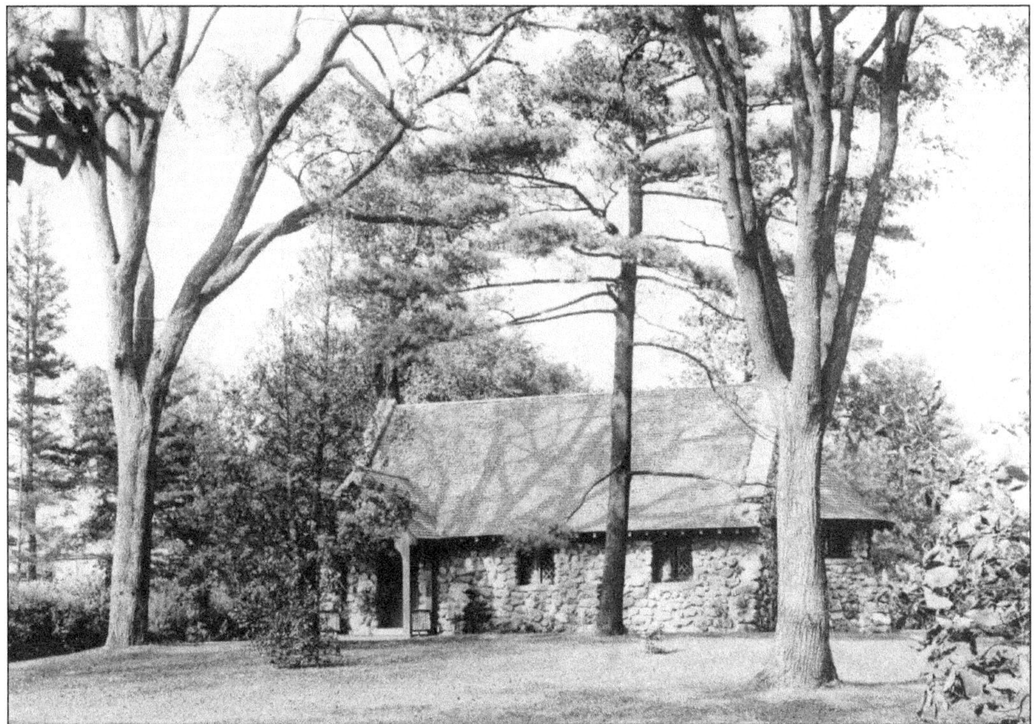

The Belmont School for Boys was begun by Benjamin Harding, the third owner of the Cushing Mansion, in conformity to the principles of the Episcopal Church. Funds for a chapel on the grounds were raised and, in 1892, construction began with the laying of the cornerstone. Payson Park Congregation and Belmont Methodist Churches first met and were organized there in 1913 and 1921, respectively.

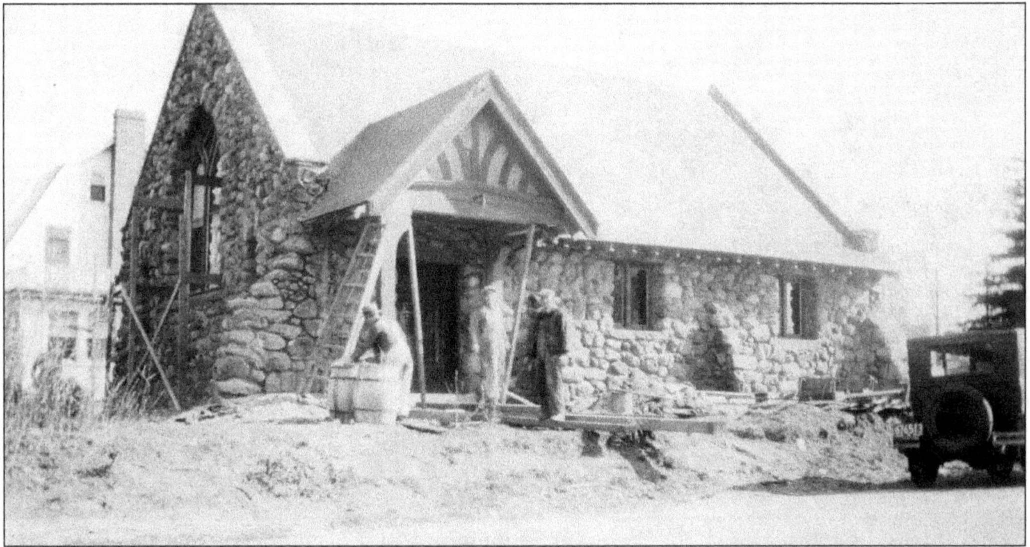

In 1930, the town meeting voted to accept the chapel and land as a memorial to Everett C. Benton, the Cushing Mansion's fourth and final owner, for use as a branch public library. The workmen pictured are renovating the building's exterior for its proposed use. The library was officially opened to the public on June 10, 1930.

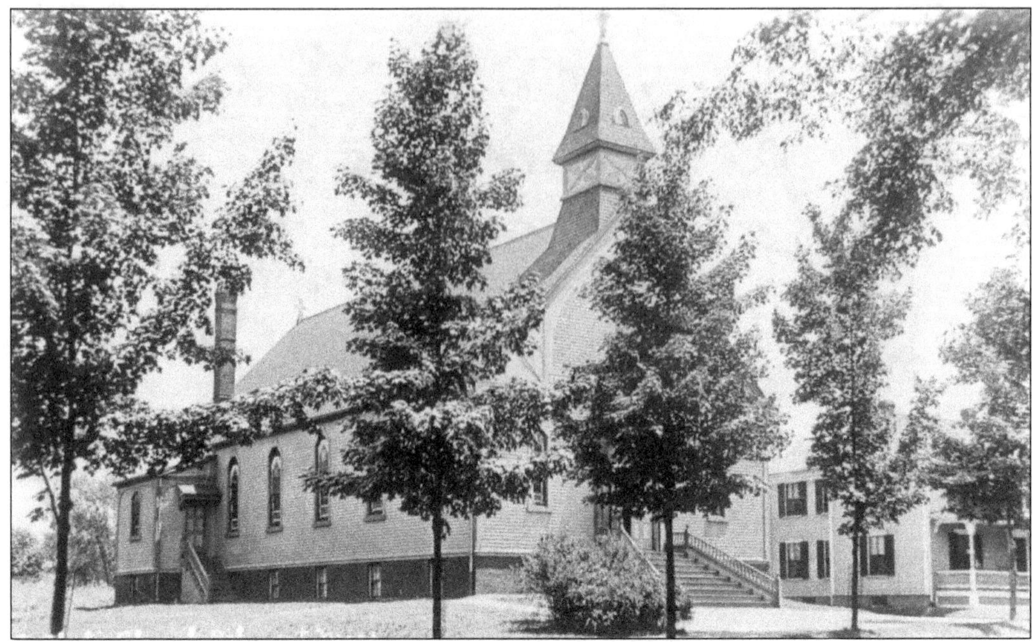

St. Joseph's was completed in 1888 when, in one of the first gestures of ecumenism, families of other faiths donated funds toward the building project. The building was used until 1912, when the present brick replacement was constructed on the site. The wooden church was moved around the corner to School Street and served as a parish house. The Belmont parish was originally a mission of St. Agnes of Arlington.

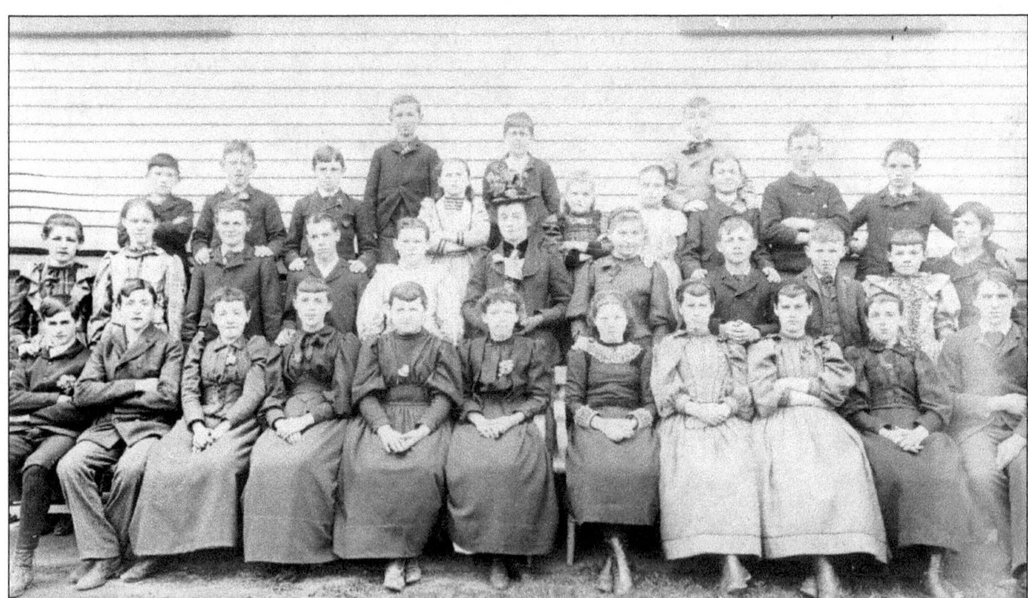

In 1900, St. Joseph's served the Belmont community of 62 families. Between 1915 and 1934, the Catholic population grew significantly and the parish was divided three times. New locations were established at St. Luke's in Waverley, Our Lady of Mercy in Payson Park, and St. Jerome's on the Belmont-Arlington line. This photograph shows the Sunday school class, *c.* 1888.

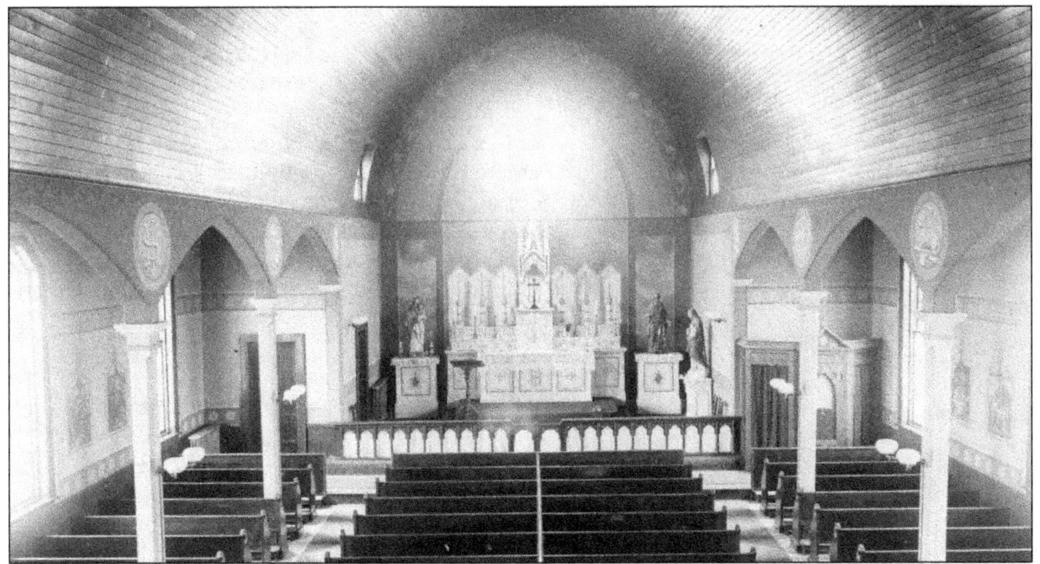

This photograph shows the beautiful interior and skilled craftsmanship of the wood ceiling in the sanctuary of St. Joseph's Church. The congregation worshiped in Arlington prior to 1887 and held services for a short time in the Belmont Town Hall, before building a permanent home off Common Street. It was in the town hall that the first choir was formed.

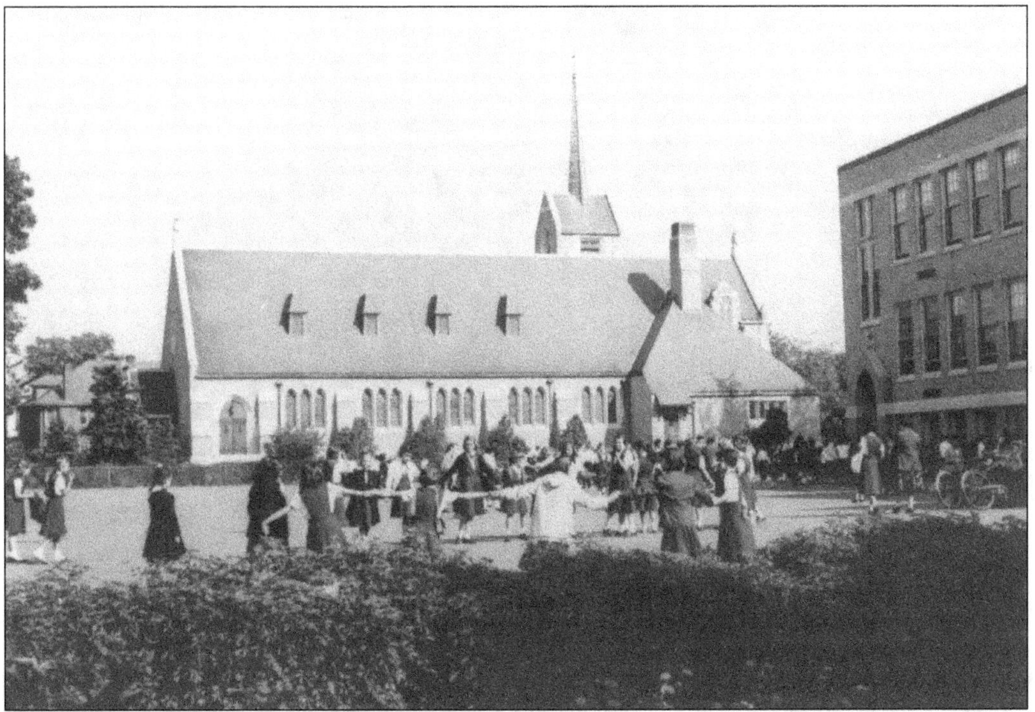

In 1926, the cornerstone was laid for the new St. Luke's Church, and the congregation celebrated the first mass in the lower level. The original wooden building, constructed in 1919 to serve the needs of Waverley, was converted and used as a social hall until it was torn down in 1929. In 1937, the Roman Catholic Archdiocese of Boston purchased additional land and construction began on the first parochial school in Belmont.

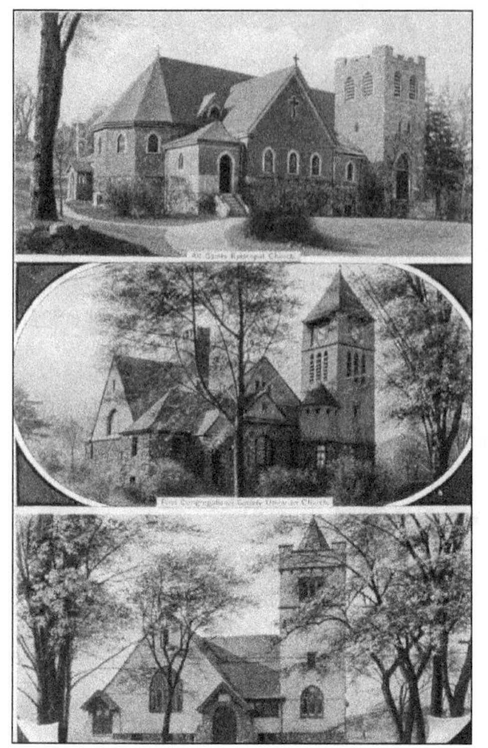

All Saints' Church was founded in 1886. The cornerstone was laid in 1896 and, in 1941, a parish hall added. First Church Unitarian was founded in 1856 on the opposite side of Concord Avenue. The new church was erected in 1889, using fieldstones gathered by congregants. Plymouth Congregational Church was founded in 1899. Services were held in the high school and at Lockhart Memorial Church on Common Street and, since 1946, on Pleasant Street.

This historical photograph commemorates the laying of the cornerstone of the Waverley Unitarian Church by the Grand Lodge of Masons on October 3, 1896. The Unitarian Society was organized in 1882 and held meetings in Waverley Hall. The church at 51 Lexington Street remains the only building in Belmont dedicated in this way. The congregation practiced a noncreedal religion until 1948, when declining membership created a merger with the First Church in Belmont on Concord Avenue.

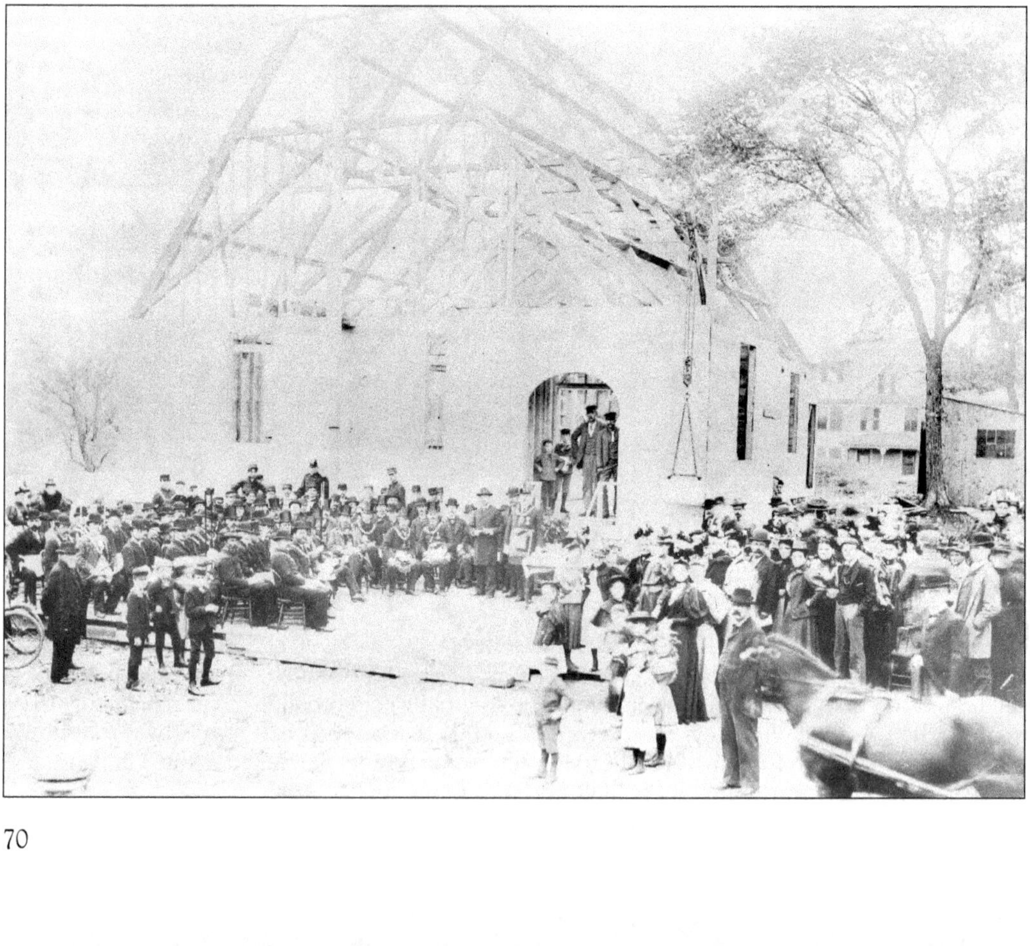

Five

Service to Town and Country

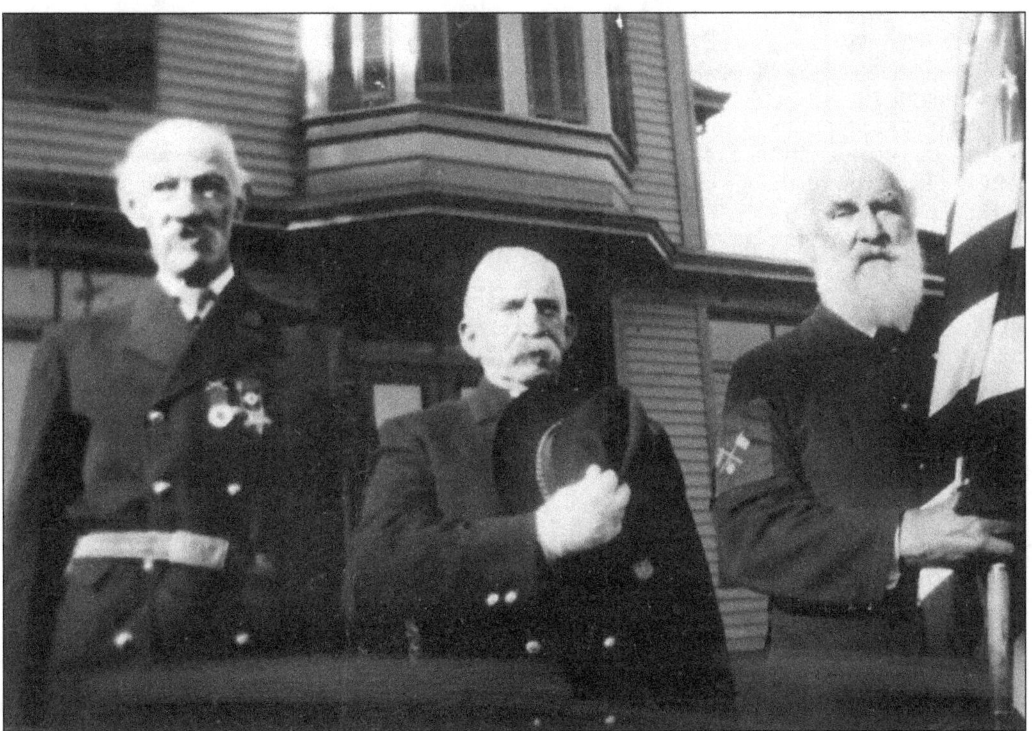

The last three survivors of the Civil War were, from left to right, Jonathan Frost, Andrew McGinnis, and David Chenery. This photograph of the three men was taken in the 1920s. Andrew McGinnis, who was 15 years old when he enlisted, outlived his comrades and died in October 1931. The three were all members of the Francis Gould Post of the Grand Army of the Republic.

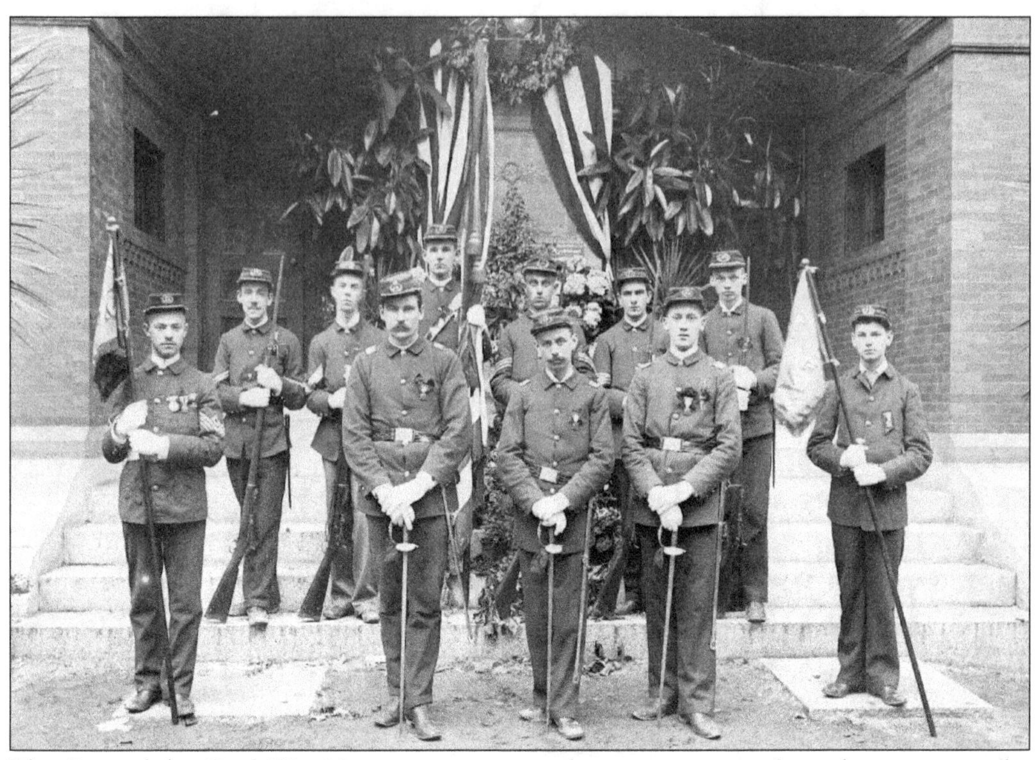

The Sons of the Civil War Veterans was an auxiliary organization formed to carry on the memories and programs of the fathers. These members are shown in front of Belmont's Civil War Plaque at the entrance of the town hall *c.* 1890. Benjamin Harris, son of Henry S. Harris, is in the front row at the far left. The original plaque was a memorial to the six men who died in the Civil War.

IN MEMORY
OF THE MEN OF BELMONT
WHO DIED TO SAVE THE UNION
1861 - 1865

LIEUT. JOHN LOCKE
Co. F. 40TH N.Y. VOLS.

ALBERT C. FROST
Co. C. 15TH REGT. MASS. VOLS.

LIEUT. JAS. McGINNIS
Co. H. 48TH REGT. MASS. VOLS

CHARLES V. MARSH
Co. C.15TH REGT. MASS. VOLS.

WILLIAM H. BENSON
Co. H. 2ND REGT. U.S.S.S.

LEWIS H. MARSH
2ND BATY MASS V. ART.

The Civil War Memorial Plaque commemorates Lt. John Locke, who died of dysentery in 1862; Lt. James McGinnis, who died of wounds in 1863; Cpl. William H. Benson, who died of wounds at Antietam, Maryland, in 1862; Pvt. Albert Frost, who died of wounds at Gettysburg, Pennsylvania, in 1863; Charles V. Marsh, who was wounded at Spottslyvania, taken prisoner, and died in Andersonville Prison, Georgia, in 1864–1865; and Pvt. Lewis H. Marsh, who died of smallpox in New Orleans, Louisiana, in 1864.

The Belmont Police Department is pictured c. 1889. Shown from left to right are John Argy, David McCabe, Frank Chant, and Jerry Ryan. Chant served as chief from 1885 to 1890. Ryan served as chief from 1890 until he died in 1917. Argy served as chief from 1917 to 1928. McCabe went on to serve as a selectman.

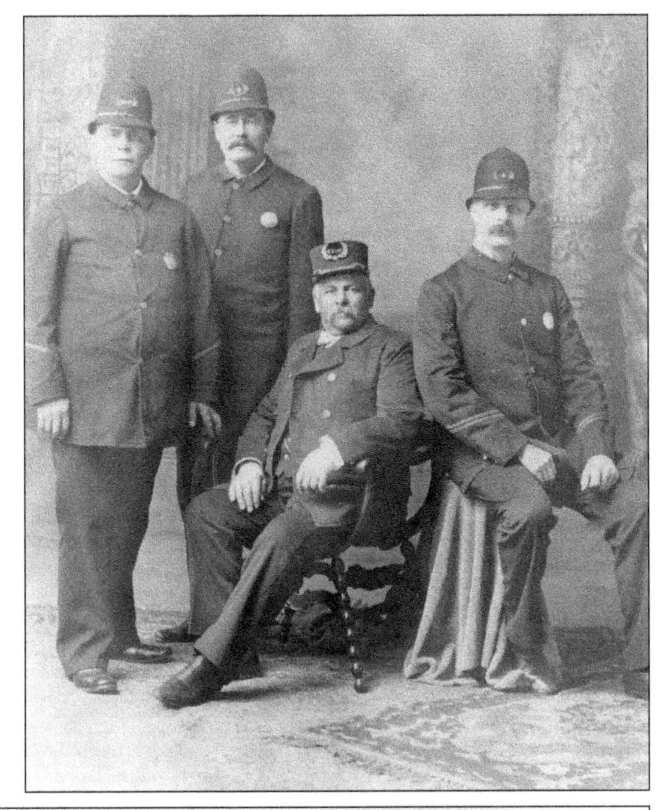

The Waverley Bucket Boys stand alongside Cushing No. 4. The fraternal group marched with this antique fire engine in the 1890 Bunker Hill Day parade in Charlestown. Everett C. Benton, on the left, owned and named the engine, which is believed to have served Watertown from 1791 to 1832. The antique engine is currently in the care of the Belmont Historical Society and the Belmont Fire Department.

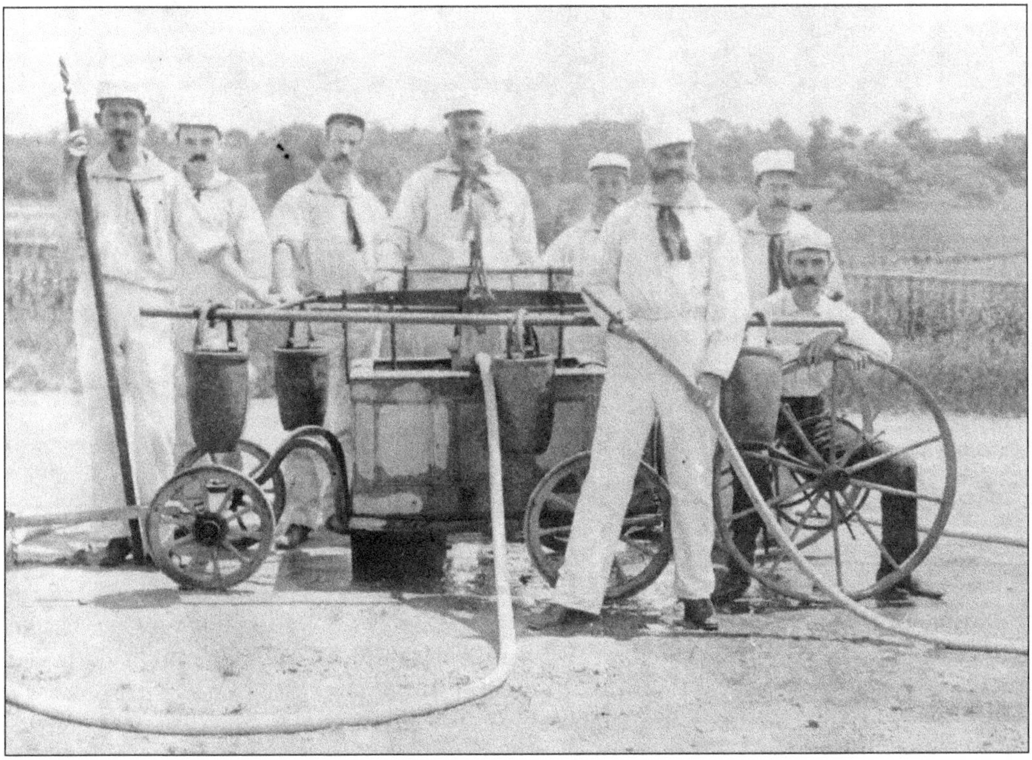

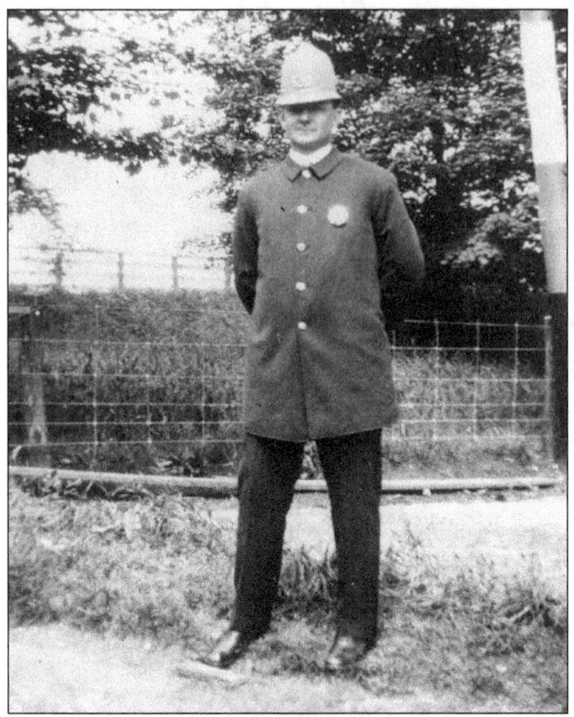

Wearing his Belmont police sergeant's uniform, Patrick J. Keenan poses for this 1906 photograph. At age seven, he and playmate John Carney were hired by renowned American artist Winslow Homer as models for his painting *Boys in a Pasture*. In 1874, the job as a model paid 75¢ a day.

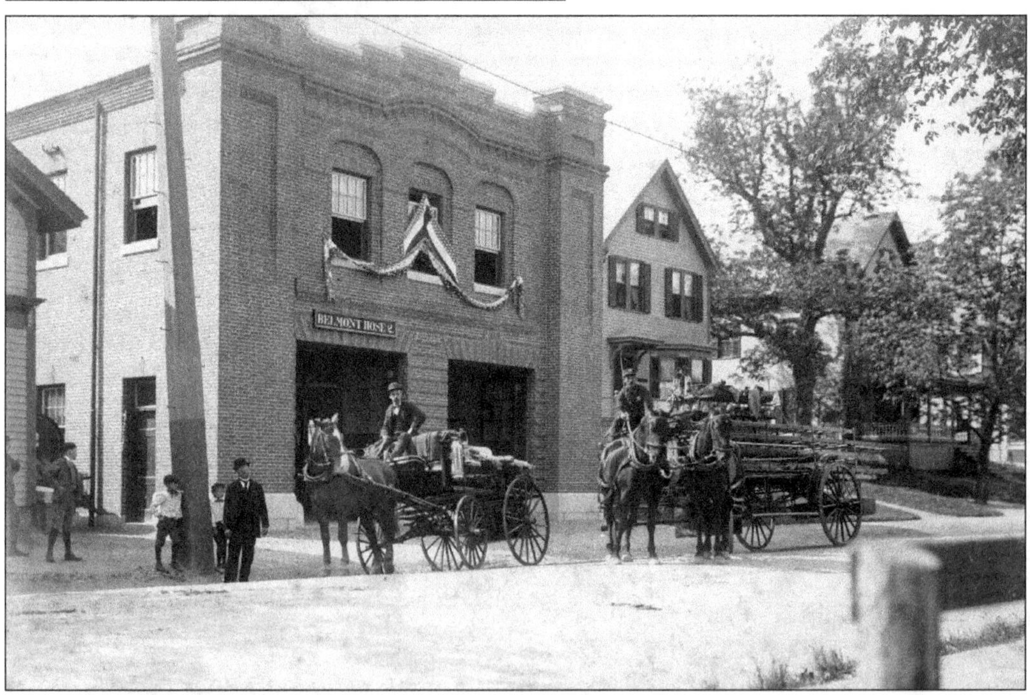

The Belmont Center Fire Station was built in late 1899 and was home to a one-horse wagon and a two-horse ladder truck, which are pictured in the early 1900s. The secondhand ladder truck cost the town $450 and the three horses cost $550. The Waverley hose wagon, (not shown) served for 24 years and never had a town-owned horse. The department borrowed a horse when needed.

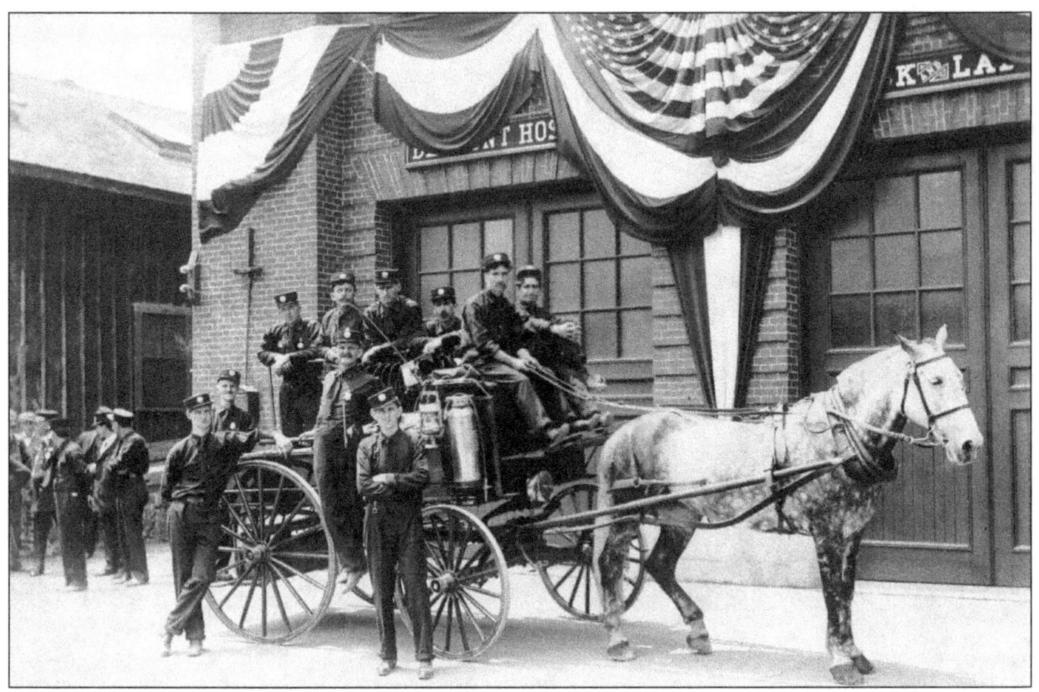

Hose Wagon No. 2 is loaded down with its volunteer company in 1909. J. McCarthy, A. Hatch, and J. Sweeney are standing; F. Parks is on rear steps; J. Lamont, T. Hughes, J. Maguire, and P. Kelly are in the wagon; Joe O'Brien is the driver, and Edward Quigley is seated next to him.

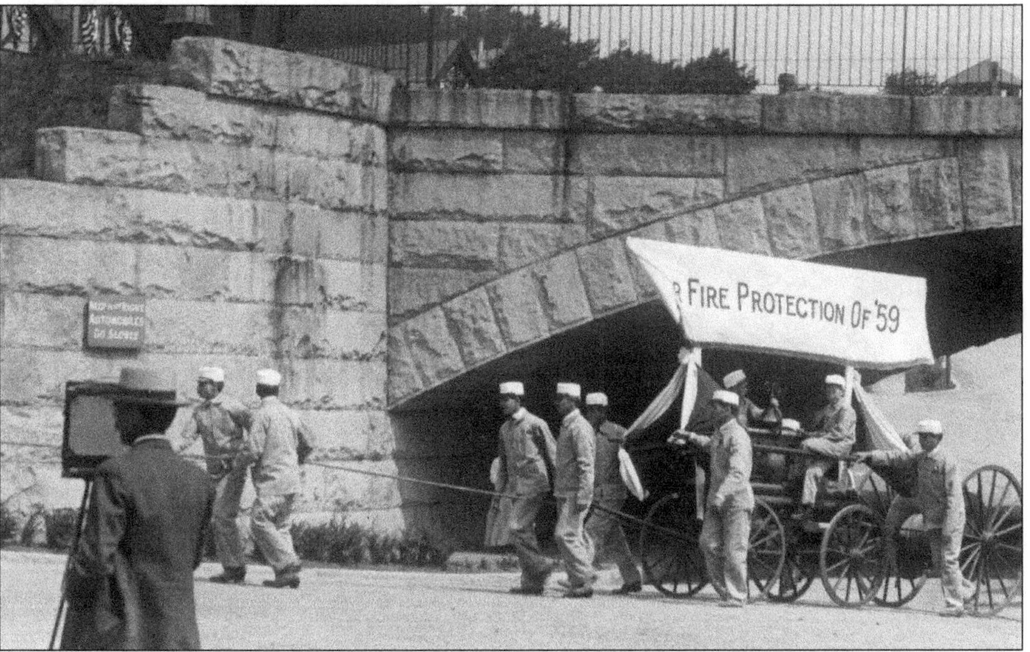

A group of firefighting enthusiasts hauled this antique hand pumper the length of the 1909 50th anniversary parade. Although the sign says "Our Fire Protection of '59," the engine was only symbolic and was never in the service of Belmont. We can only wonder who the photographer in the foreground is.

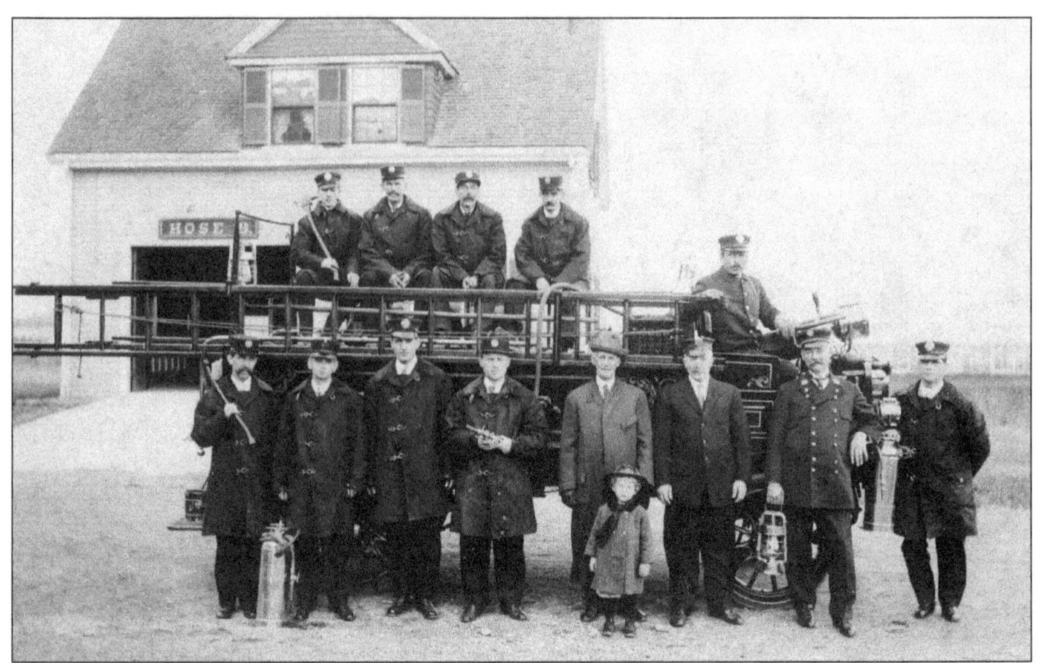

In 1908, the town voted to erect a new fire station on Fairview Avenue, improving fire protection in the Harvard Lawn area. The station housed Belmont's first piece of motorized fire equipment, which is seen in this 1910 photograph. The time of hand-drawn tubs and horse-drawn wagons had passed. The small wooden building originally held a company of six men who operated two hand reels and 700 feet of hose.

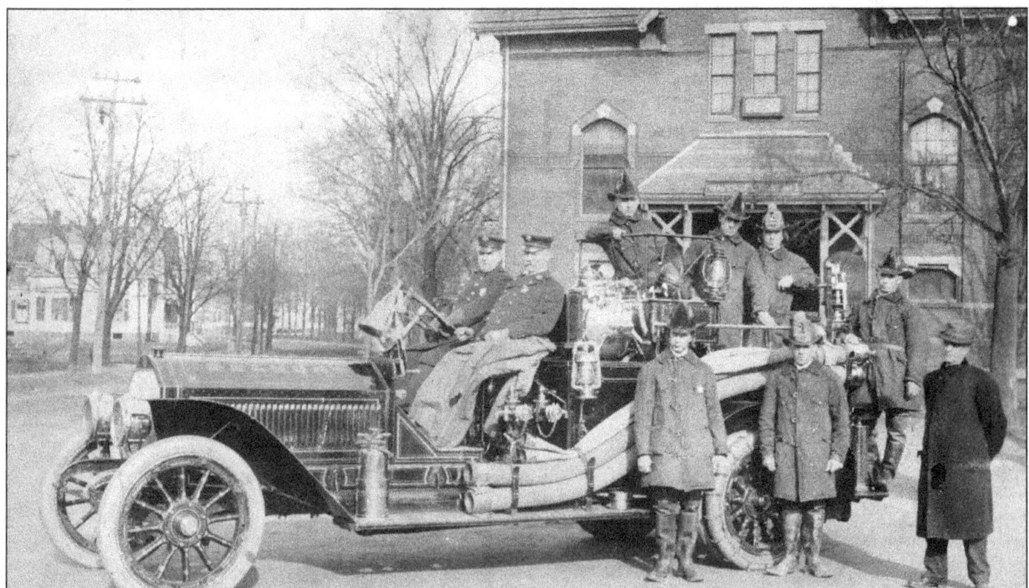

The crew poses in full gear in front of the Waverley fire station in this 1913 photograph. In the driver's seat is Chief John F. Leonard, and at the far right, dressed in a long coat, is engineer Herbert H. Russell. The arrival of the first triple-motorized fire truck was celebrated throughout town, and the local newspaper reported, "You can be sure that all the kids (and grown-ups, too) were on hand when this snappy outfit rolled into Belmont."

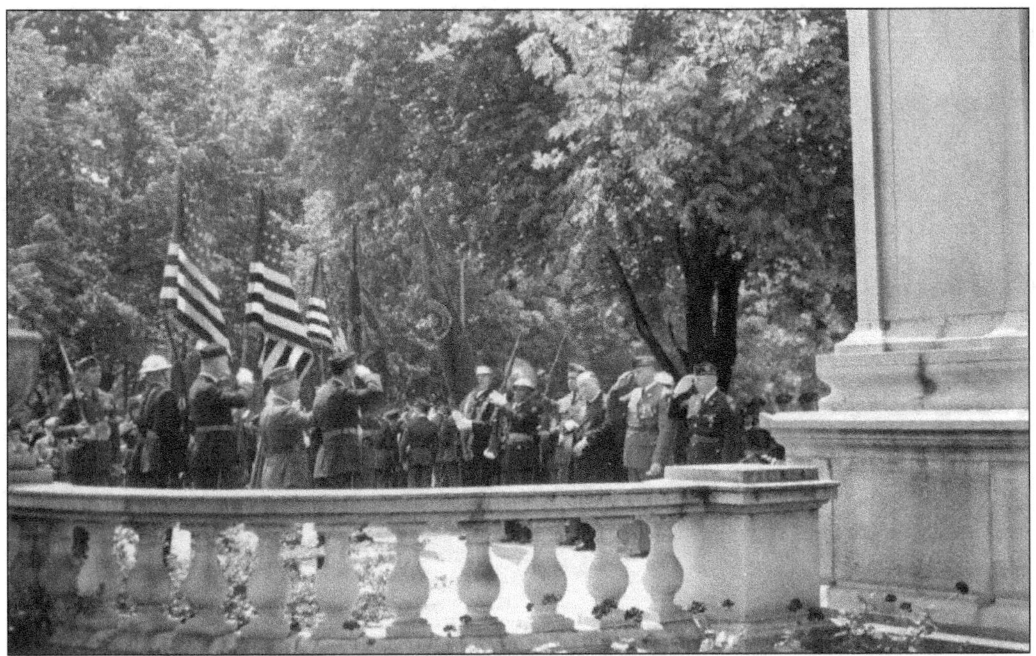

On Memorial Day in 1941, veterans of "the war to end all wars" (World War I) salute their fallen comrades in front of Belmont's World War I Memorial on the delta in front of the railroad station, now the Lions Club.

Private JOSEPH CIRINO

Lieutenant V. RALEIGH CRAIGIE

Lieutenant W. CLIFFORD FINN

Private FRED K. LINCOLN

Private DEARBORN J. McALEER

Lieutenant HUGH W. NIMMO

Corporal CARLETON M. PATRIQUIN

Mechanic WILLIAM H. SMITH

Private LEON A. TRUE

Nine men from Belmont gave their lives in World War I. In addition to the monument on the delta, nine oak trees were planted in front of Belmont High School on Orchard Street.

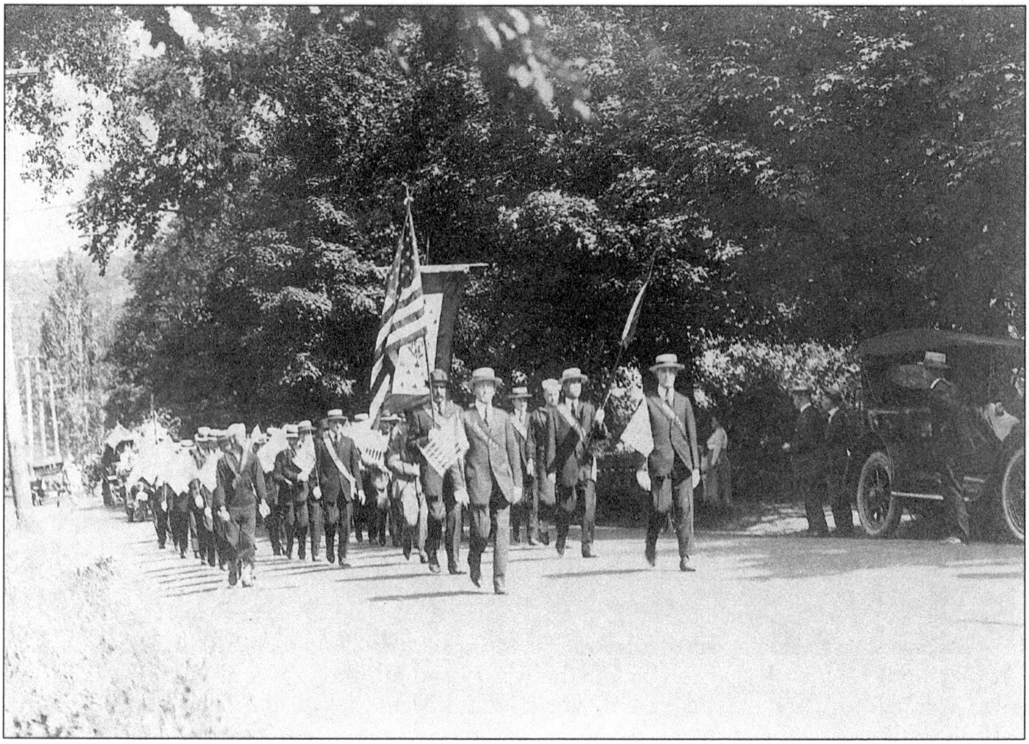

This parade was held to help raise money for Liberty Bonds during World War I. Both citizens and servicemen can be seen marching up Common Street for that worthy cause.

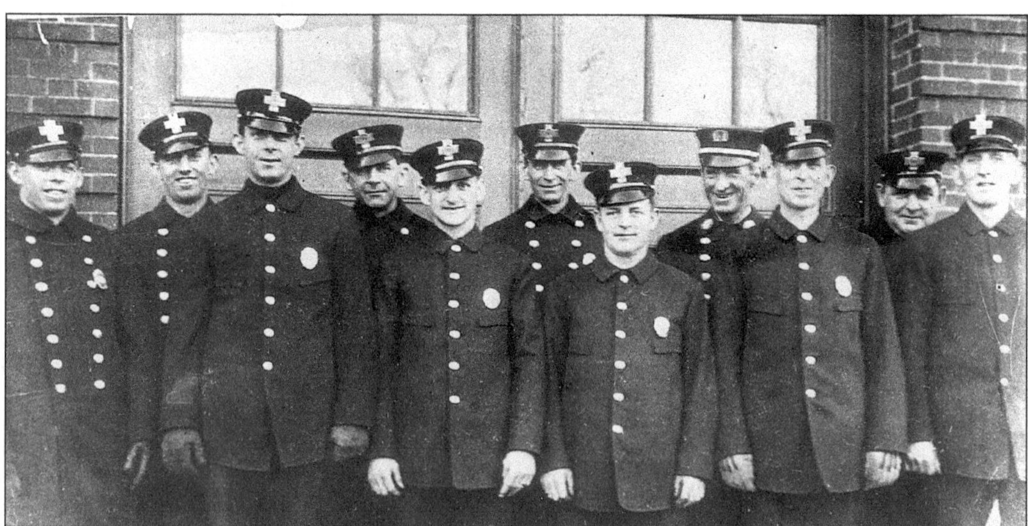

The Belmont Fire Department in 1926 was a family affair, with several sets of brothers serving the town. Pictured are, from left to right, George Brennan, Joseph Brennan, John Brennan, Walter Lynch, Alvah Hatch, Edward Lynch, Oliver Mahoney, Capt. James Maguire, Prescott Buckley, Edward Maguire, and Daniel Buckley.

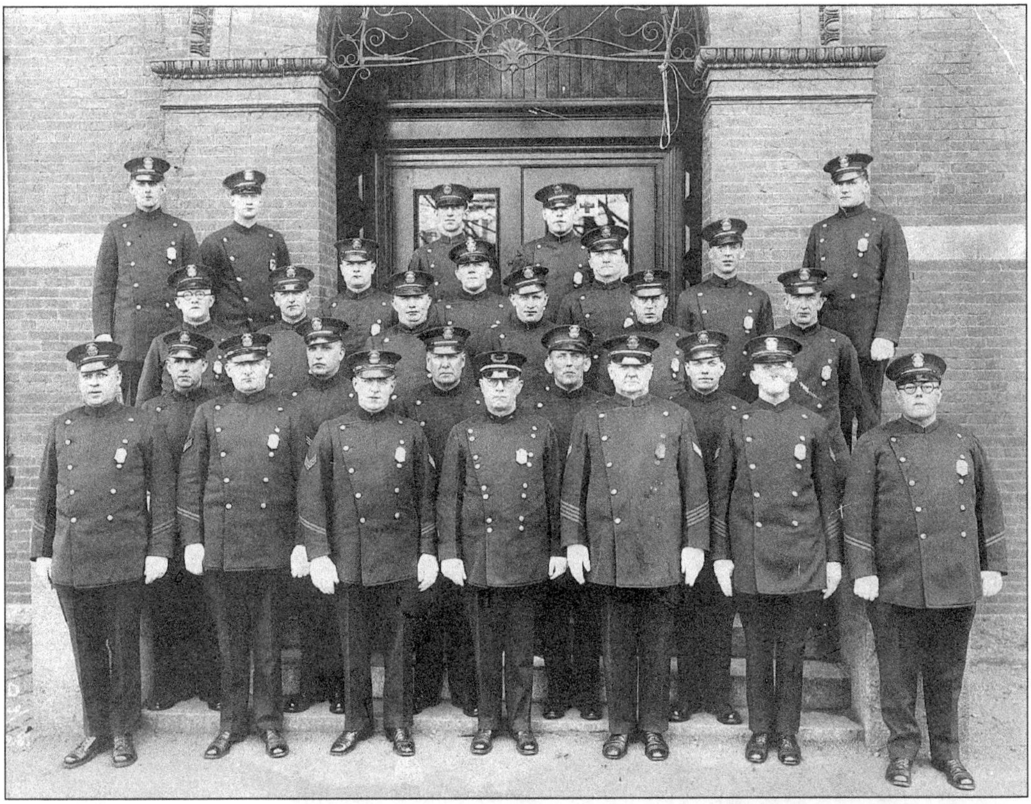

In 1929, this group from the Belmont Police Department poses on the steps in front of the Homer School. The department was quartered in the town hall until the new station opened in 1931.

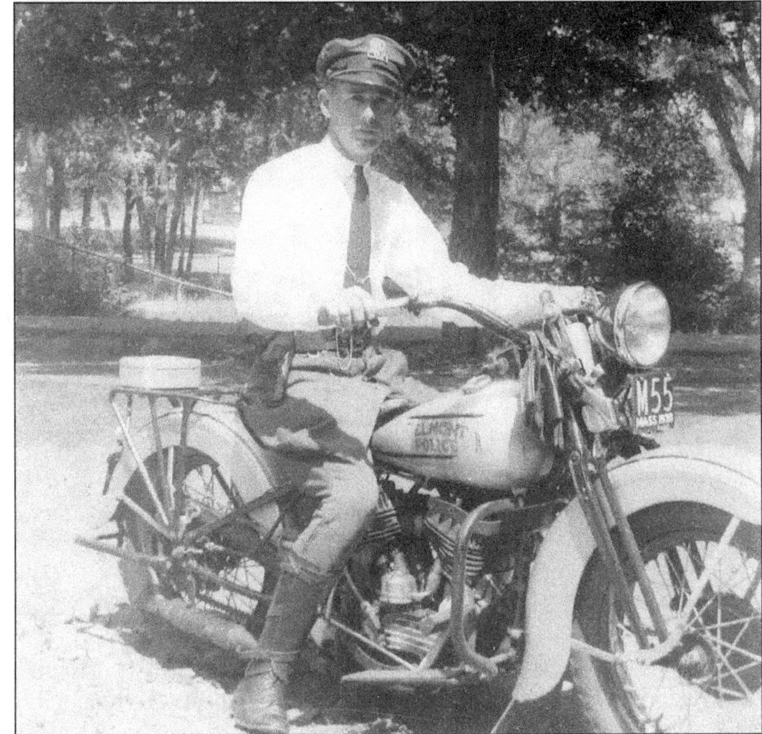

Pictured here on the police motorcycle in 1939 is officer Edwin L. Marsh.

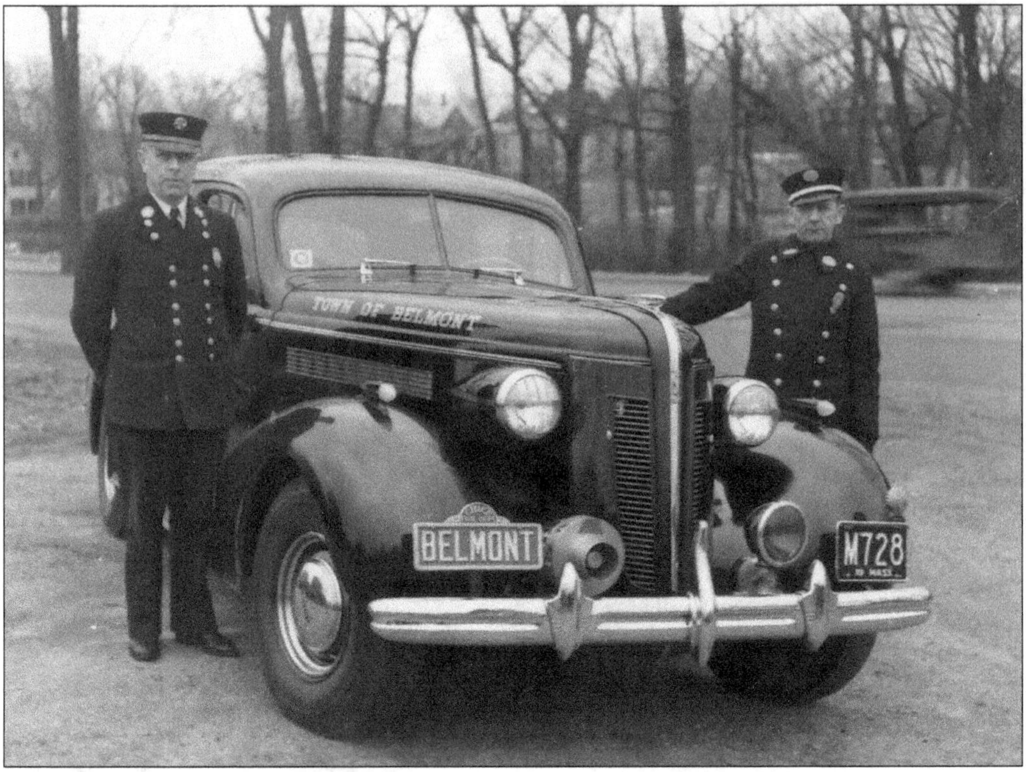

Fire Chief Hill and his driver proudly stand by the latest chief's car in 1939. The car was parked in the Concord Avenue gasoline station opposite the future site of the Belmont Memorial Library.

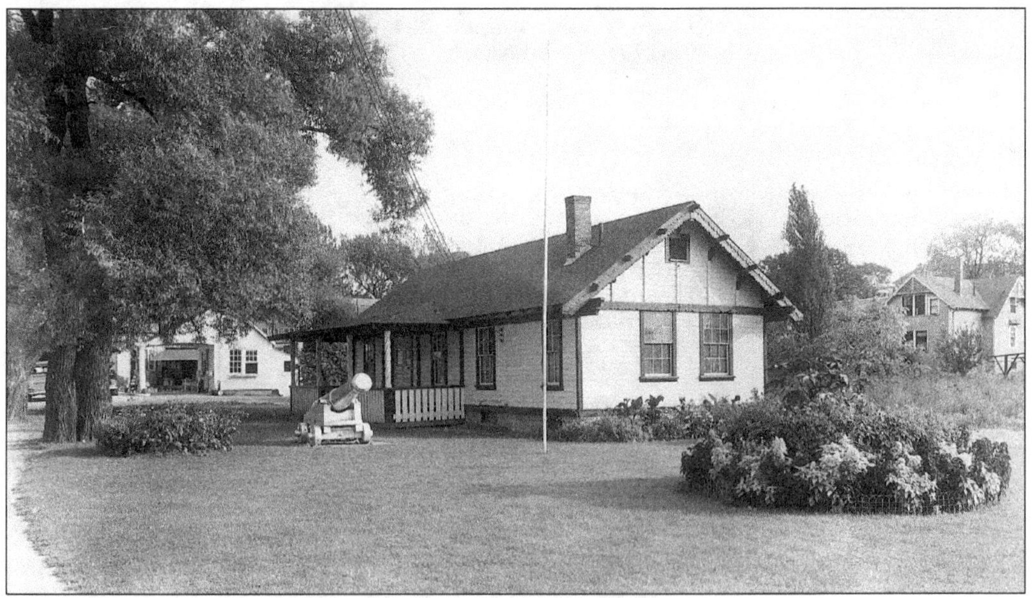

The "Shack" was moved from the town field in 1925 to Cushing Square, where it became the home of Post 1272 of the Veterans of Foreign Wars (VFW). The small building was originally constructed in 1903 by high school students. The posts on the porch were carved by the ninth-grade students as a class project.

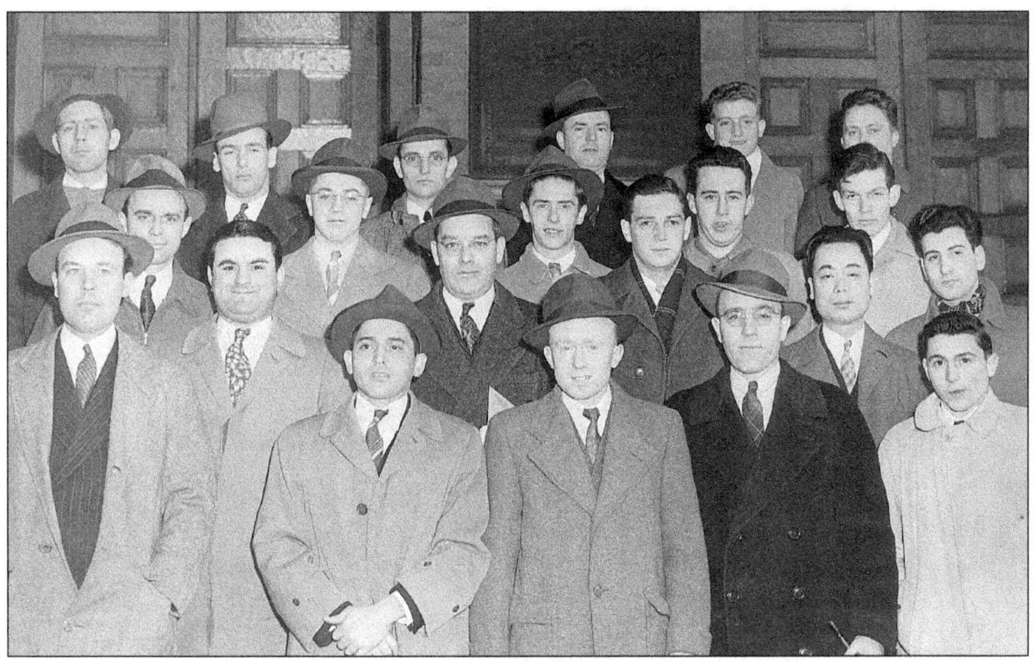

Three days before Christmas in 1943, these young draftees gather on the steps of the town hall ,awaiting transport to Fort Devens. Shown, from left to right, are the following: (first row) L. Shaughnessy, G.Terrasi, Jack Haley, W. Pratt, and R. DiGiovanni; (second row) A. Swanson, P. Agrillo, Joseph Haley, J. Tracy Jr., Y. Shew, and C. Adler; (third row) F. Maurer, R. Marsh, R. Fitzgerald, and J. Yee; (fourth row) J. Nestor, A. Dodge, D. Smallman, A. Tutein, A. Cardillo, and J. Dailey. Fortunately, all of them returned from the war.

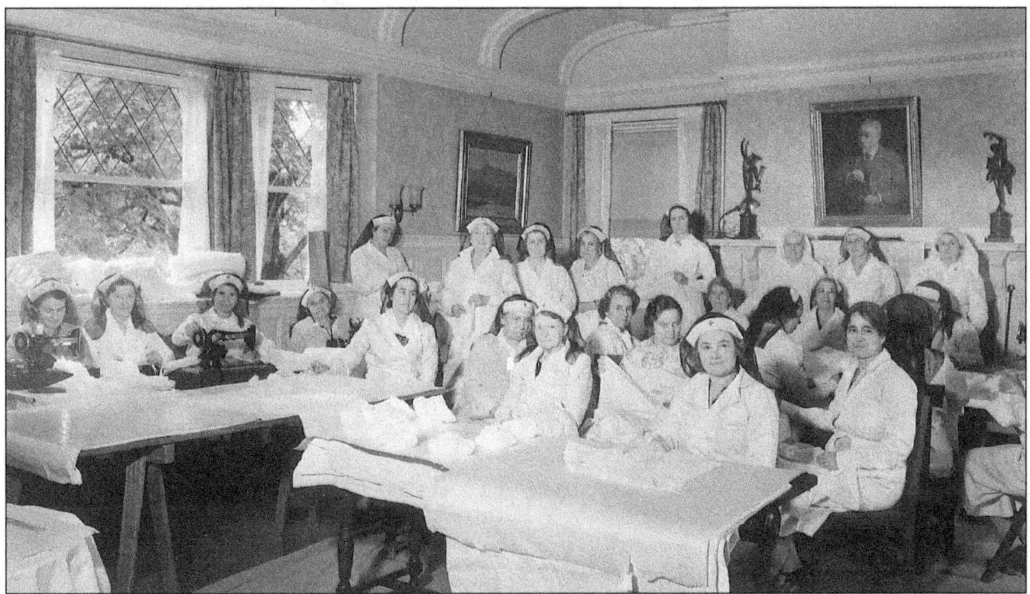

Women of the Belmont Red Cross diligently work to roll bandages in this makeshift workshop at the Concord Avenue home of Mrs. Edwin Atkins. The Red Cross production unit began in January 1940 and continued to meet until August 1945. Pictured third from the left, behind the sewing machine, is the familiar face of Isabelle Betts.

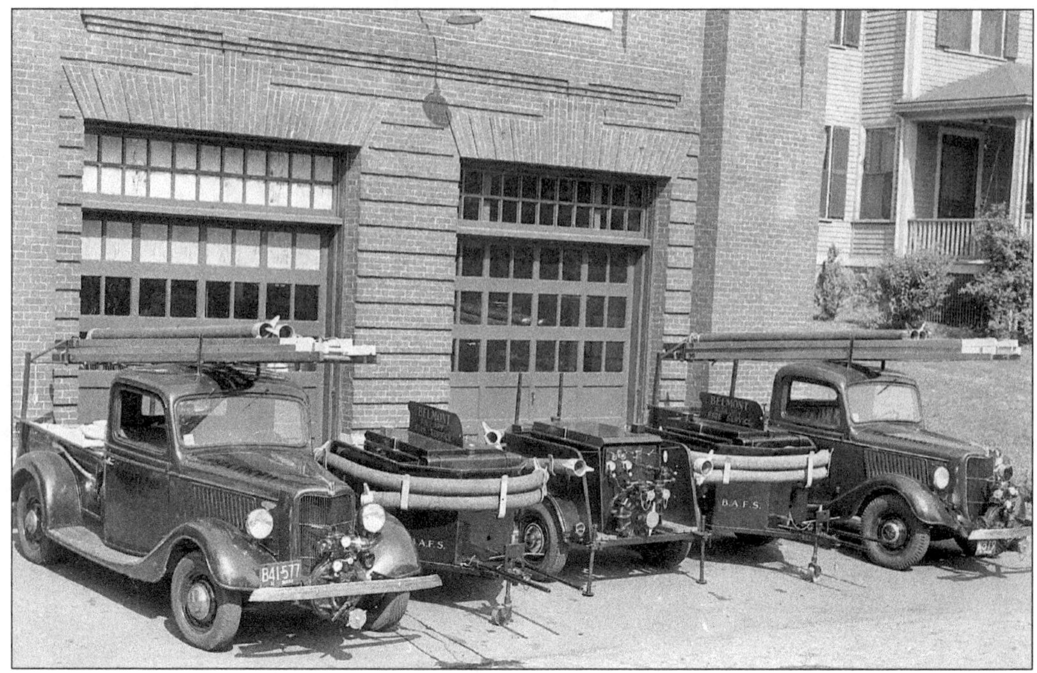

The World War II auxiliary fire department displays some of its outdated but still serviceable equipment in front of the center fire station.

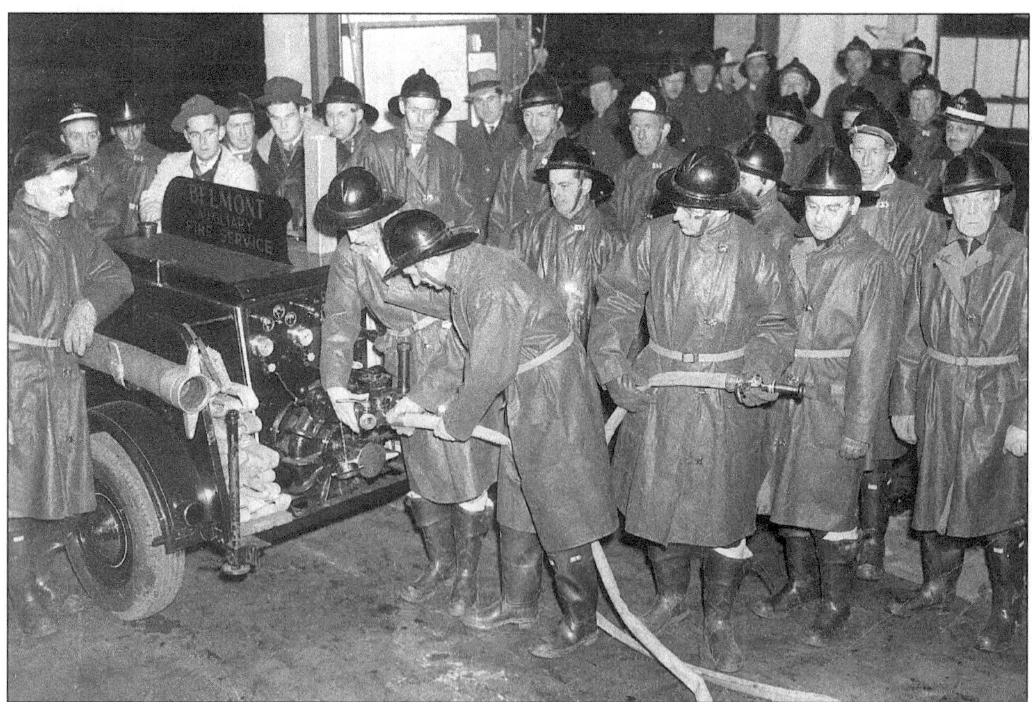

Under the watchful eyes of their peers, auxiliary firemen practice attaching the hoses to the outlet on the back of the portable engine.

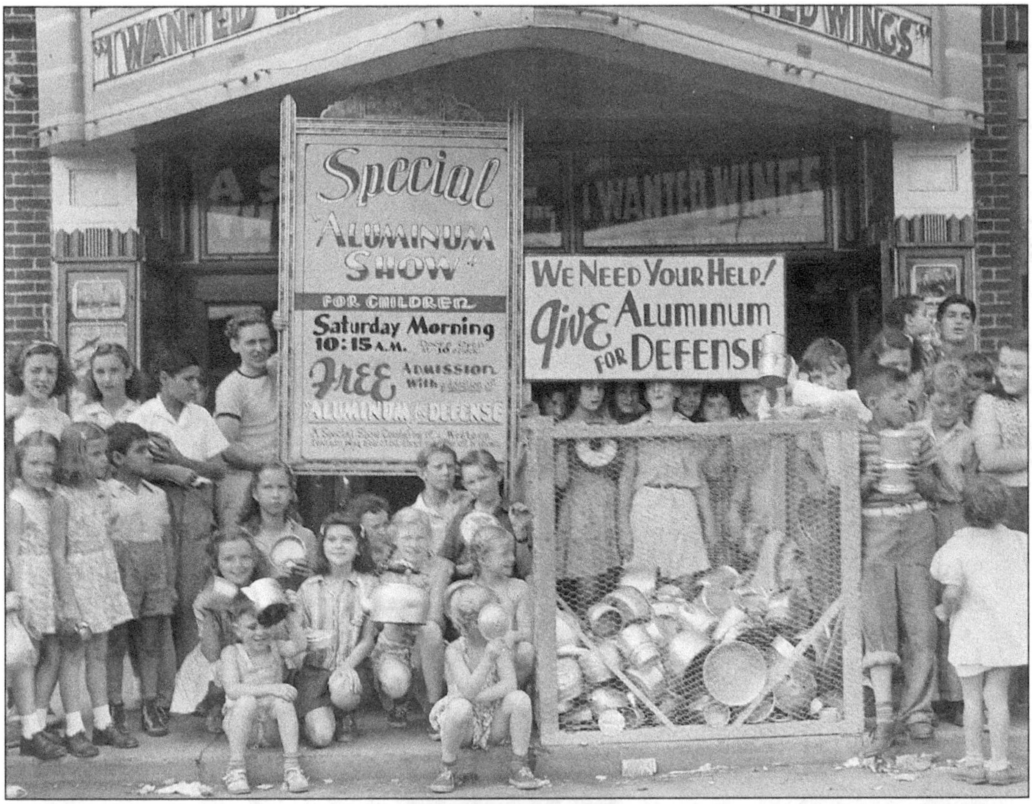

This 1942 photograph shows the early recycling of aluminum, which was in short supply during World War II. Children in front of the Studio Theatre (locally known as "the Barn") were offered free admission to a special matinee with an aluminum donation. Committee Chair and Selectman Charles Betts set up bins in various locations around Belmont for collection.

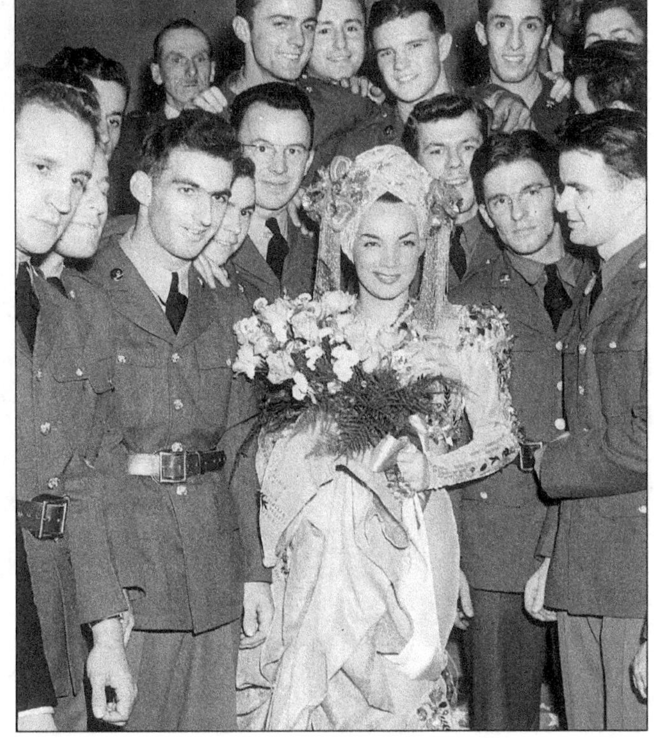

In 1941, the Veterans of Foreign Wars sponsored a ball with the entire proceeds benefiting the Belmont branch of the American Red Cross. One of the major attractions was popular singer Carmen Miranda. Sewing machines were purchased for the war effort.

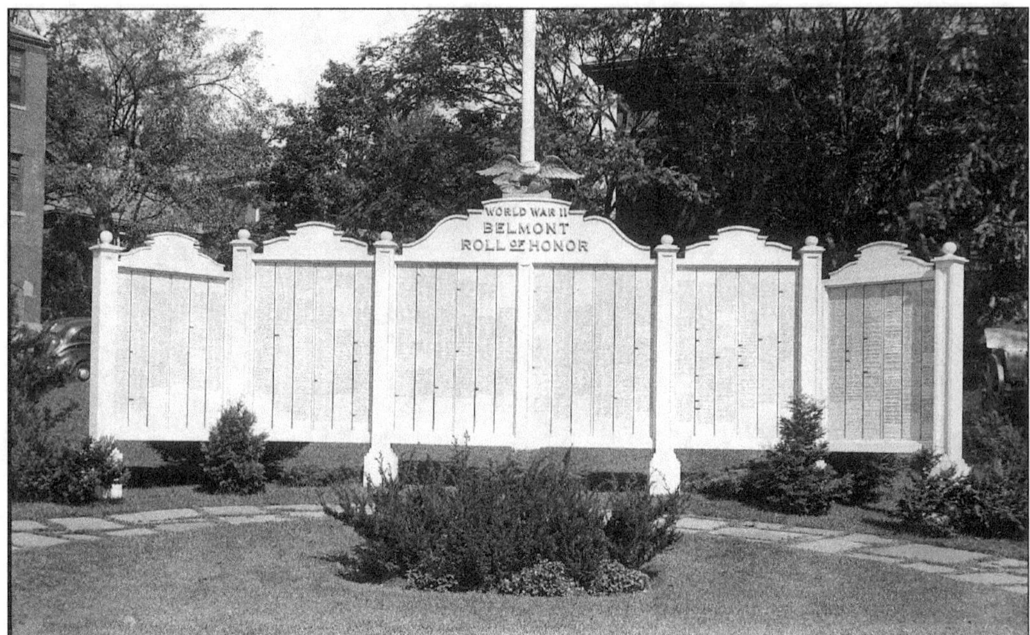

The Belmont Roll of Honor was located along Concord Avenue on the town hall lawn. When dedicated in July 1943, it included the names of nearly 2,200 men and women of Belmont who served their country in all parts of the world. In 1946, additions to the list brought the total to more than 3,600.

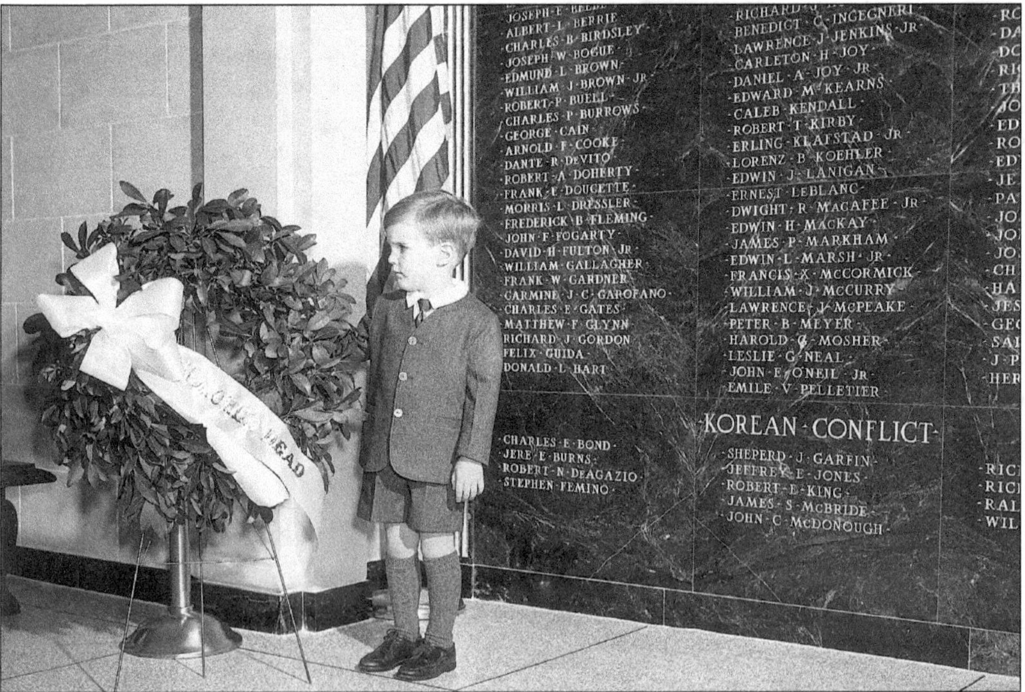

Ralph Burns Jr. helps place a wreath in front of the Memorial Wall during the dedication of the Belmont Memorial Library. The ceremony was to honor the men who sacrificed their lives for their country in World Wars I and II and the Korean War.

Six

Belmont's Women

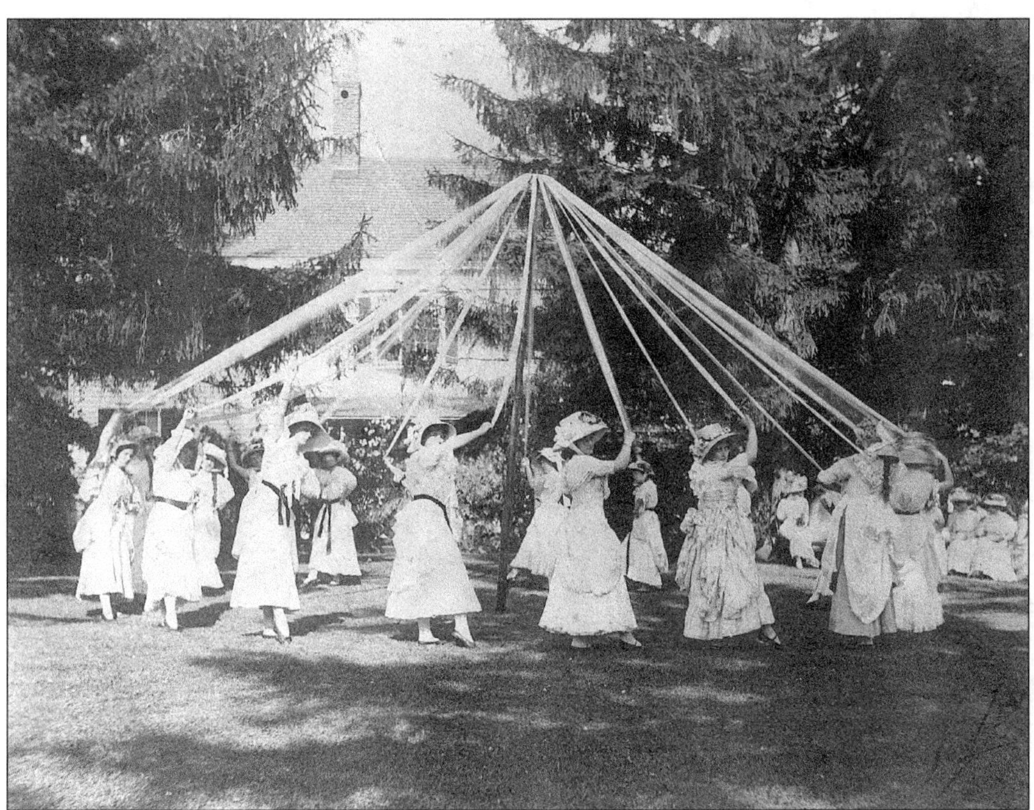

At the beginning of the 20th century, Belmont women gather to celebrate the arrival of spring with a Maypole dance. Throughout the town's history, from incorporation to today, women's influence has been felt strongly. Even the image on the town seal depicts women's prominence. (Courtesy of the Wellington family.)

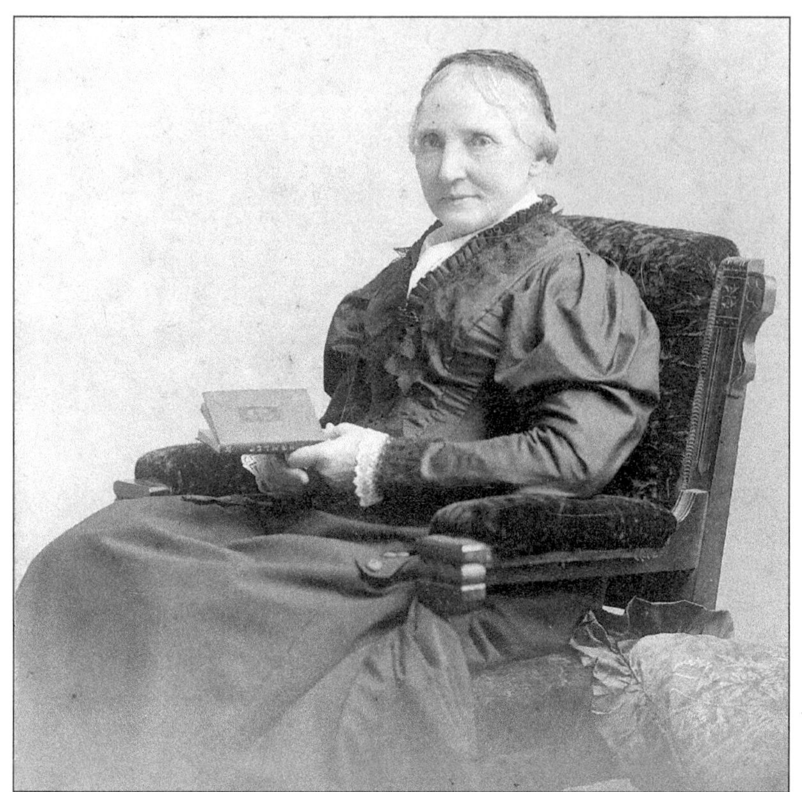

Sarah Wellington, a sixth-generation descendant of original settler Roger Wellington, was a teacher and a pioneer in the women's suffrage movement. She was one of the first women to vote in the state of Massachusetts, which was the 13th state to allow votes for women.

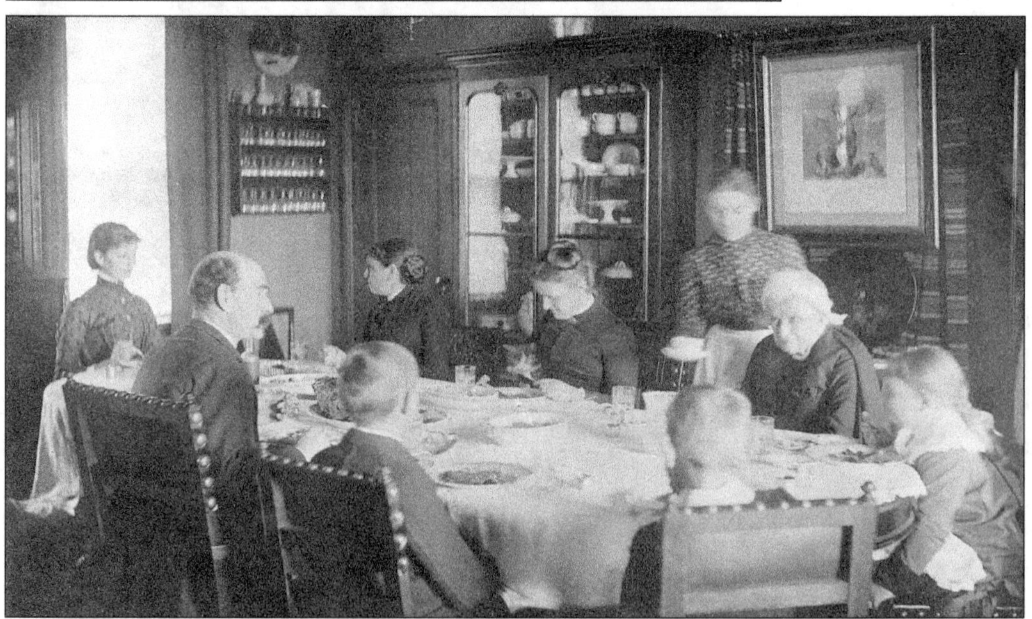

This photograph captures an informal look at the Hartshorne house dining room. James H. Hartshorne purchased the property on Pleasant Street *c.* 1860. The home, with its wide veranda overlooking Boston, was a favorite place for the family to gather. In later years, the building was used as a parish house for the Plymouth Congregational Church. It was finally torn down when the church put on the last of its additions. (Courtesy of the Weeks family.)

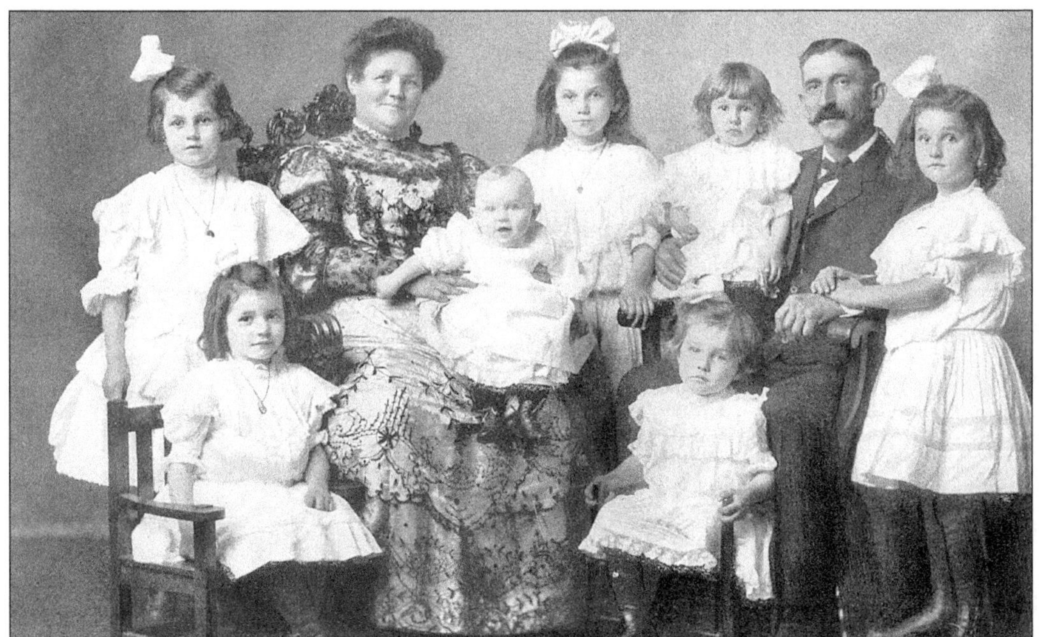

In 1865, Mary Ellen Purcell married Edward Francis Skahan. Her husband and his brother John Skahan owned and operated two of Belmont's original farms and became among the most successful market gardeners in the state. She was one of the founders and the first president of the Payson Park Teachers Association. In 1942, she sold the 16-room family residence at 91 Grove Street to Belmont, which allowed the town to enlarge the cemetery.

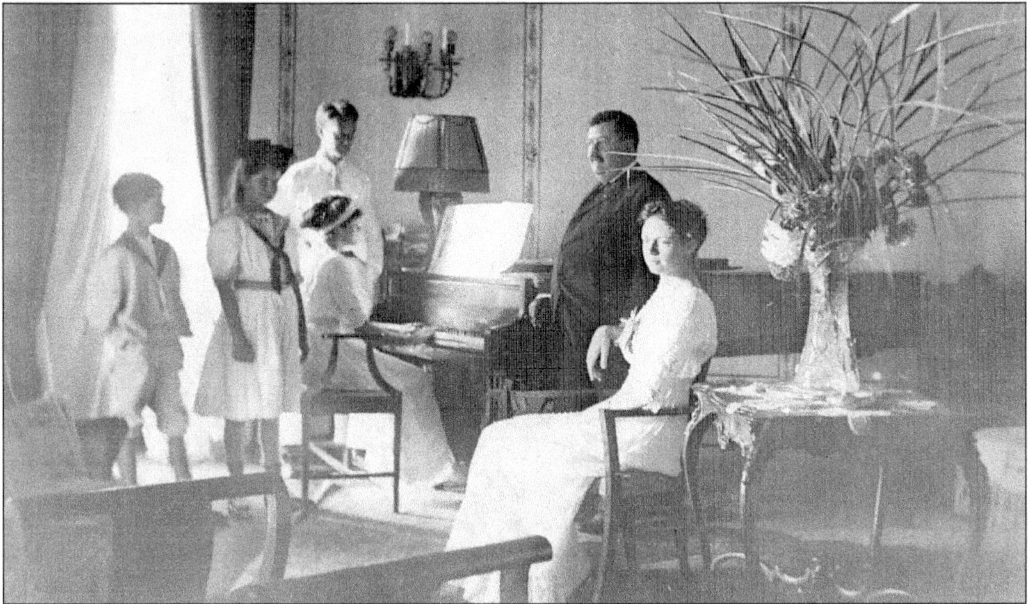

On a Sunday afternoon *c.* 1908, the Benton family relaxes at home. The setting for this rare look at the Victorian interior of the Belmont mansion is the large oval music room on the first floor, directly off the circular rotunda. Gathered around to listen to the peaceful sounds of the piano are, from left to right, Josiah, Hannah, Jay, Dorothy (at the piano), Uncle Jay Bayard Benton, and Blanche Benton.

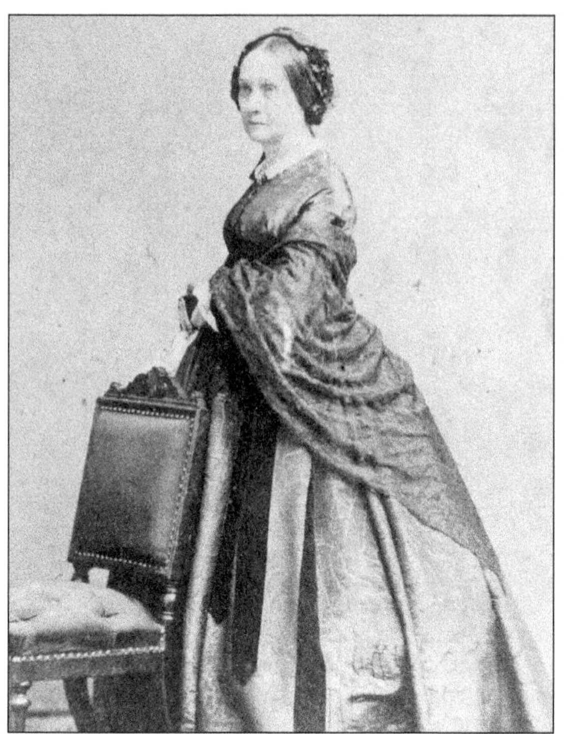

Adeline Wellington Homer was described by her family as "a woman of great energy and activity." She inherited from her mother, Elizabeth Loring, a love for nature, which could be seen in her extensive cultivation of flowers and shrubs.

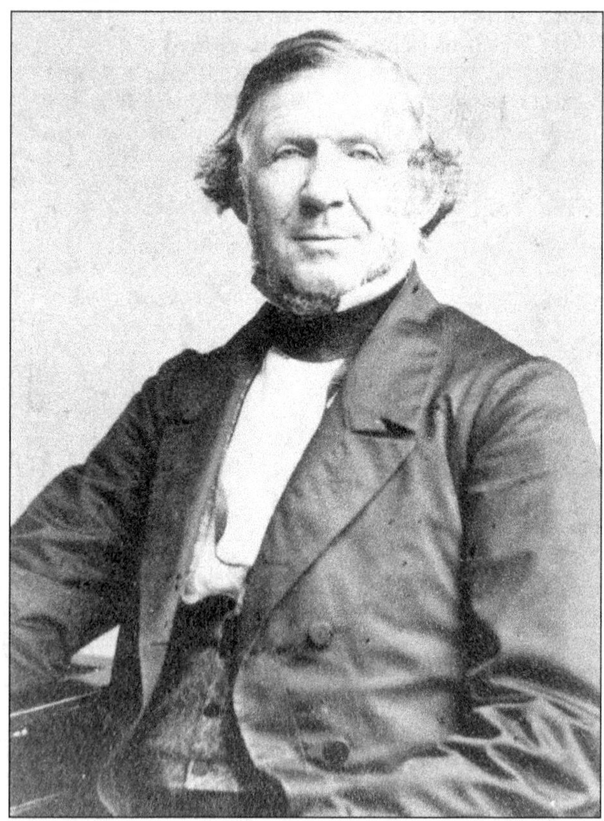

In 1836, William Flagg Homer, a wealthy Boston merchant, purchased the 2 acres of land at the corner of Concord Avenue and Pleasant Street from Samuel O. Mead, on which he later built his fashionable summer residence.

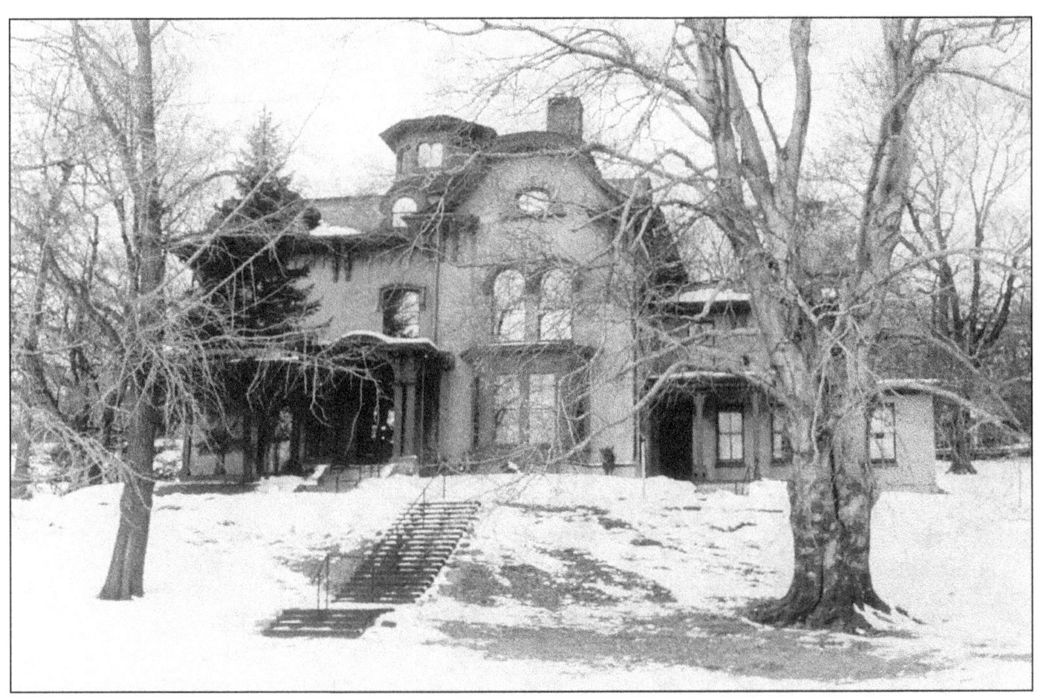

The William Flagg Homer House was built in 1853 in the Italianate style by the uncle of the renowned artist Winslow Homer. The famous painting *The Croquet Scene* is set on the front lawn of the property. Winslow Homer's influence helped to develop the image of the active American woman through his artistic social commentary of the 1800s.

Lillian Russell owned the estate at 661 Pleasant Street in 1893. It remained home to her husband, Joseph Russell, and family until 1904. The property changed hands several times and was saved from destruction by the Belmont Women's Club, the owner of the historic house since 1927.

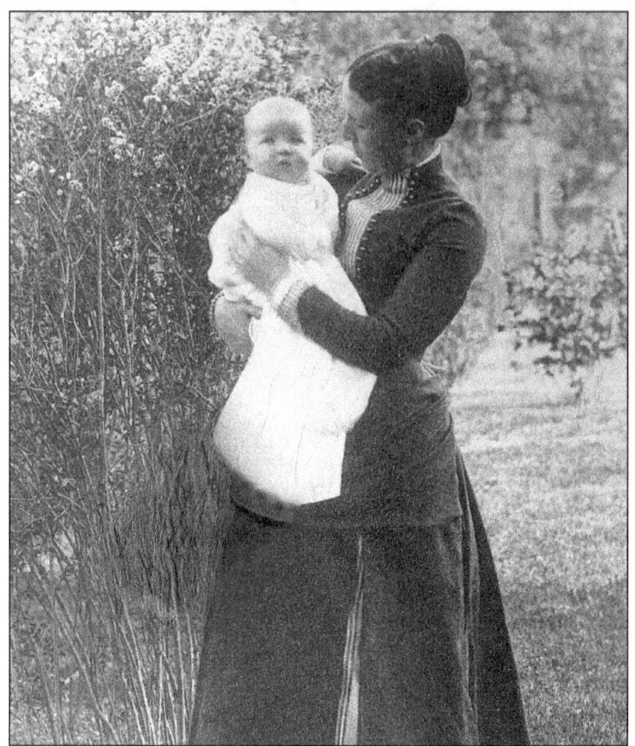

Jennie Cushing married Henry Oliver Underwood, the eldest son of William James Underwood and Esther (Wellington) Mead, in 1884. Jennie's sister Ida Cushing married Henry's brother William Lyman Underwood three years later. (Courtesy of Helen Underwood.)

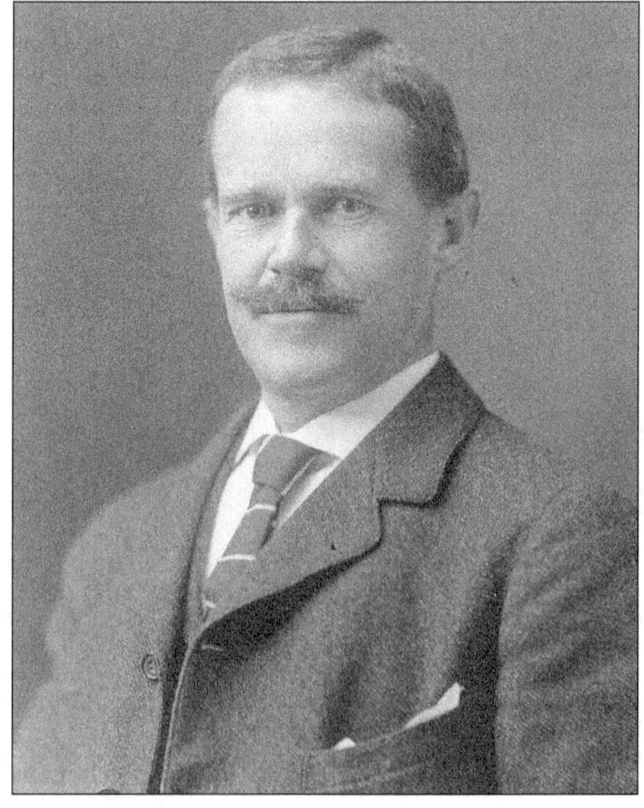

Henry Oliver Underwood was the grandson of William Underwood, founder of the Underwood Company in 1822. From 1880 to 1922, Henry Underwood served as president of the family-owned business, which held the oldest registered food trademark in the country. Brother William Lyman Underwood worked to pioneer the art of preserving food in canisters.

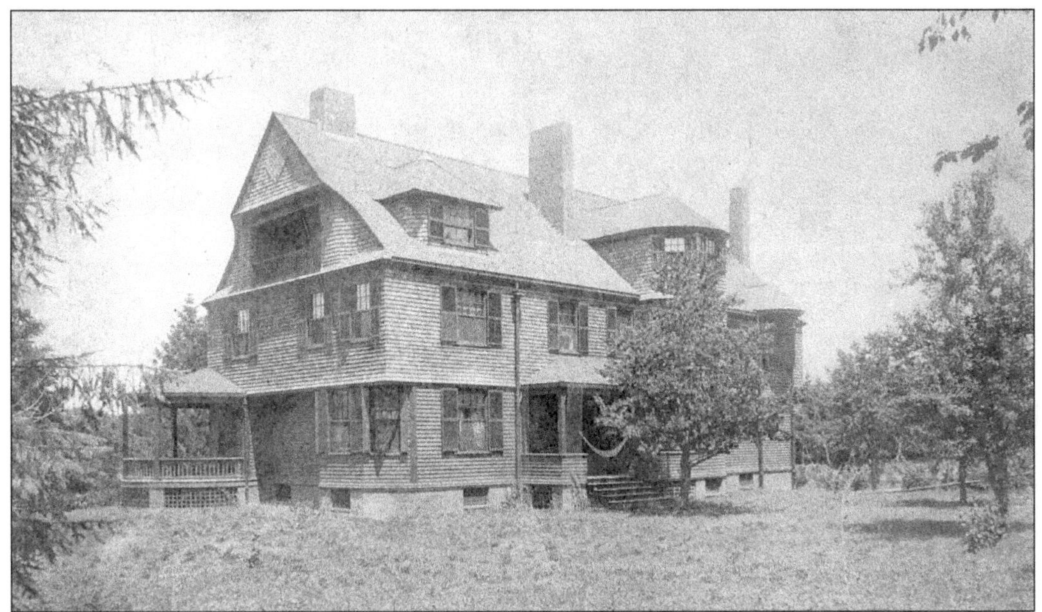

The shingle-style H.O. Underwood house was designed in 1885 by architects Hartwell and Richardson on the property commonly known as the Underwood Estate. Brothers Loring Underwood, a landscape architect known for his design of many local areas like Underwood Pool and Clay Pit Park, and William Lyman Underwood, scientist and forerunner in the art of photography, also had houses on the property.

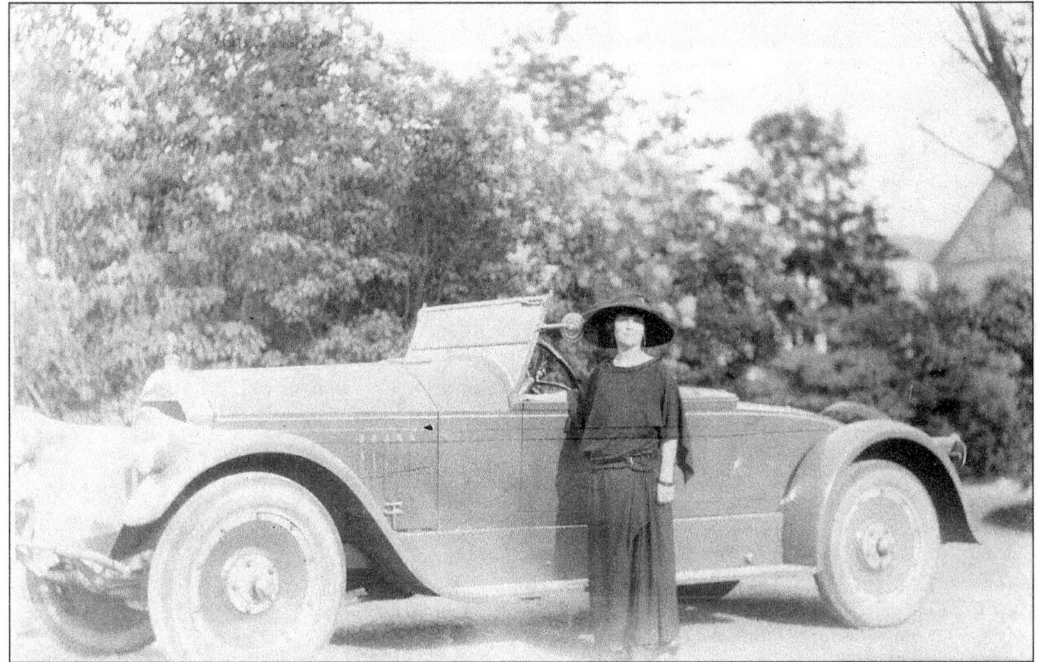

Margaret Underwood Davis also made the family residence at 100 Common Street home with her husband, Francis Davis. Her husband, who maintained a workshop on the grounds, was the inventor of power steering in automobiles; she poses in front of the first automobile to be equipped with the new mechanical wonder.

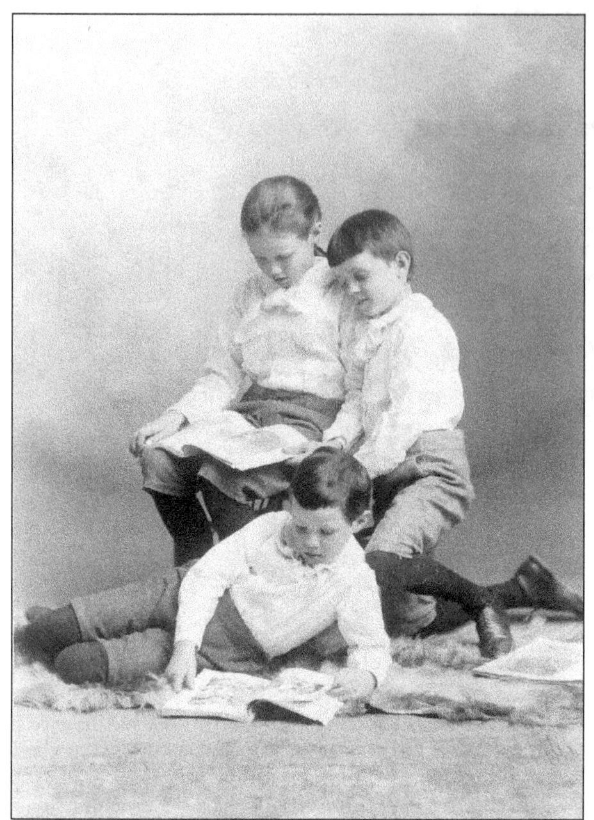

The three young daughters of Henry Oliver Underwood and his wife, Jennie Cushing Underwood, sit for this formal 1893 portrait. Helen, Margaret, and Alice are shown, from front to back.

Helen Underwood married Charles Oliver Wellington in 1912 on the Underwood Estate, and these prominent Belmont families' ancestries crossed a second time. The family tree also extends to include branches of the Hill, Mead, and Homer families, to name a few. Photographed, from left to right, are the following: (front row) bridesmaids Emily and Dorothy Wellington, maid of honor Margaret Underwood, best man Henry Wellington, the bride, the groom, and Barbara and Ruth Wellington; (back row) two ushers, Mrs. and Mr. Jeduthan Wellington, Mr. and Mrs. Henry Underwood, and two ushers. (Courtesy of Helen Underwood.)

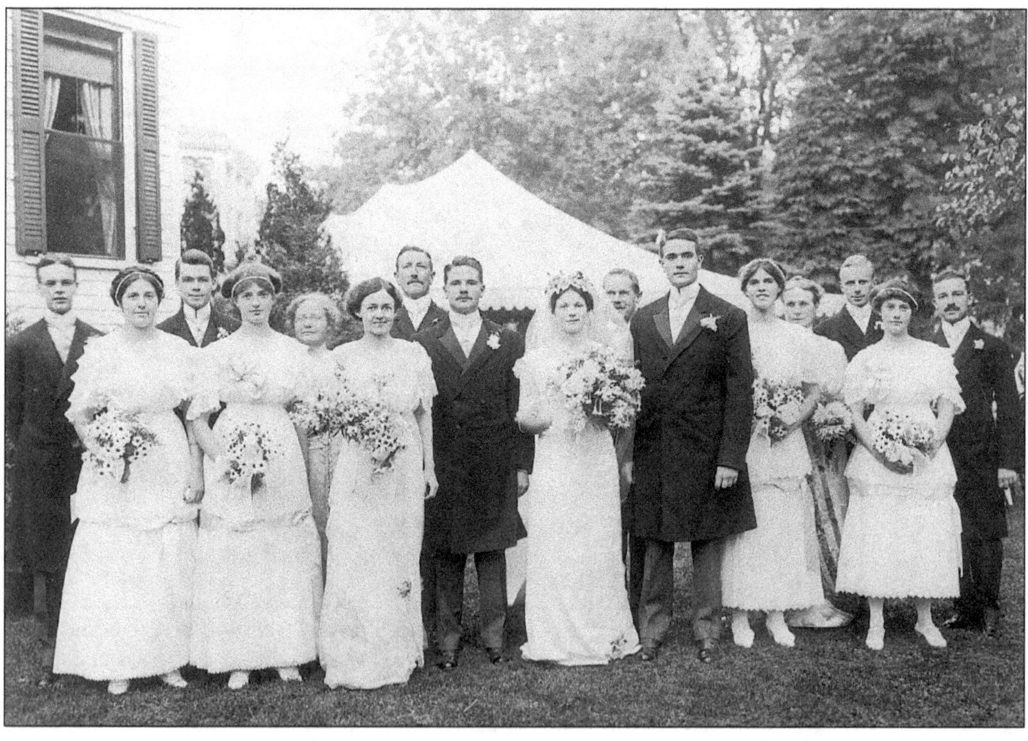

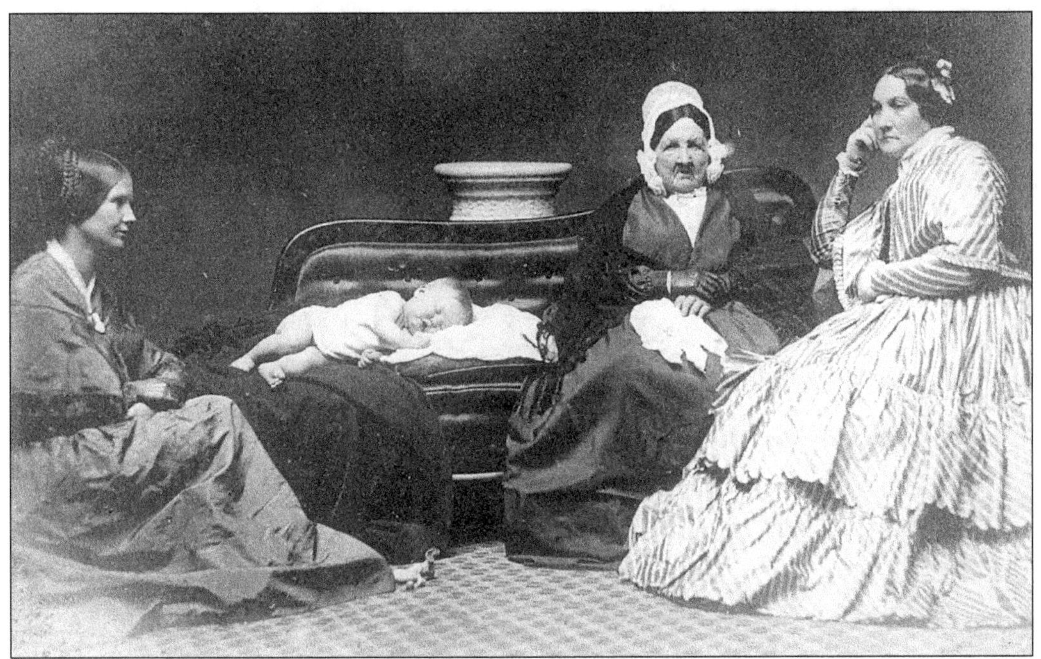

Mead family descendants of many generations are pictured in this *c.* 1860 photograph. Maria Mead, wife of Samuel O. Mead, was described as "a most active enterprising woman, kindhearted and charitable. Her tastes were social and her beautiful home was always opened to her large circle of friends." The Mead's first house was moved up the hill on Concord Avenue when the Pleasant Street property was purchased by William Flagg Homer. Their second home at 346 Concord Avenue still houses descendants. (Courtesy of the Wellington family.)

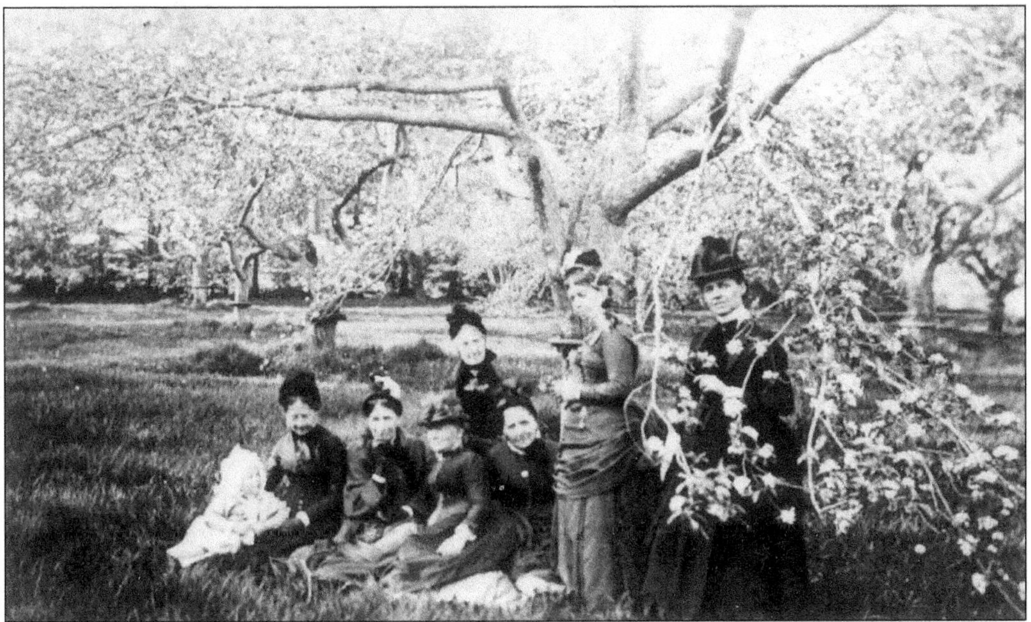

Women pose beneath a flowering tree on a spring afternoon at the Cushing Mansion, *c.* 1880. The 200-acre estate Bellmont included a conservatory and 14 greenhouses devoted to the cultivation of trees, plants, and shrubs.

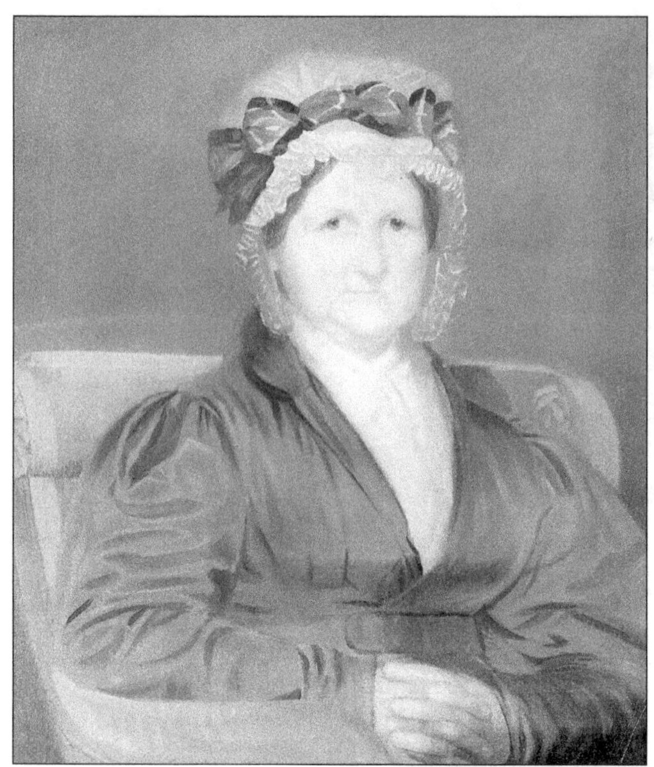

Elizabeth Loring was the second wife of Colonel Jeduthan Wellington. Remembered by those who knew her as never idle, she spun and wove linen and household cloth, and her busy fingers fashioned ornamental and useful articles that found ready sale in Boston. Her thrift and industry added much to the comfort of her family, by whom she was idolized.

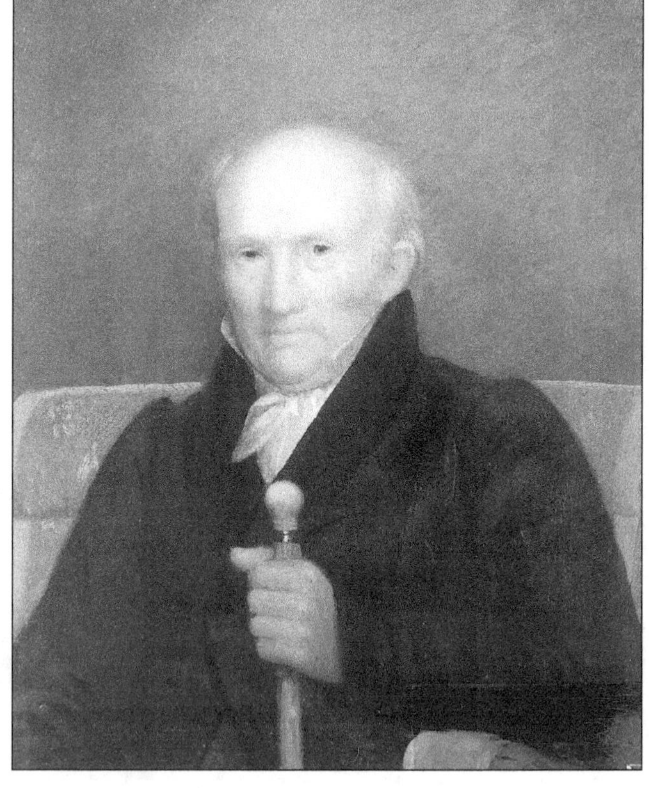

Jeduthan Wellington, born in 1750, was a private at the Battle of Bunker Hill and rose to the rank of colonel by the early 1800s. He was a descendant of early settler Roger Wellington. In 1825, Colonel Wellington was visited by French General Lafayette, under whom he had served. The general arrived traveling a route known as the Concord Turnpike, which Wellington had laid out as surveyor and overseer of public highways.

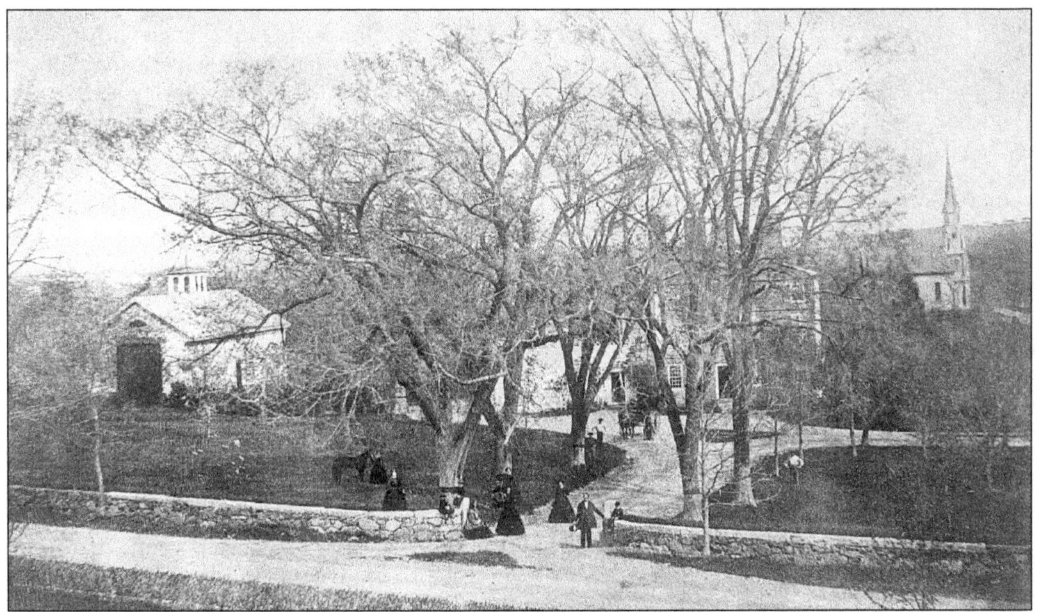

The Wellington Homestead and Tavern was home to Col. Jeduthan Wellington and his large family and was a popular stopping place for travelers between Boston and Concord. Located at the base of Belmont Hill, Wellington kept a team of oxen ready to assist in climbing the steep slope. The buildings were demolished in 1897, and the Homer School built on the site.

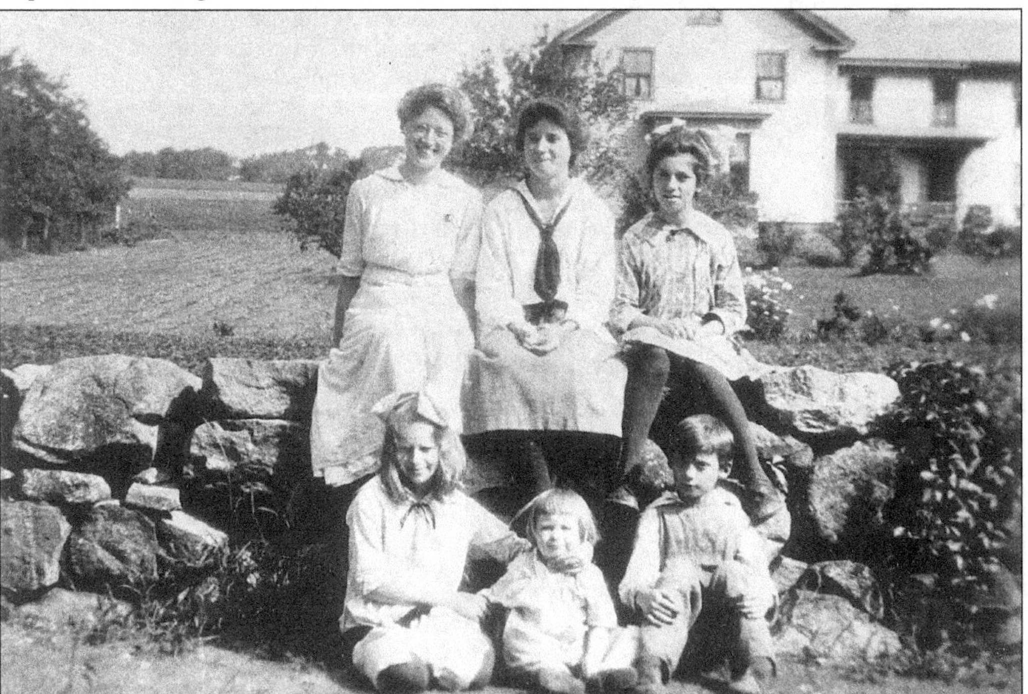

The Richardson children pose in front of the family farmhouse on 24 Richardson Road. Father Henry Richardson owned two farms along Washington Street. The Richardson-Hill farm remains the last working farm in Belmont. The original land grant by King Charles I of England to Abraham Hill dates from 1633.

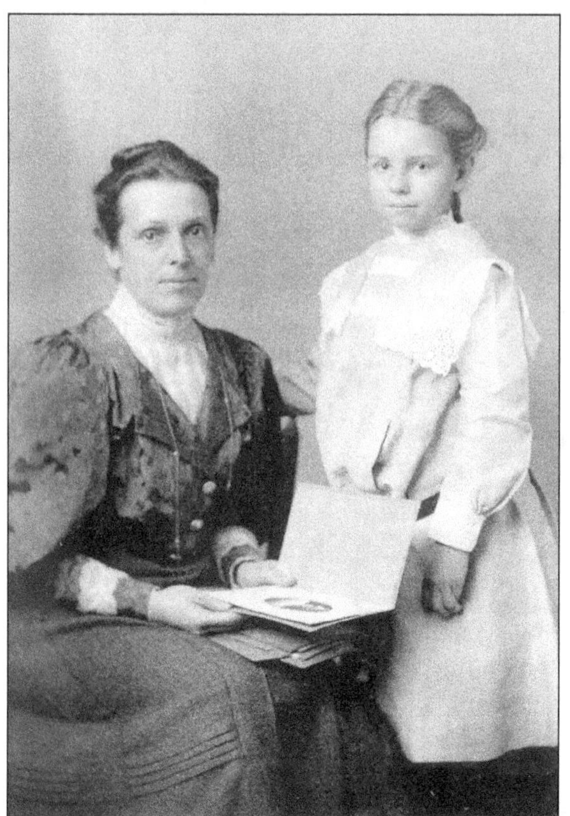

Katherine Wrisley Atkins is shown with her daughter Helen Atkins. Born in Boston in 1860, Katherine spent many summers as a young girl at the home of her grandparents Mr. and Mrs. James Hartshorne. In later years her benefactions to Belmont and its citizens were numerous. She was described as a woman of great activity. Linked with the early history of the town, her strong influence for the good of its people and broad vision for the years to come contributed largely to its growth. (Courtesy of the Weeks family.)

This is an intimate look at Katherine Atkins and a friend in the living room at 580 Concord Avenue. Before Katherine was married in 1882, her husband-to-be, Edwin F. Atkins, purchased the Ware house on Belmont Hill, which he and his bride soon named Hilholme. Atkins was successful in the family business and became known as the "dean of the Cuban sugar industry." (Courtesy of the Weeks family.)

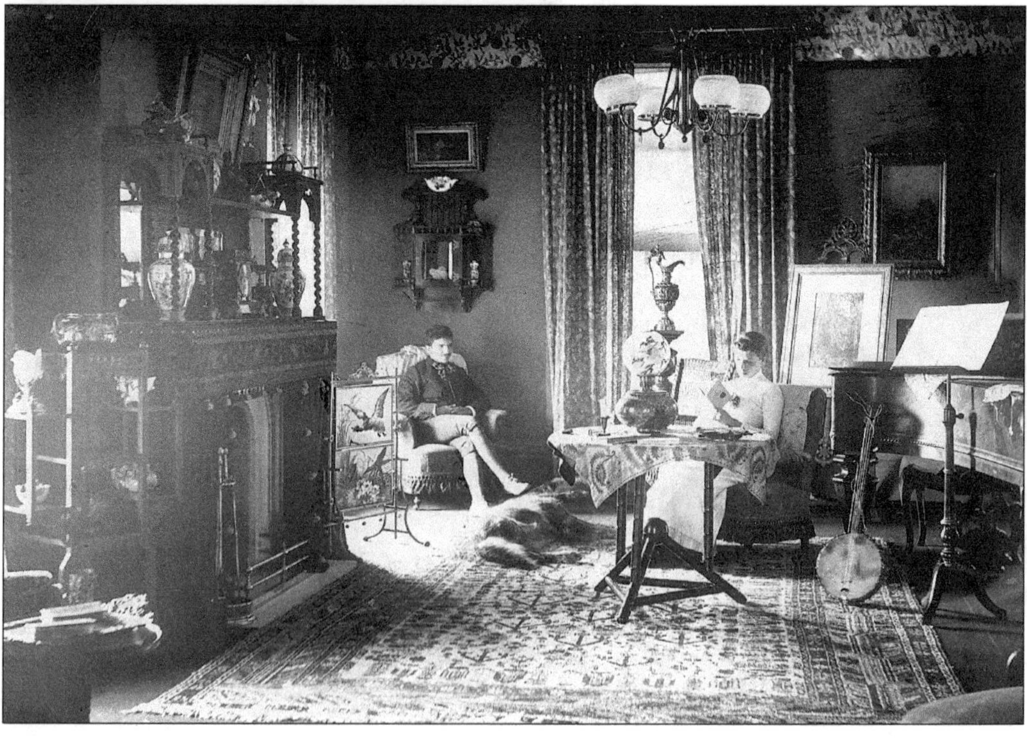

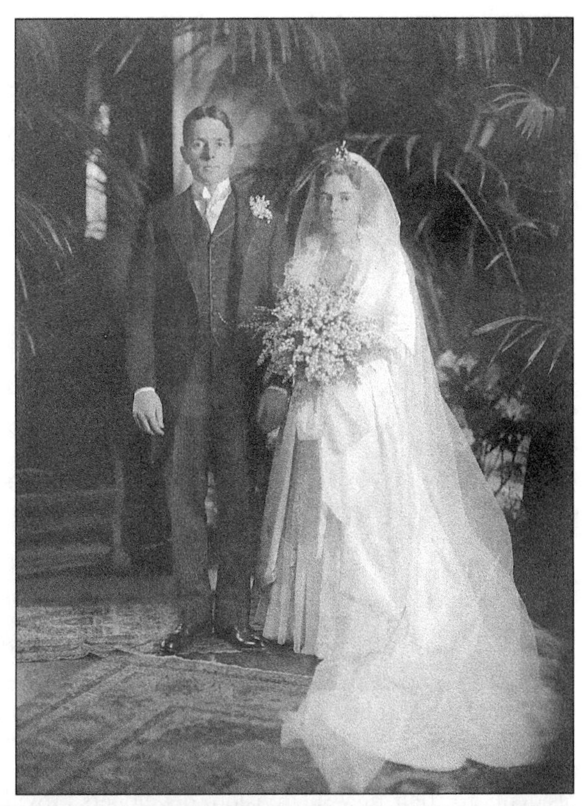

Mr. and Mrs. Edwin Farnsworth Atkins announced the marriage of their daughter Helen to William Henry Claflin Jr. The wedding took place on Saturday, April 21, 1917, in Belmont. The Claflins carried on the elder generations' generosity and service to the town throughout their lives. Helen Claflin helped form the Belmont Historical Society and donated a furnished room in the Belmont Memorial Library as a home for the society and its extensive archival collection. (Courtesy of the Weeks family.)

The Leonard twins of Sunnyside Place graduated from Belmont High School in 1922. Margaret and Mildred Leonard were daughters of John F. Leonard, who was employed by the Atkins family on their Belmont estate. John Leonard served both as a town meeting member and chief of the fire department in its volunteer days.

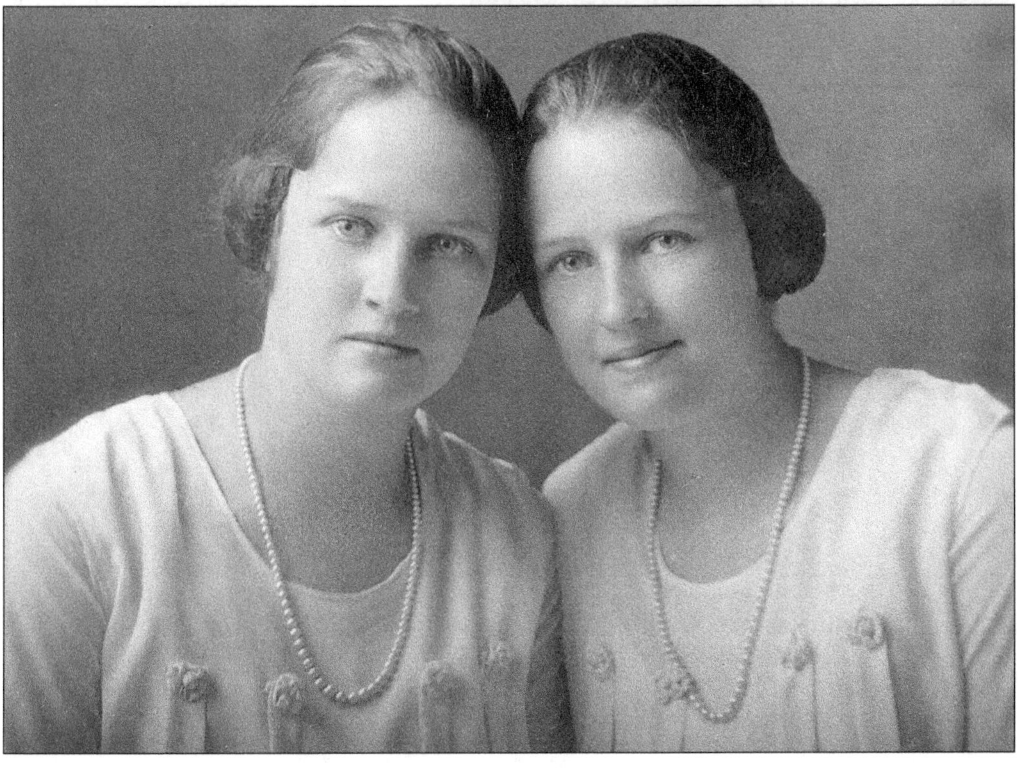

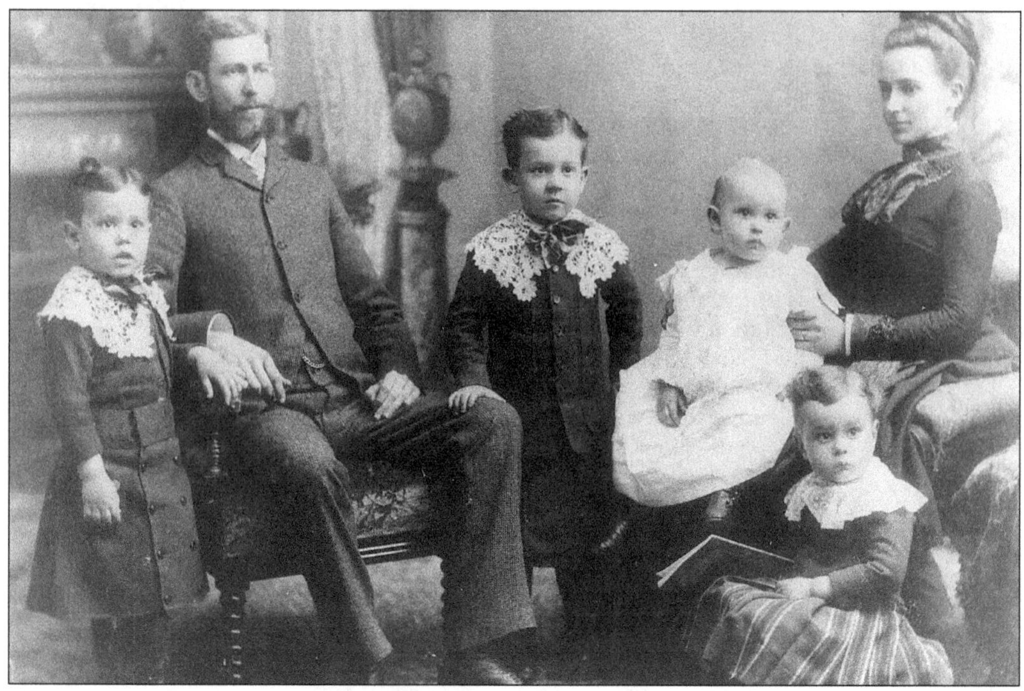

Eva Georgiana Andrews purchased the Burnham house at 43 Burnham Street in Waverley. She and her husband, Edward Andrews, and their children are representative of early families in the area prior to the major development in the 1870s by the Waverley Land Company. To attract residents to their new subdivision, developers provided free railroad passes to Boston, on the Fitchburg line, to those constructing homes near Plympton's Crossing.

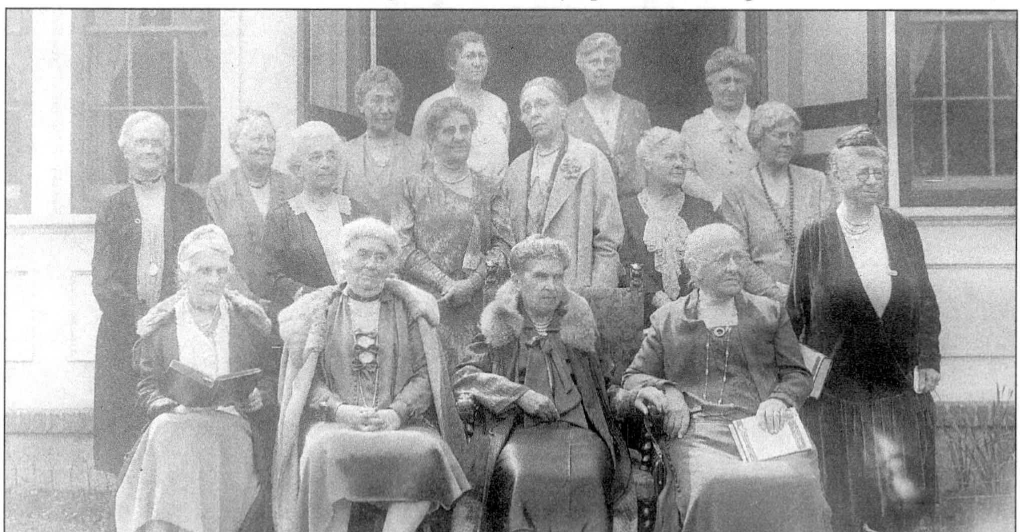

The Thursday Club began in 1890 when the Robbins sisters started to read aloud together and soon decided to include friends. The membership grew to 20 women, who gathered for the "reading and discussion of literature of permanent worth." Pictured in 1930 are Mrs. W. Chenery, Mrs. Marsh, Miss Chenery, Mrs. J. Wellington, Miss Richardson, Miss Cunningham, Mrs. Howe, Mrs. Castle, Mrs. A. Wellington, Mrs. Vaughn, Mrs. G. Chenery, Mrs. Jeffers, Mrs. N. Chenery, Mrs. Jenny, and Mrs. James.

Seven

SCHOOL DAYS

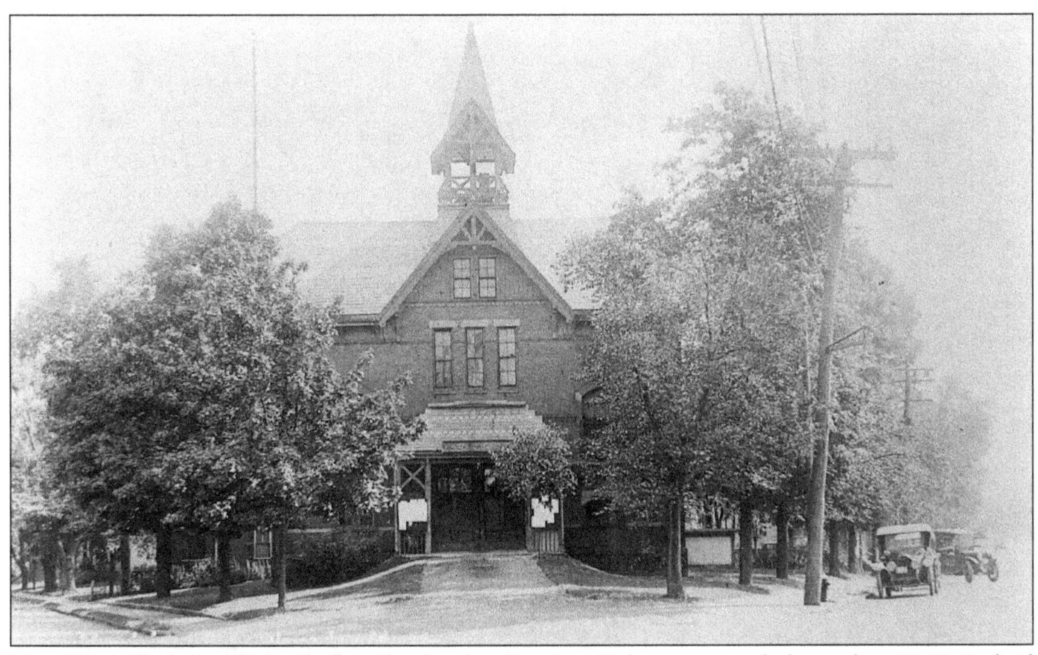

The New Waverley School, the first brick school in Belmont, was dedicated in 1873. It had one room on the first floor for the school and a hall on the second floor. A two-room addition was completed by 1895, and the school was renamed the Daniel Butler School. This building continues to serve the town as a fire station and a branch library. (Courtesy of John Garrity.)

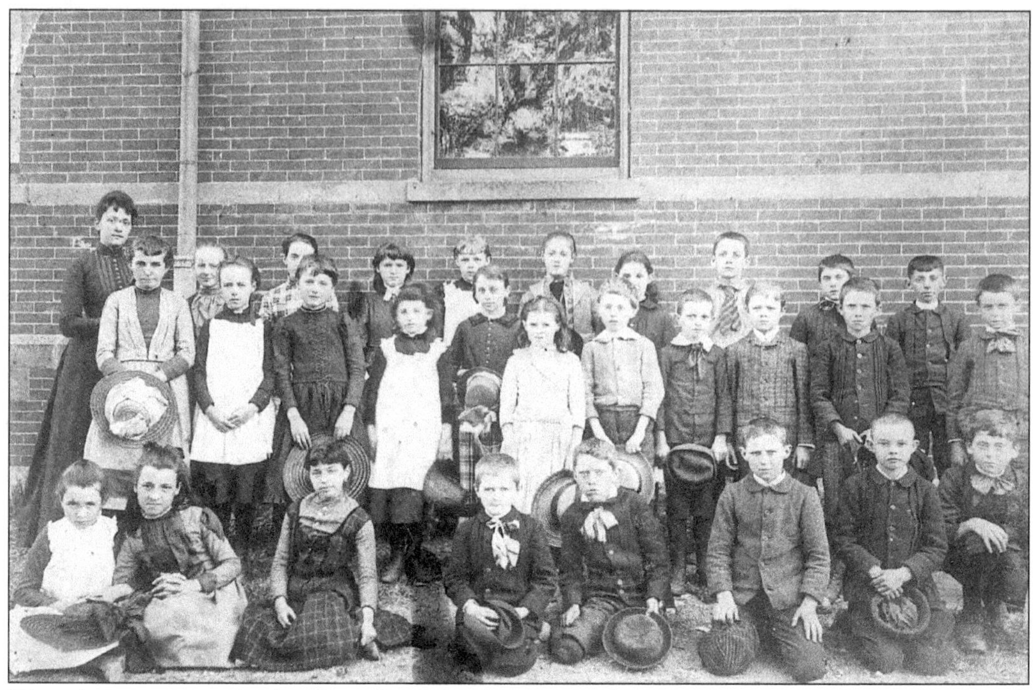

This class poses outside the Waverley School in 1889. There were two entrances to the school, one for boys and one for girls. Ellen Welsh is in the first row at the far left; her sister Katherine Welsh is in the second row, fifth from the left, wearing the light dress. They were the daughters of Maurice Welsh, the Waverley gatekeeper. (Courtesy of Barbara White.)

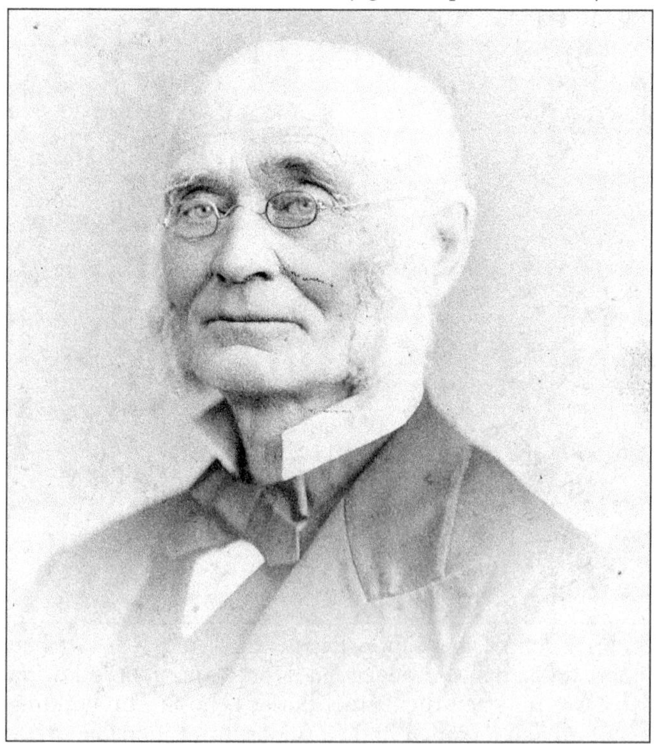

Rev. Daniel Butler, a Congregational minister for whom the school was named, moved to Waverley in 1865 and lived on the corner of Sycamore and White Streets. He served on the school committee from 1871 to 1877 and represented Belmont in the state legislature in 1883. He was well known and highly respected. His son, Henry Butler, was principal of the high school from 1871 to 1877.

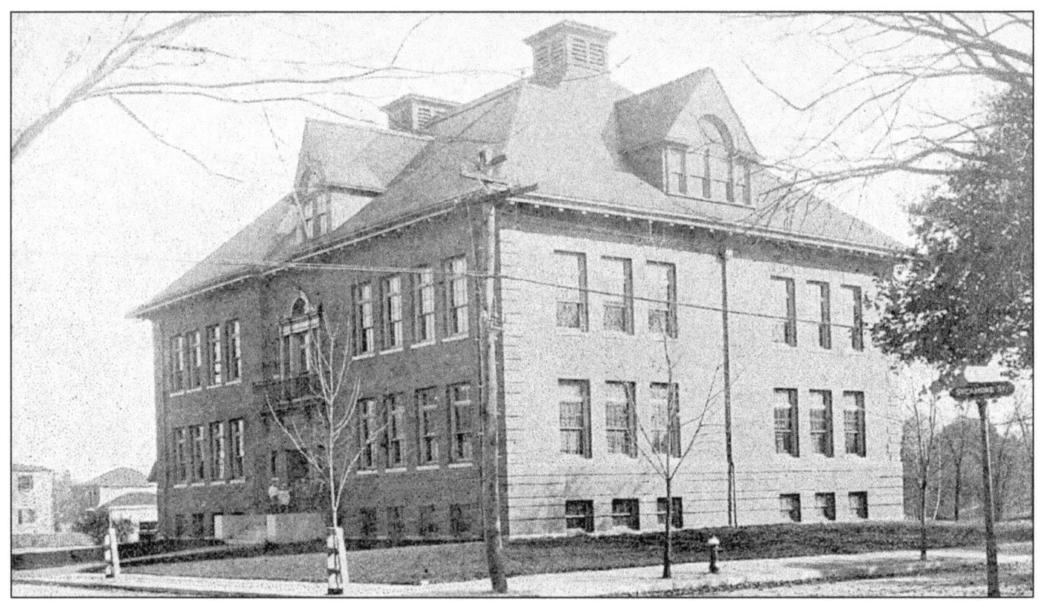

Construction was started in 1900 on a new Daniel Butler School. The new building originally had eight classrooms, with an assembly hall on the third floor. The rooms and corridors were planned so that the building could be enlarged to 16 rooms without detracting from its beauty. (Courtesy John Garrity.)

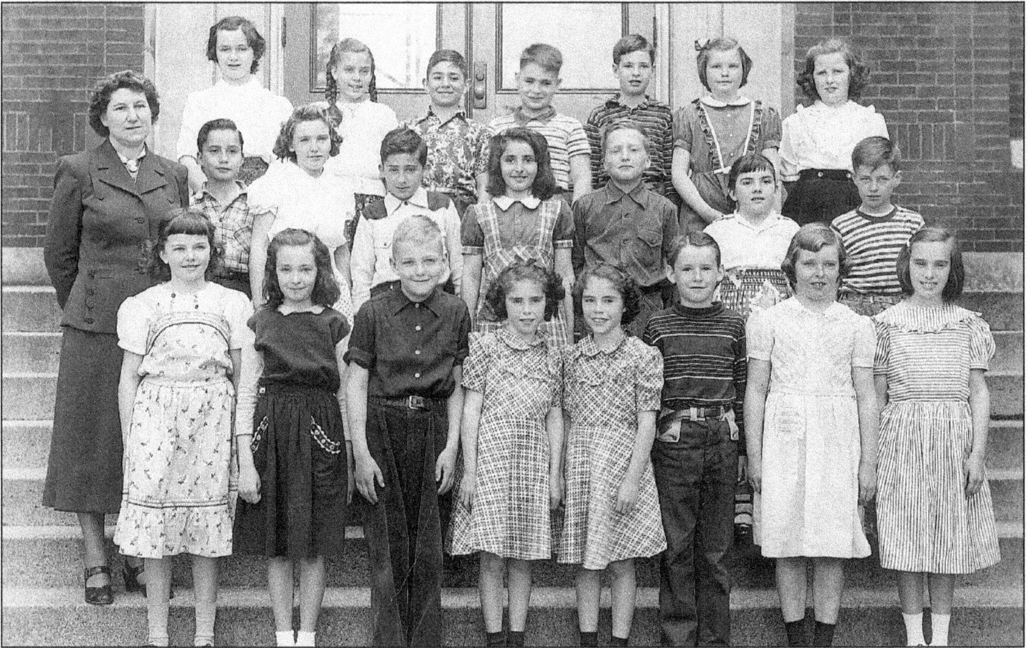

Helen Foss, a highly esteemed teacher, poses with her sixth-grade class on the steps of the Daniel Butler School in 1950. The students, from left to right, are as follows: (first row) C. Gifford, P. O'Hara, F. Millet, M. Millet, two unidentified students, and P. Whitney; (middle row) A. Spilios, two unidentified students, M. Coluccio, unidentified, S. Bere, and unidentified; (back row) S. Bryant, N. Jaynes, G. Alcock, G. Ruiz, G. Hagopian, S. Elso, and J. Sullivan.

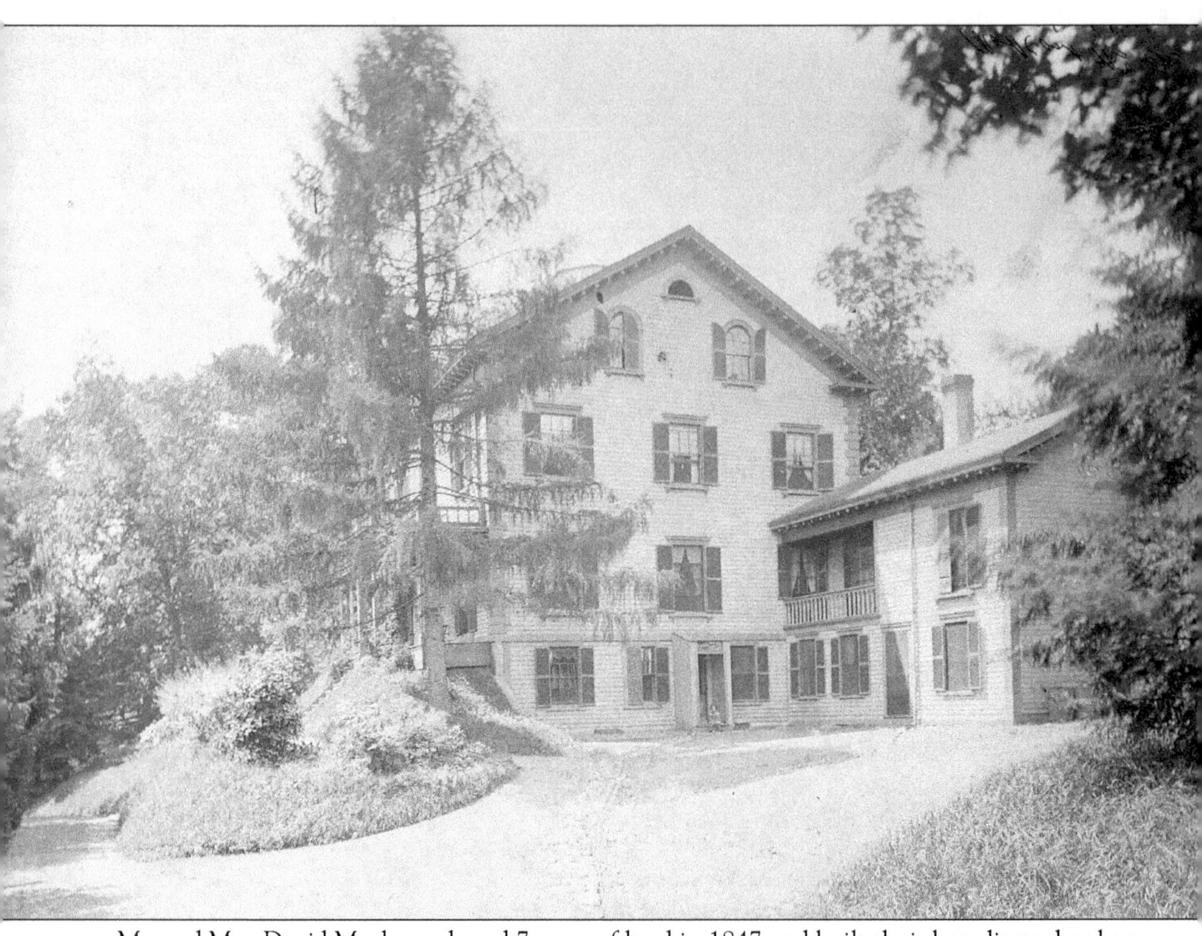

Mr. and Mrs. David Mack purchased 7 acres of land in 1847 and built their boarding school on a steep hill covered with cherry, pear, apple, and quince trees. The Orchard Hill School stood on the steep side of Pleasant Street, across from the Clark Street Bridge. The establishment, furnished with bathing accommodations and a bowling alley, was situated in a delightful region abounding with pleasant walks. It combined every facility for exercise and health. The school's enrollment dropped during the Civil War because many of its students were from the South. However, it accepted day students and remained open until David Mack's death in 1878.

Dr. David Mack, a graduate of Yale, was chairman of the building committee for the First Church and was instrumental in founding the public library in 1869. He served as the first librarian in the old town hall on School Street; at the time the library was to be opened for delivery of books one hour a week. This photograph shows him, his wife, Lucy Mack, and three of their children, Laura, Isabella, and David Jr.

The advertisement for the Orchard Hill Boarding School informed parents of the costs and types of instruction. Pupils were expected to furnish their own towels, silver fork, and napkin ring. Every article of clothing was to be distinctly marked in some conspicuous place. Tuition, board, and washing amounted to $320. Some of the extras included music and use of piano for $25 and cultivation of the voice for $30. Letters, newspapers, and packages always had to be prepaid. Students were instructed to take the Fitchburg train to Wellington Hill Station.

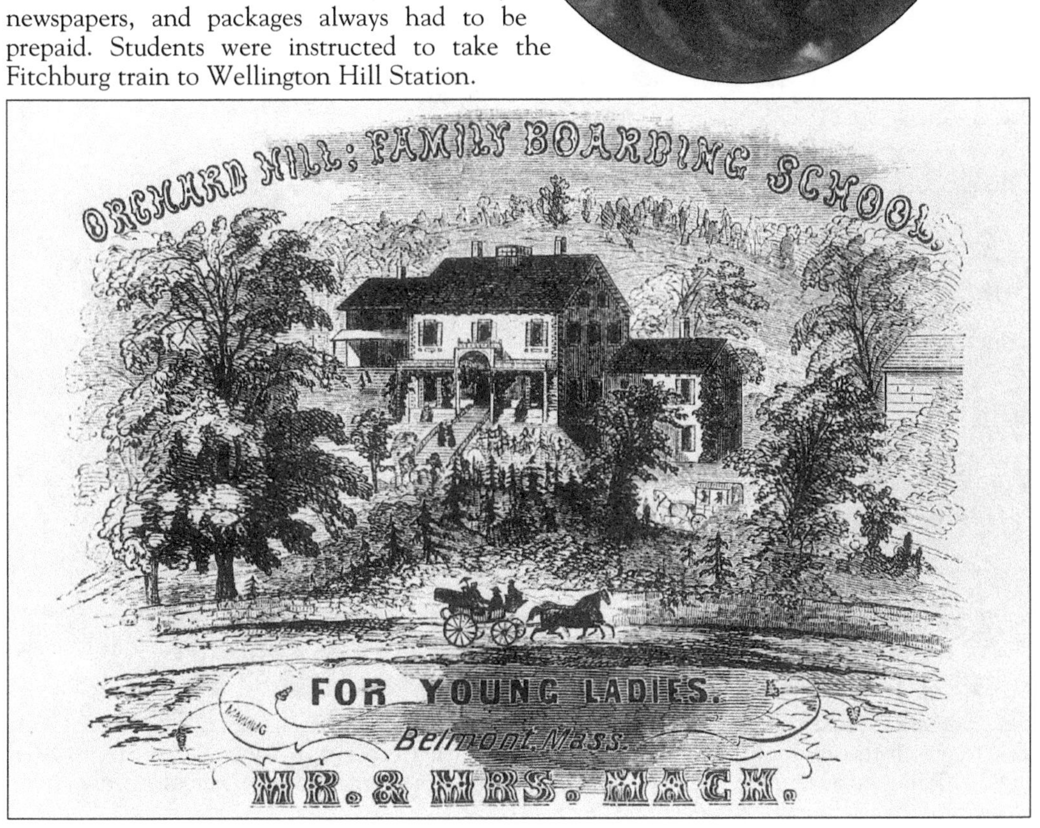

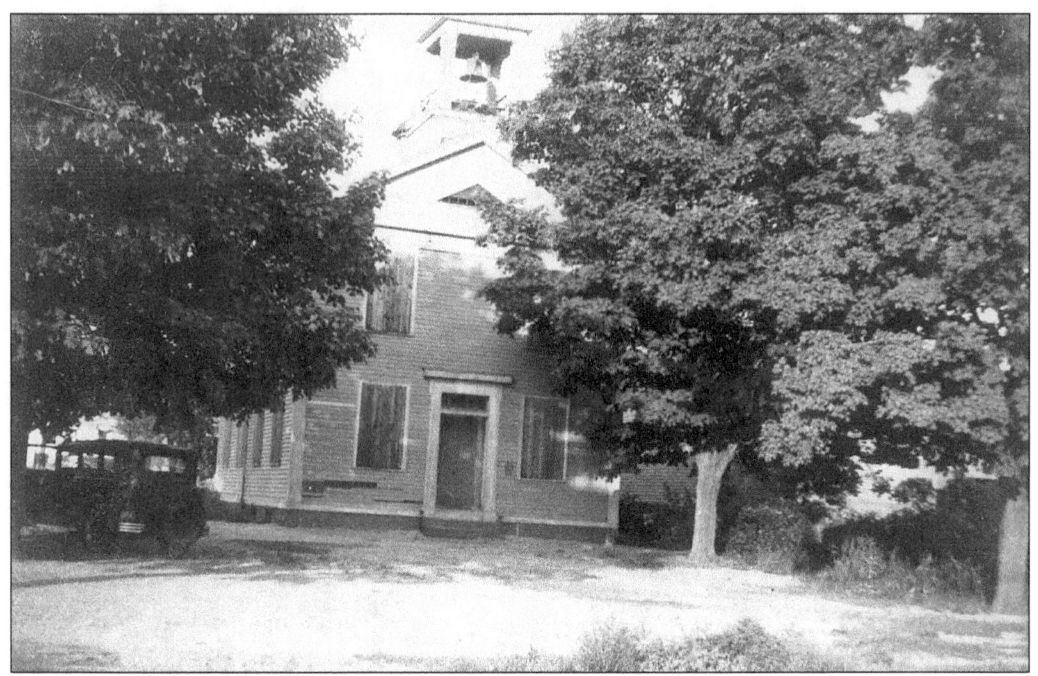

The Brighton Street School was built in 1842 in West Cambridge. It came to Belmont when the town was incorporated. It had neither plumbing nor electricity. Thirsty children used a tin dipper hanging next to a wooden pump. In September 1921, the school was closed and students moved to the Homer School.

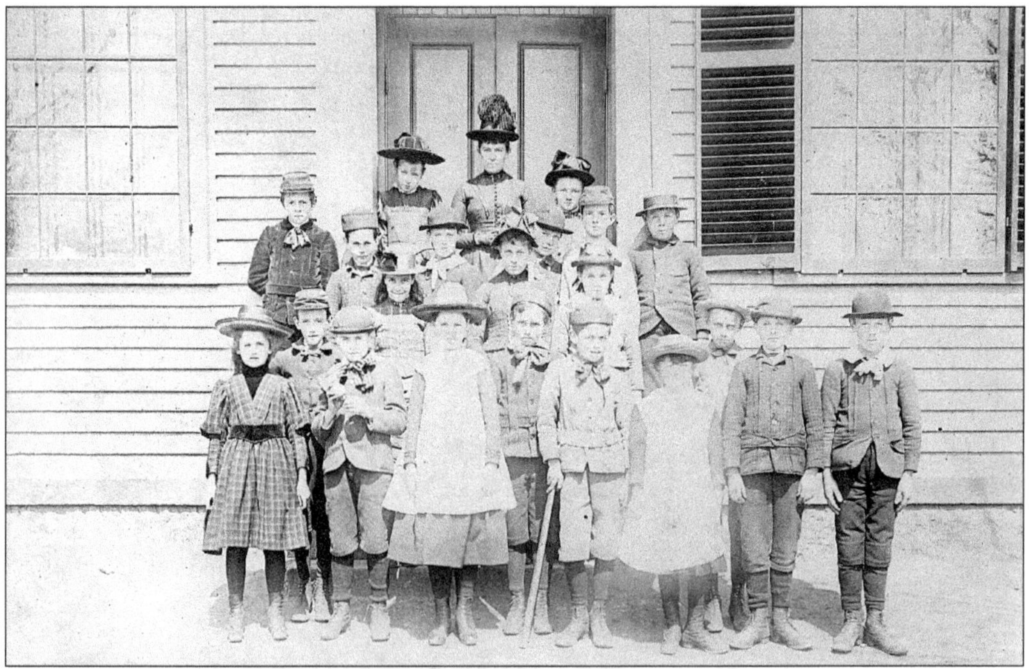

The pupils of the Brighton Street School pose with their teacher, Kitty L. Beran, in 1883. In the 1800s, before automatic washers and wrinkle-free clothing, children always dressed well for school and never thought to question the dress code.

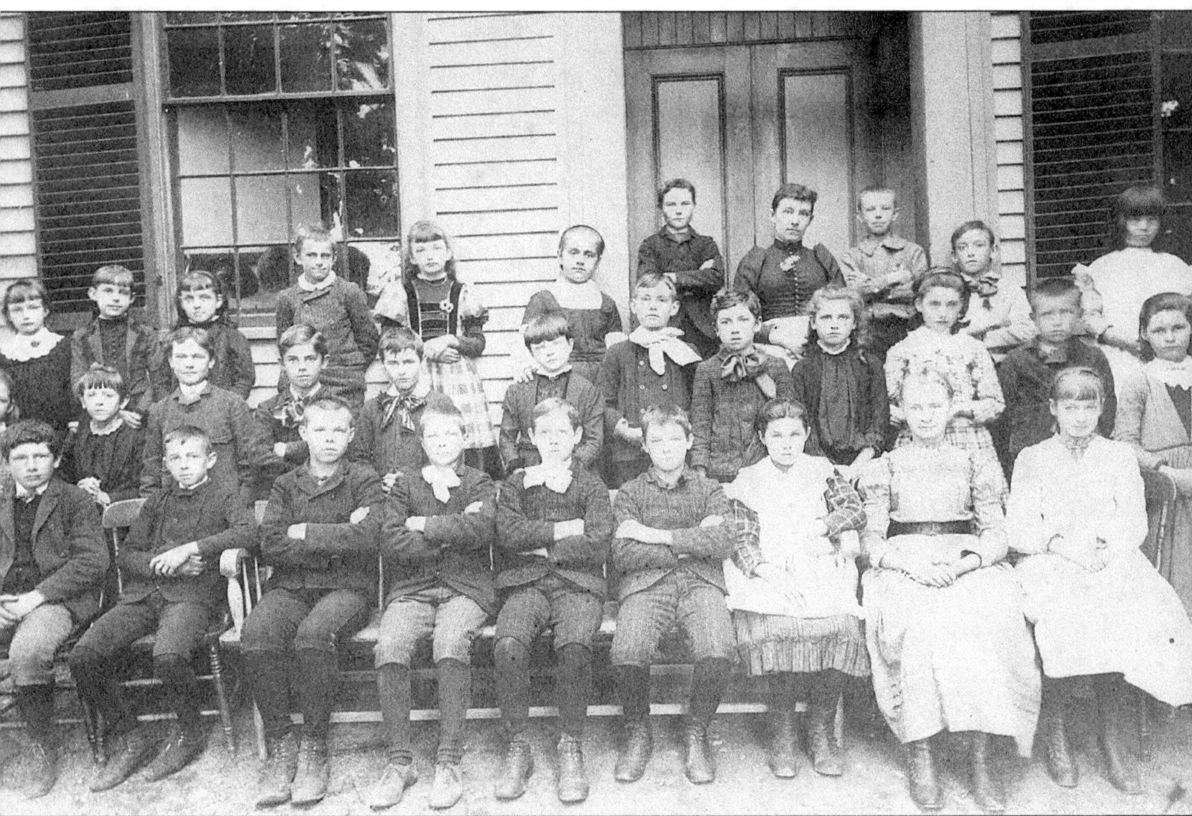

In 1895, outside the Brighton Street School, this group waited for the photographer to finish his work. When there were snow days and school had to be closed, children anxiously listened for the no-school signal, which was blown on the whistle of the piano key factory of the Tower Manufacturing Company on Concord Avenue.

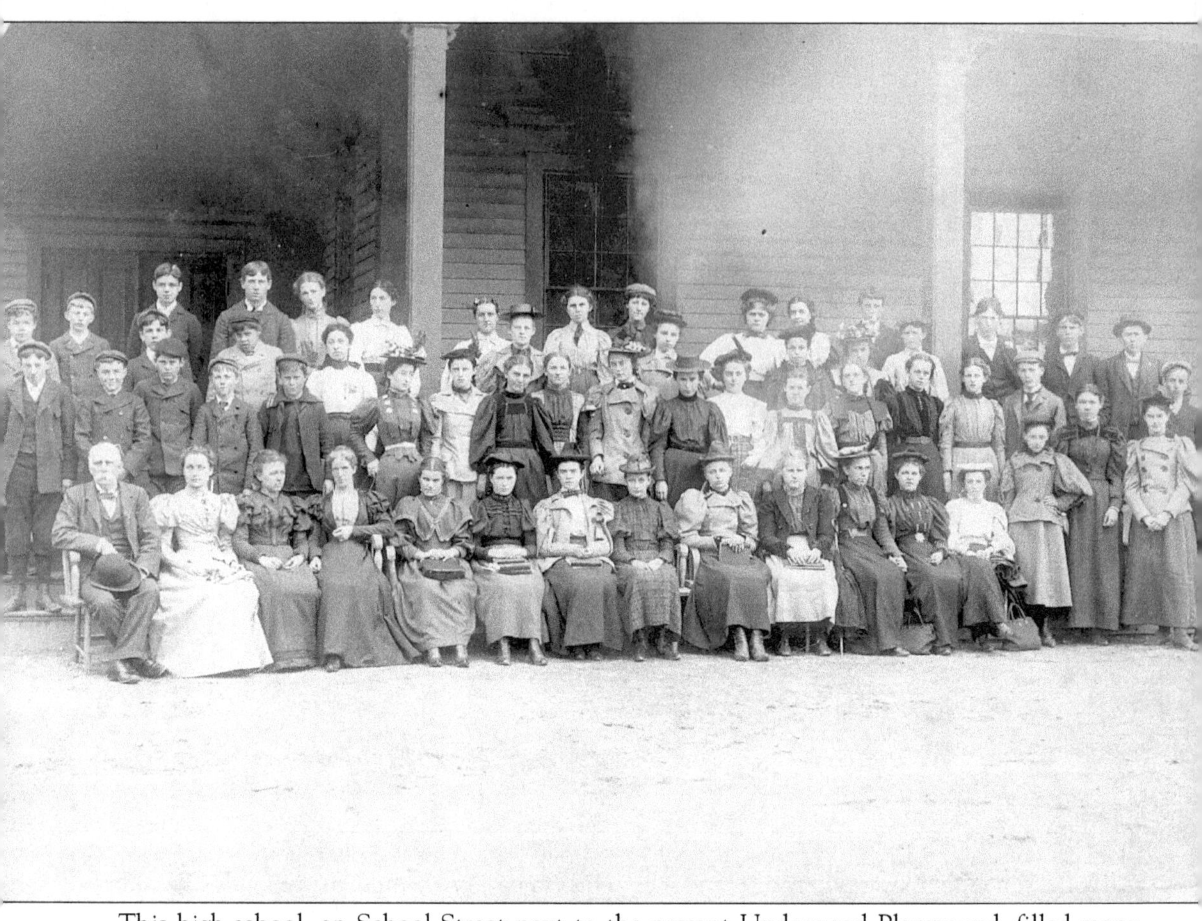

This high school, on School Street next to the present Underwood Playground, filled many needs. At one time it served as the town hall, and the Congregational church started here. The high school was held on the second floor, and the seventh and eighth grades were held in one large room downstairs. The pupils and faculty of Belmont High School posed in front of the building in 1898. Seated in the front row is Henry Butler, principal, and teachers Edith May, Miss Denny, and Mary Lee Burbank.

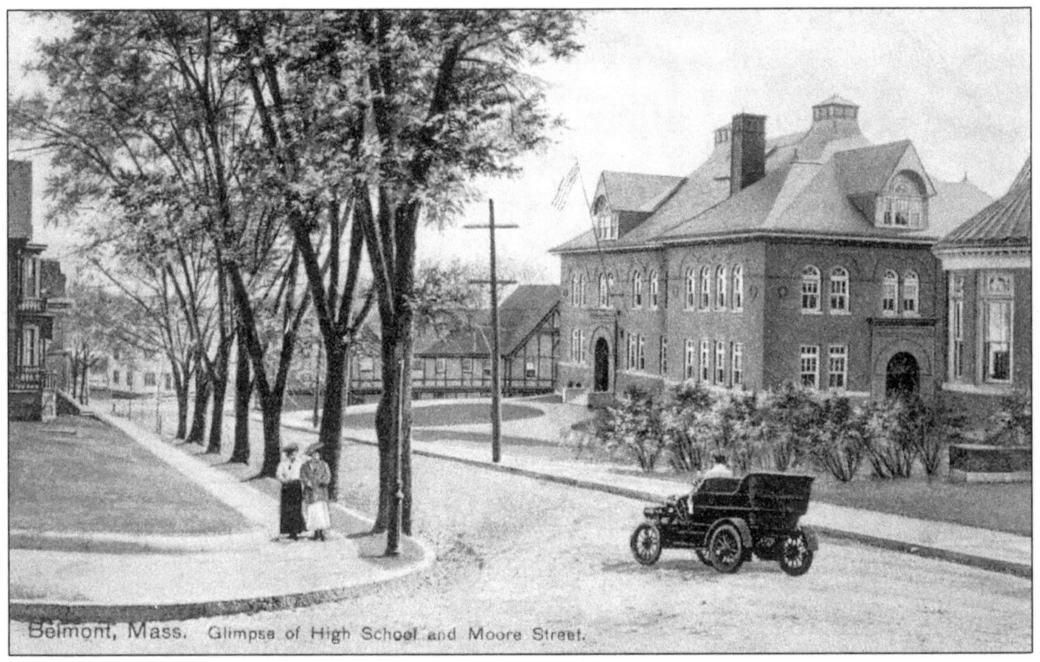

The second high school in Belmont graduated its first class in 1899. Built on Moore Street, on the site of the Homer homestead, it was renamed the Homer School. In 1935, this building was no longer needed as a school and was used as an annex to the town hall.

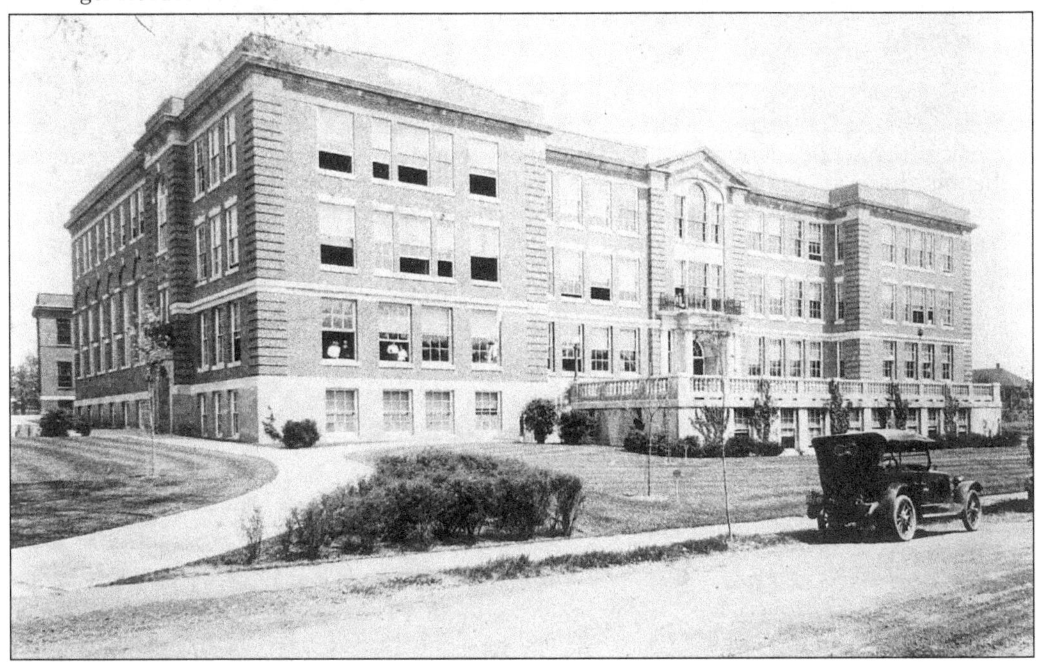

The Atkins and Underwood families donated money toward the land purchase on Orchard Street for the new high school, which opened in 1917. In 1923, the high school was connected to the Roger Wellington School through a 12-room addition. In 1938, a cafeteria was added, and in 1939 came a new gymnasium which, with Mel Wenner as coach, developed years of great basketball teams.

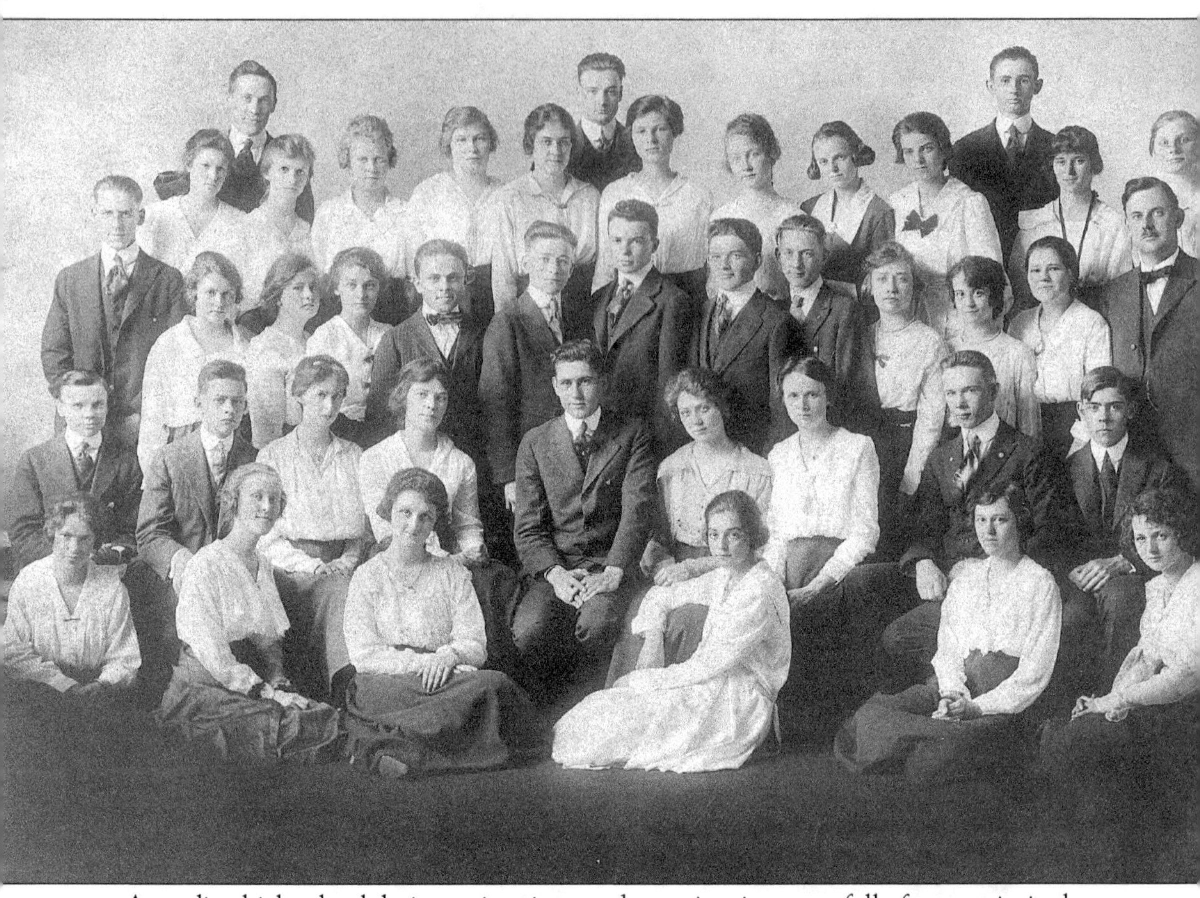

Attending high school during trying times and experiencing years full of uncertainties because of the war, this class graduated in 1918. Much of the program for the graduation and Class Day exercises was war-related. Frank A. Scott, the principal when this photograph was taken, later became the superintendent of schools.

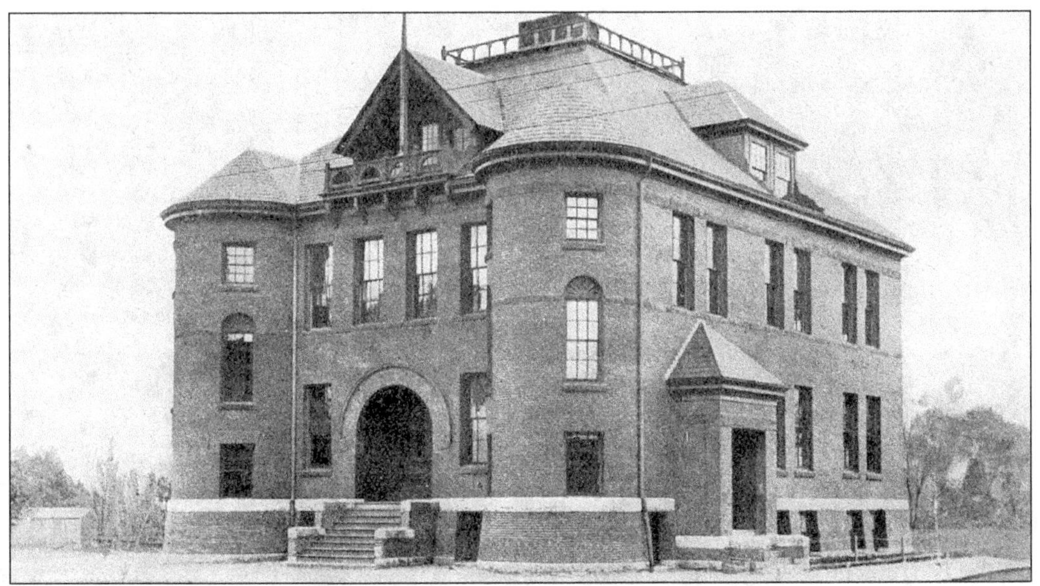

The Roger Wellington School was originally opened as a four-room school in 1892. Below are the two new wings, which were added in 1908. Part of the curriculum for the seventh-grade and eighth-grade girls included the hemming and marking of roller towels for use in the school. (Top photograph courtesy of John Garrity.)

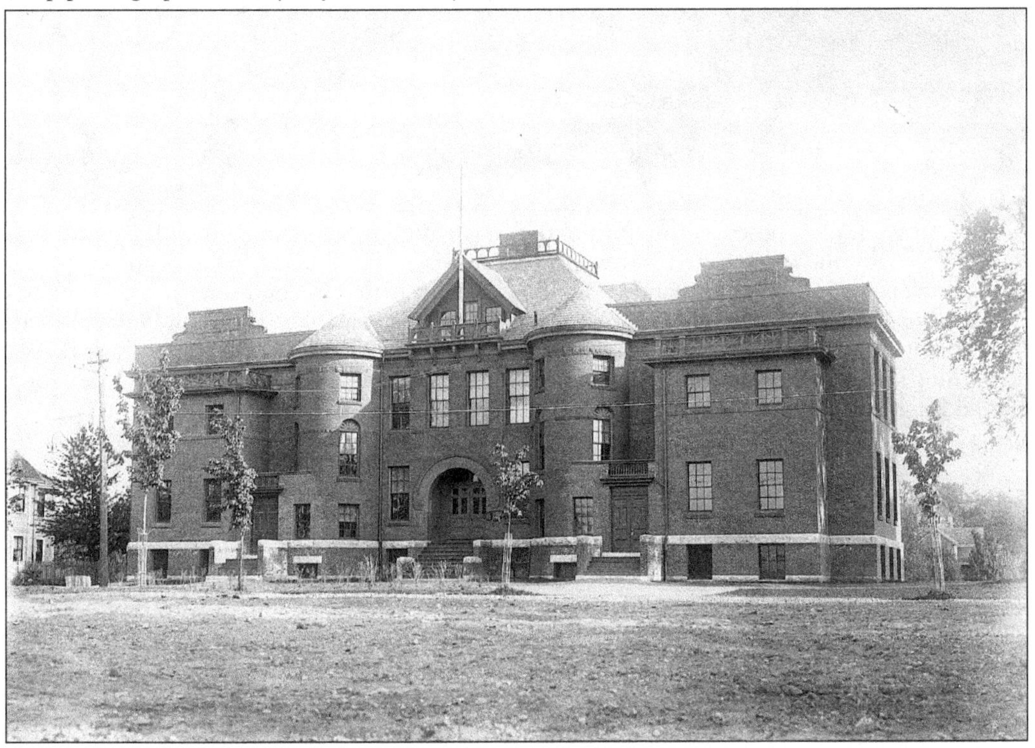

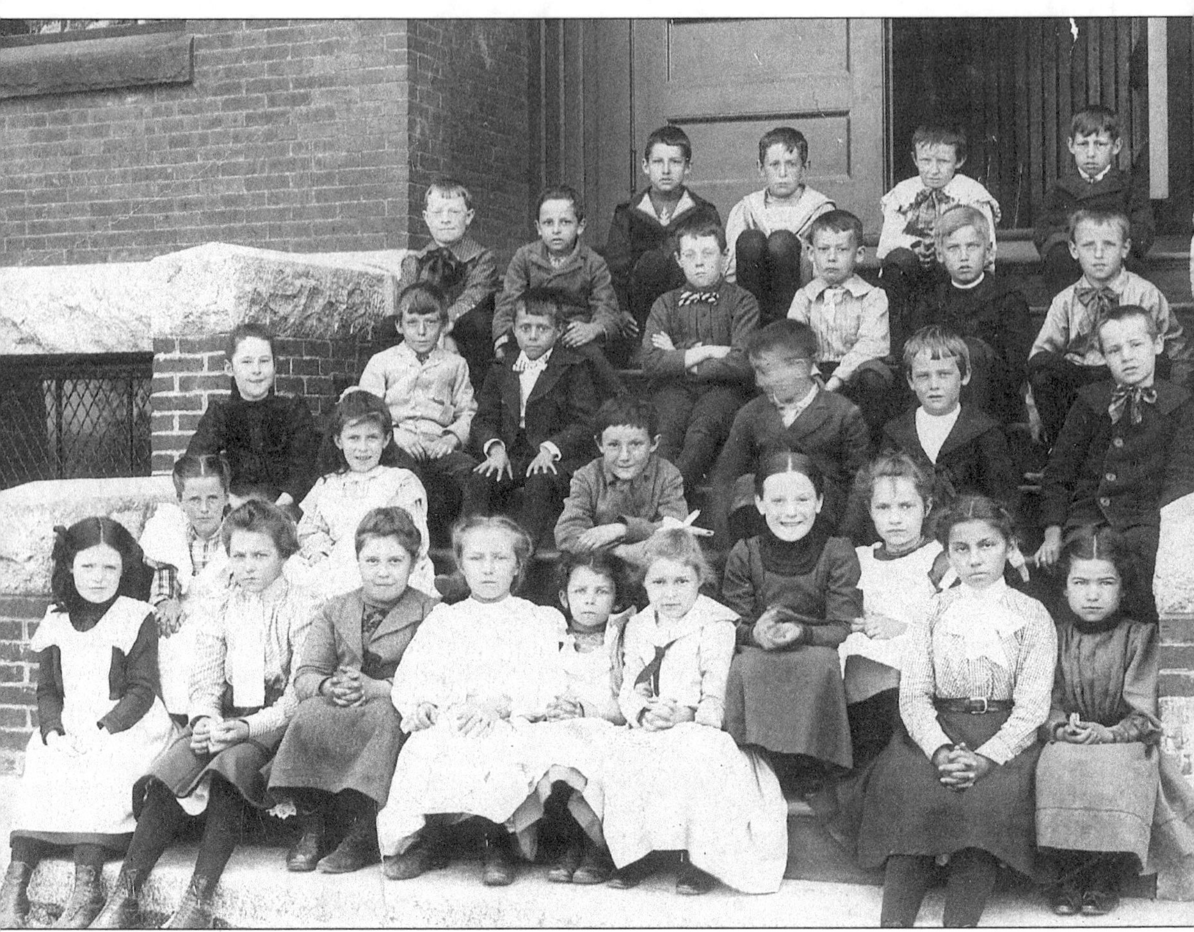

The fourth-grade class poses on the stairs of the Roger Wellington School in 1900. Shown are, from left to right, the following: (first row) Rebecca Carson, Ethel Slade, Ethel Bean, Katherine Joyce, unidentified, Marie Elias, and two unidentified students; (second row) Jessie Donahue, Helen Haggerty, unidentified, Mary Carson, and Constance Lincoln; (third row) unidentified, Joe O'Brien, Alex Husband, unidentified, Albert Blaikie, and Frank Bennett; (fourth row) Ava Poole, Jim Brown, unidentified, Guy Robinson, Bill Hallowell, and unidentified; (fifth row) Harold Birch, unidentified student, Tim Griffin, and unidentified.

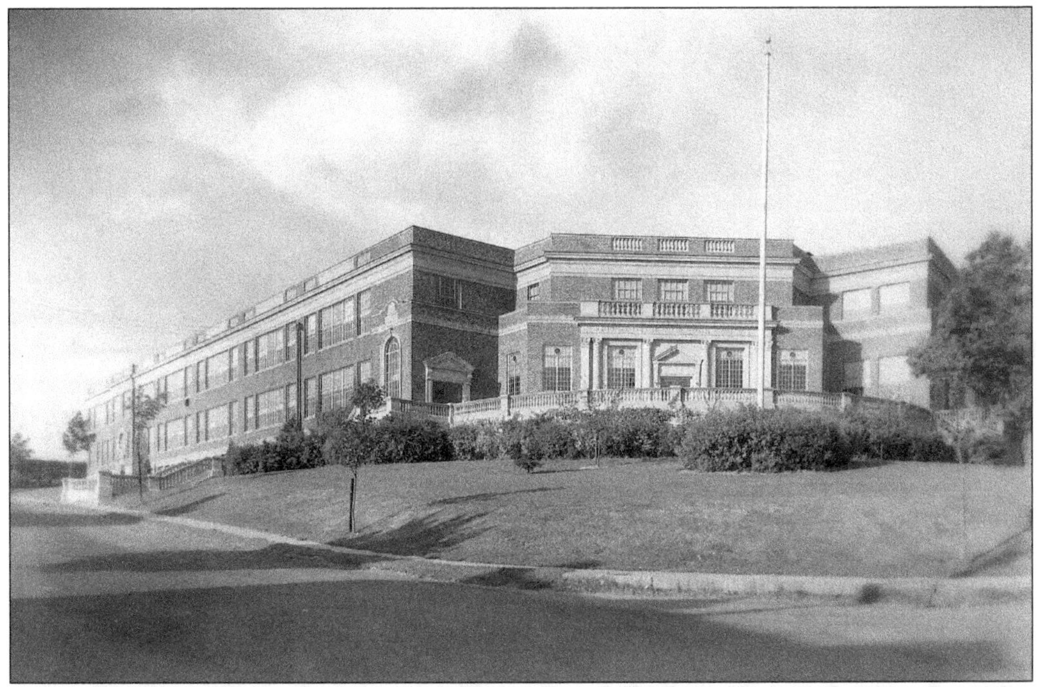

A building boom brought more homes and therefore more families to Belmont, so more space was needed in the schools. Housing for 415 families was added to the town in 1924 and for 437 families in 1925. The Belmont Junior High School opened in 1926.

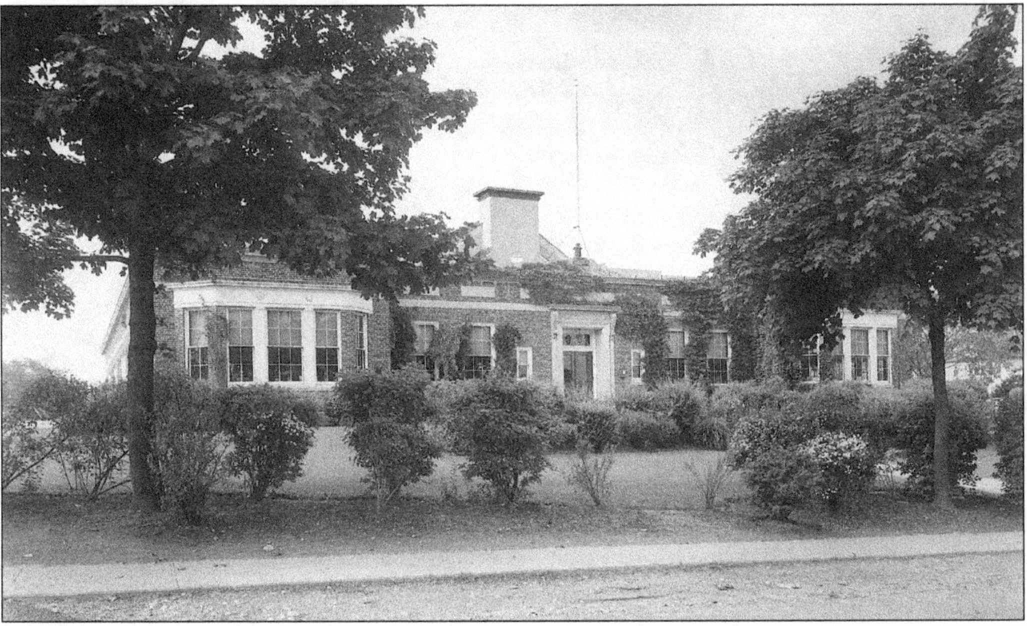

When the Winthrop L. Chenery School opened in 1924, it was considered the safest grade school in the country. It was one-story with an assembly hall in the center. Each classroom had a direct exit to the outside. It was named for Winthrop L. Chenery, in recognition of service to the town in public affairs, serving as representative to the state legislature, on the school committee, as town treasurer, and for 35 years as town clerk.

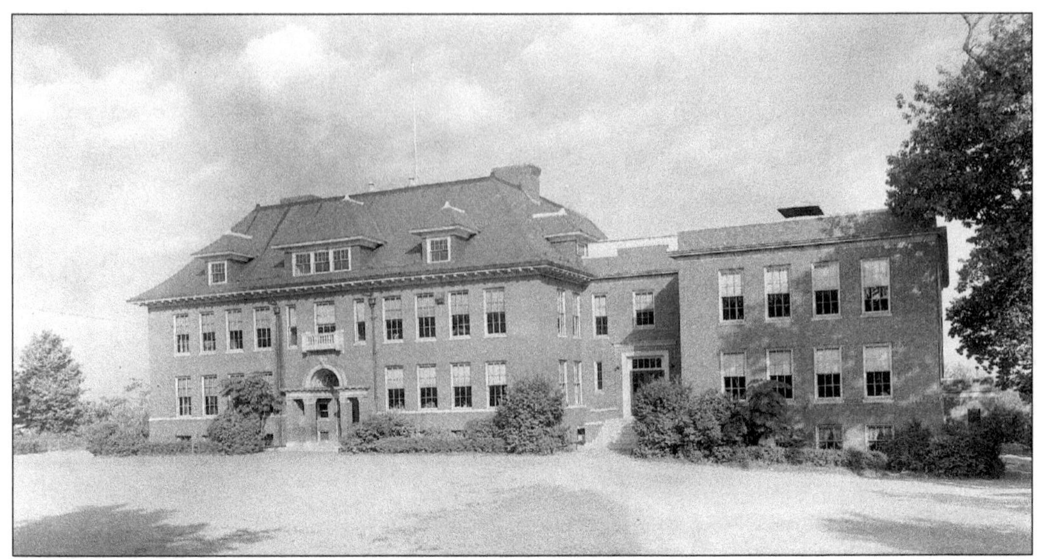

In 1905, the Payson Park School was built with four of the eight classrooms completed, making room enough for 99 pupils. Typical of the early schools, the auditorium was on the top floor. It was also the custom to finish a fraction of the rooms in new schools, and then from time to time two or more additional rooms would be completed.

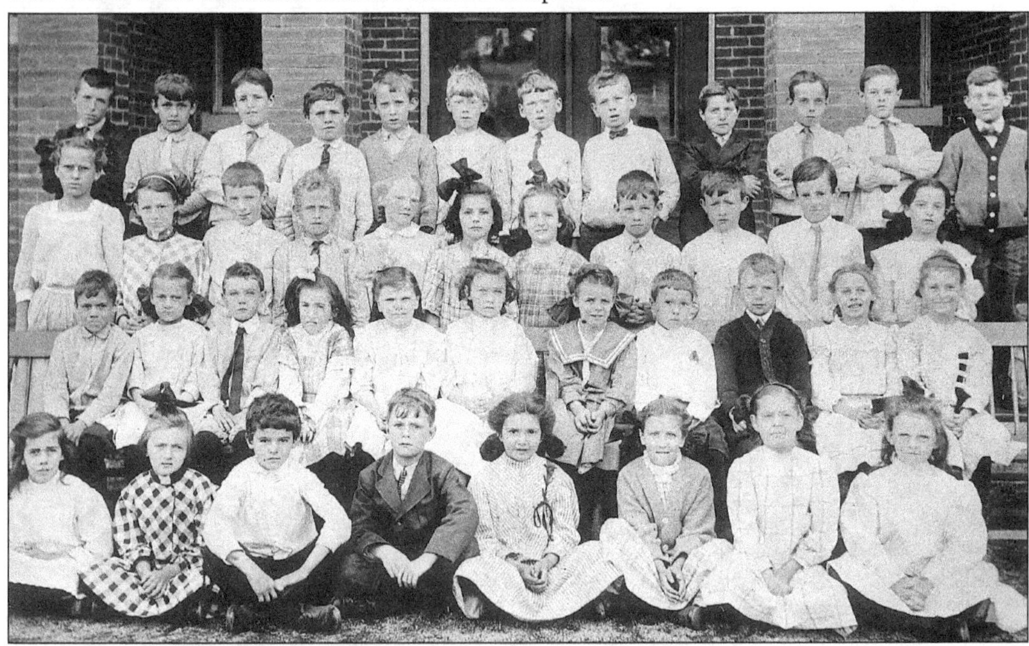

Shown in this 1911 photograph of Payson Park School students are, from left to right, as follows: C. Rose, M. Clark, J. Greelish, J. Benton, E. Haley, M. Blennerhasset, unidentified, and M. Burns; (second row) ? Haagland, unidentified, T. Tierney, ? Hall, E. Johnson, S. Skahan, F. Conley, two unidentified students, ? Tierney, and R. Caulfield; (third row) ? Pollard, ? Campbell, ? Fitz, M. Conley, two unidentified students, K. Grant, C. Dennis, unidentified, M. Keefe, and H. O'Brien; (fourth row) E. McArthur, F. Wright, J. Tierney, J. Millett, H. Gallagher, H. Johnson, A. Doyle, unidentified, A. Morse, G. VanWyck, unidentified, and Ralph Burns.

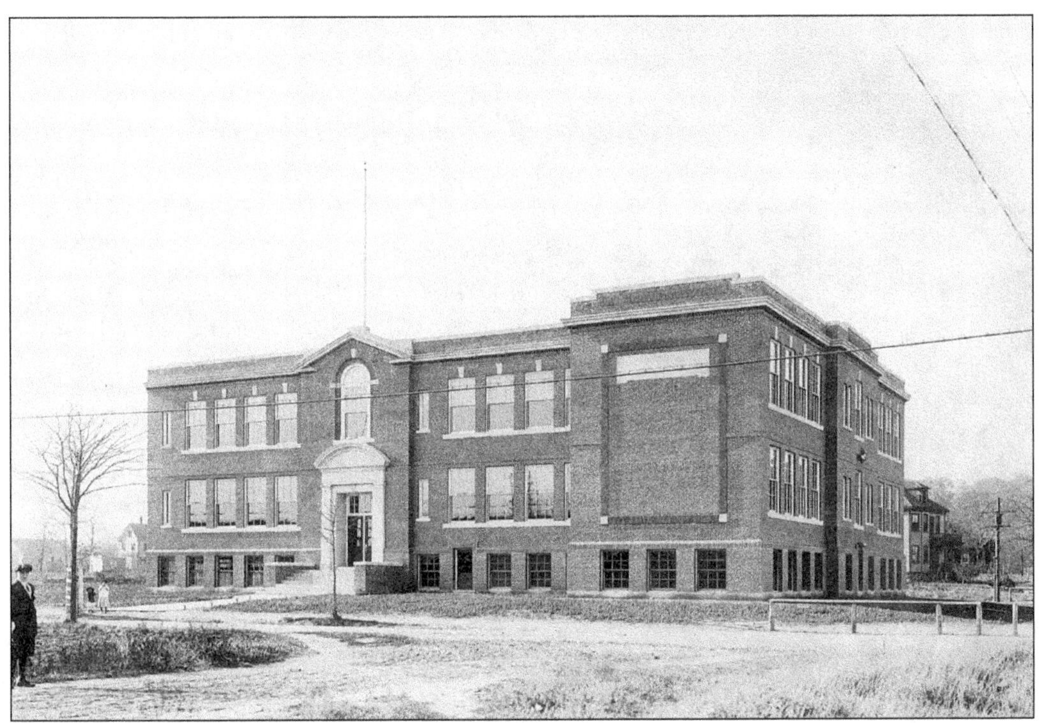

The Josiah S. Kendall School opened in 1915 with eight classrooms and an assembly hall. It was built so that an addition could be added later and still make the building look symmetrical and complete. For many years, the ground and gardens in front of the school were a big attraction, ably cared for by Oscar Duncan, the custodian with the green thumb.

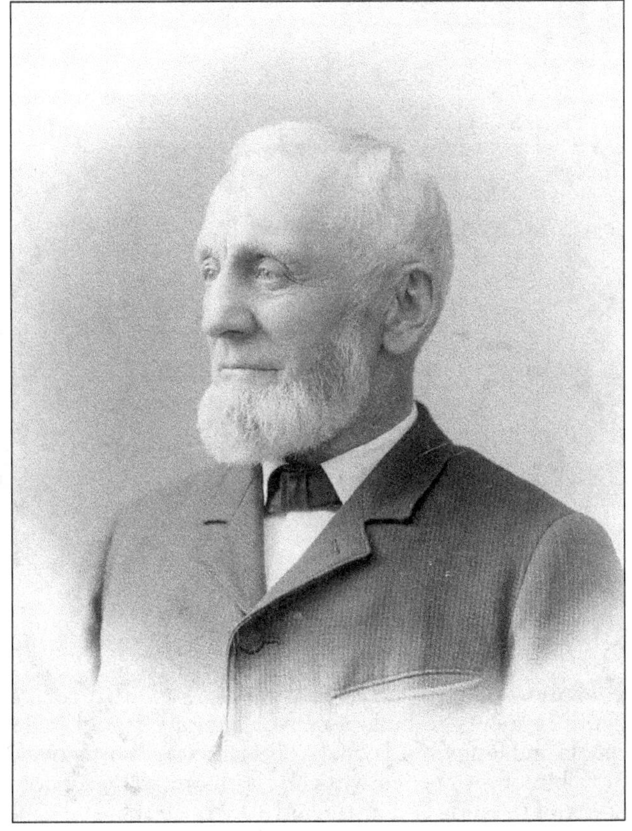

Josiah Shattuck Kendall was born and died in the family homestead on Mill Street. His service to the town began in 1862, when he was elected to the school committee; he later served as assessor and selectman, serving the town for 42 years. His father and uncle ran a mill on Beaver Brook. They also ran a 120-acre farm, which he took over and turned into a successful dairy farm.

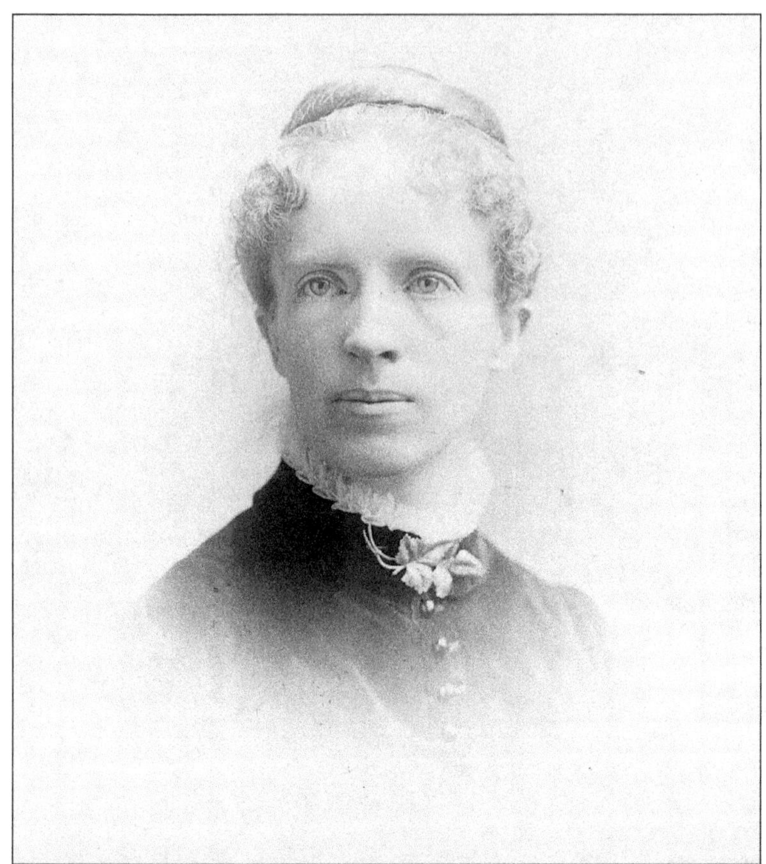

The eldest of seven children, Mary Lee Burbank, born in 1860, was the daughter of Prof. Levi and Margaret Russell Burbank. At age 18, she started teaching in Belmont as an assistant teacher at the high school on School Street. She taught algebra, geometry, French, and German and retired in 1921 after 40 years of service.

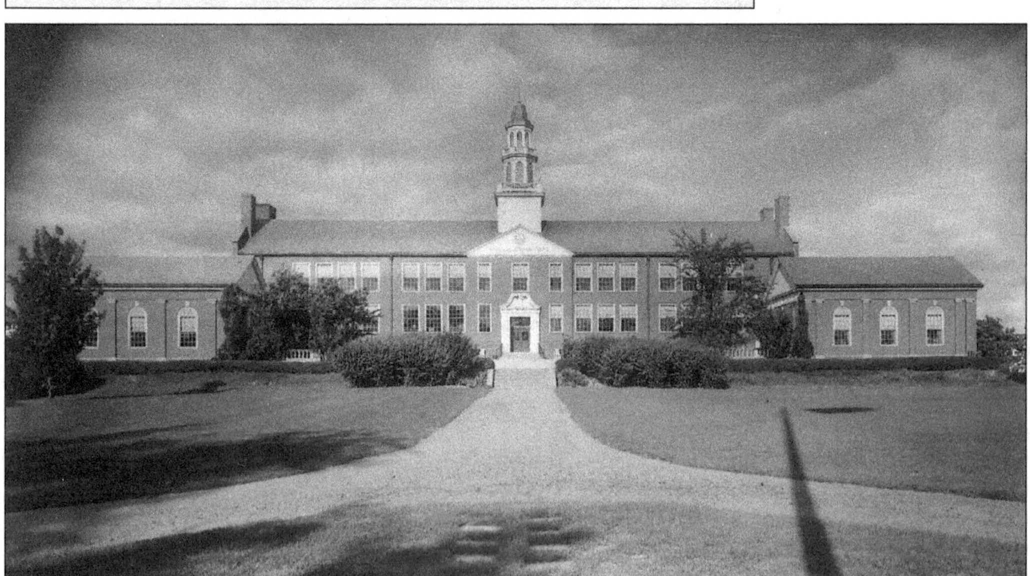

It was necessary to build a new elementary school in 1931. This attractive building, with its cupola and long front lawn, has been admired by many. Designed by Belmont architect George E. Robinson, it opened with 17 classrooms. The school was named for Mary Lee Burbank, in honor of the long and distinguished service that she gave the town.

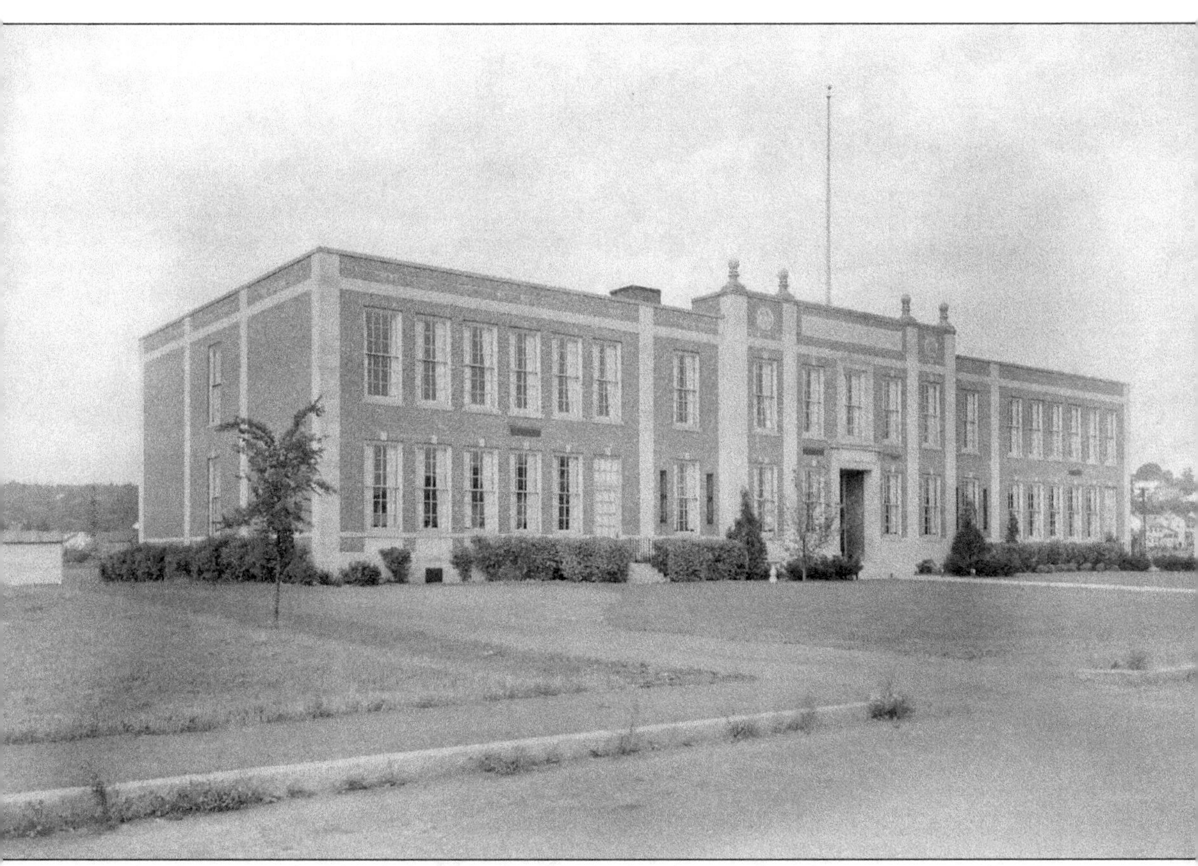

When the Winn Brook School opened in 1935, the teachers and students were transferred to the new building. As the town continued to grow and the farms were developed into house lots, additions were constructed and school officials continued to seek needed space. In the 1940s and 1950s, the sixth-grade classes and their teachers were transported to the Mary Lee Burbank School. Incidentally, the year Winn Brook was opened, the janitor's fee was $2 an hour up to 11:00 p.m. If snow shoveling or extra cleaning was required, an extra 75¢ was paid.

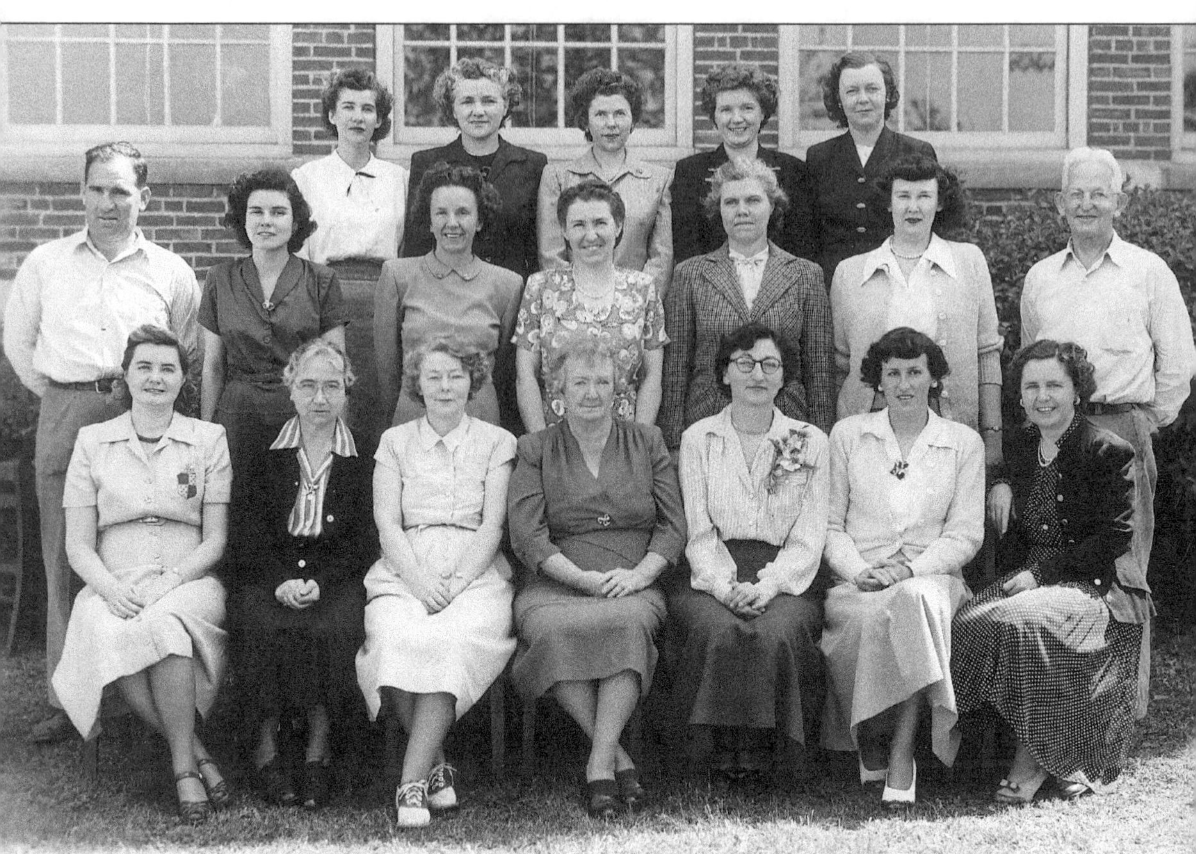

Belmontians have always taken pride in their schools and have been fortunate in attracting dedicated teachers. In 1949, this group staffed the Winn Brook School. The principal, Eva Burns, also served at the Brighton Street School and the Homer School. Shown are, from left to right, the following: (first row) Gladys Mahoney, Blanche Greener, Ellen O'Clare, Eva Burns, Lillian Kales, Betty Enright, and Kay O'Brien; (middle row) John Quigley, Betty Carolyn, Marion Ryder, Dorothy Gibb, Barbara Jack, Rita Tracy, and Mr. Gardner; (back row) Hildegarde Ditchett, Florence Hargrove, Kay Hennessey, Alice Good, and Fran Conley.

Eight

Recreation and Celebration

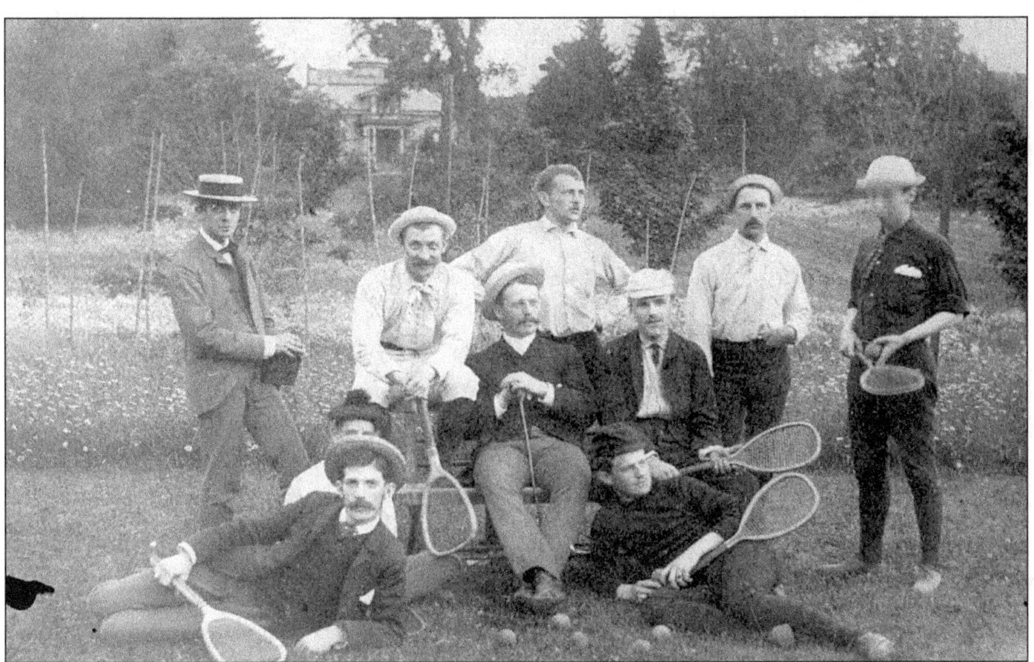

At the beginning of the 20th century, tennis was a popular sport and there were several courts around town. This photograph shows members of the Belmont Tennis Club before the clubhouse was built. The Blake-Kilburn house is visible in the background. The Belmont Tennis Club is believed to be the second oldest in the country.

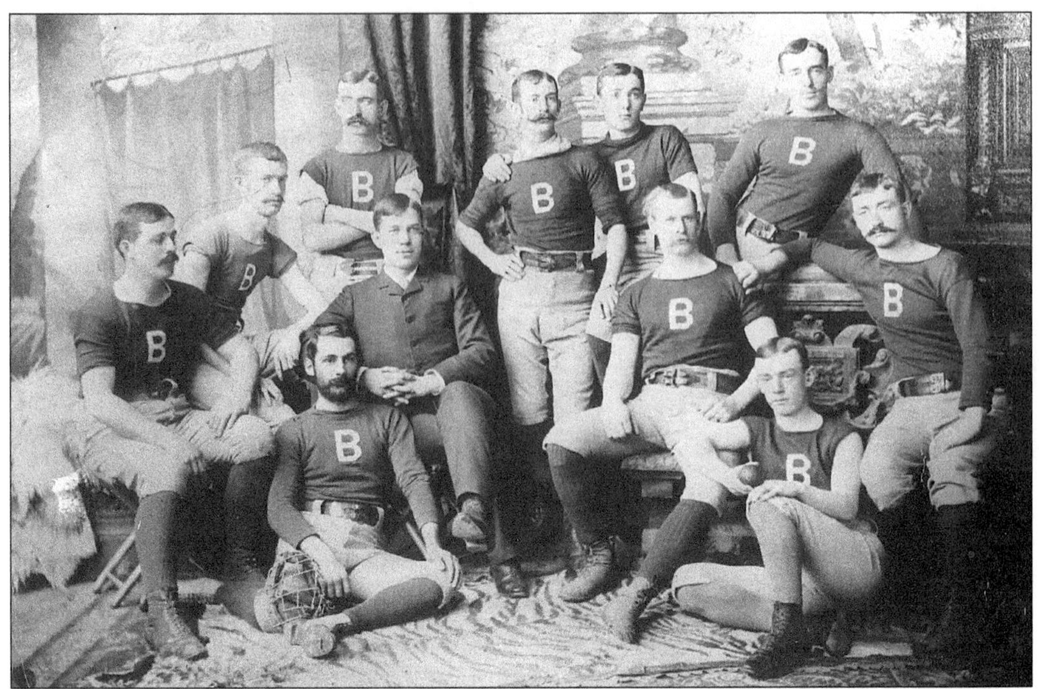

There was always fierce competition between the Waverley and Belmont town teams. Members of the 1897 Belmont Base Ball Club are, from left to right, as follows: (front row) Vedetto (catcher) and Fowler (pitcher); (middle row) Murphy (left field), White (center field), T.D. Hill (manager), Apollonio (third base), and Cadigan (first base); (back row) Burke (pitcher), Deane (second base), Poor (shortstop), and Ellison (right field).

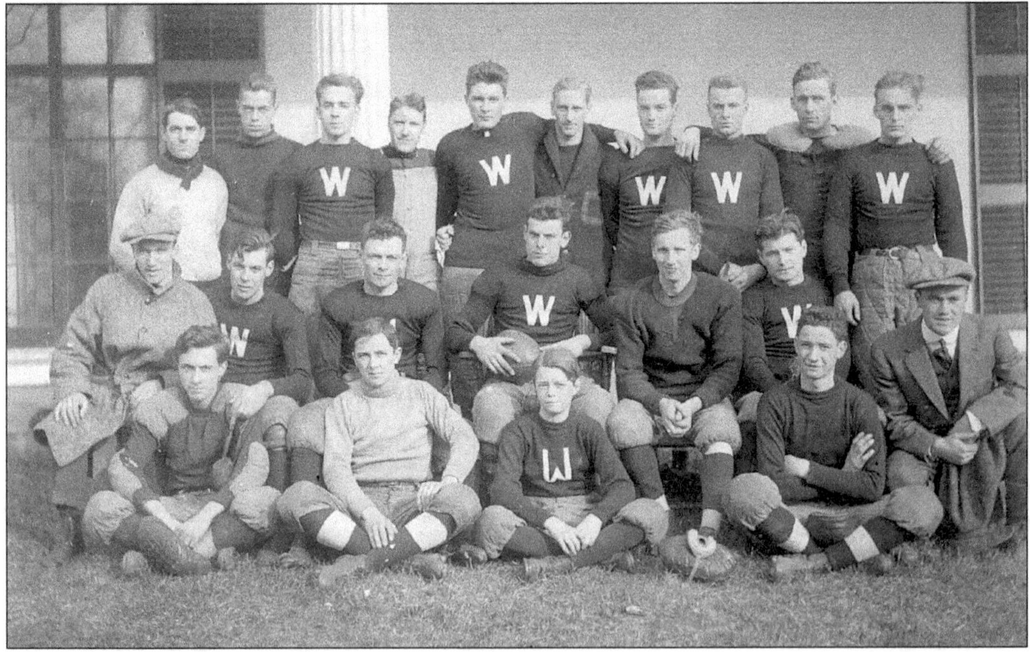

In 1914, the Waverley town team members were the proud winners of the Thanksgiving Day football game. This photograph shows them gathered in front of the Benton Estate.

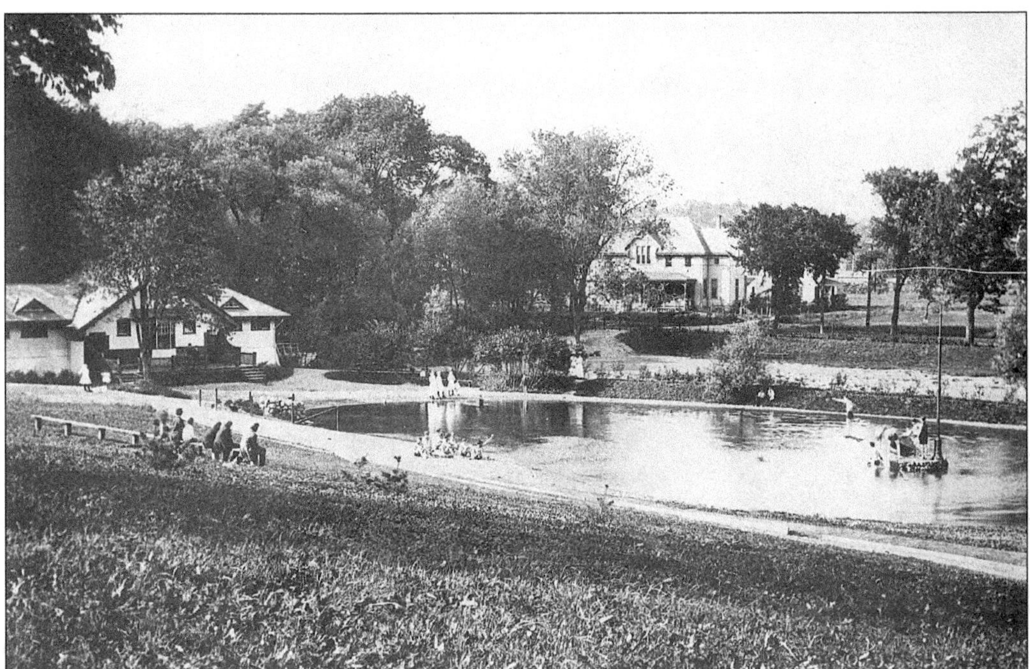

In 1911, Belmont voted to trade several lots of land with H.O. Underwood when he offered to develop a playground with a swimming pool. Loring Underwood designed the area with swings, teeters, and sandpits for small girls and boys. The Underwood Pool was the first public outdoor pool in the country. The house in the background was once the railroad station, moved from Belmont Center.

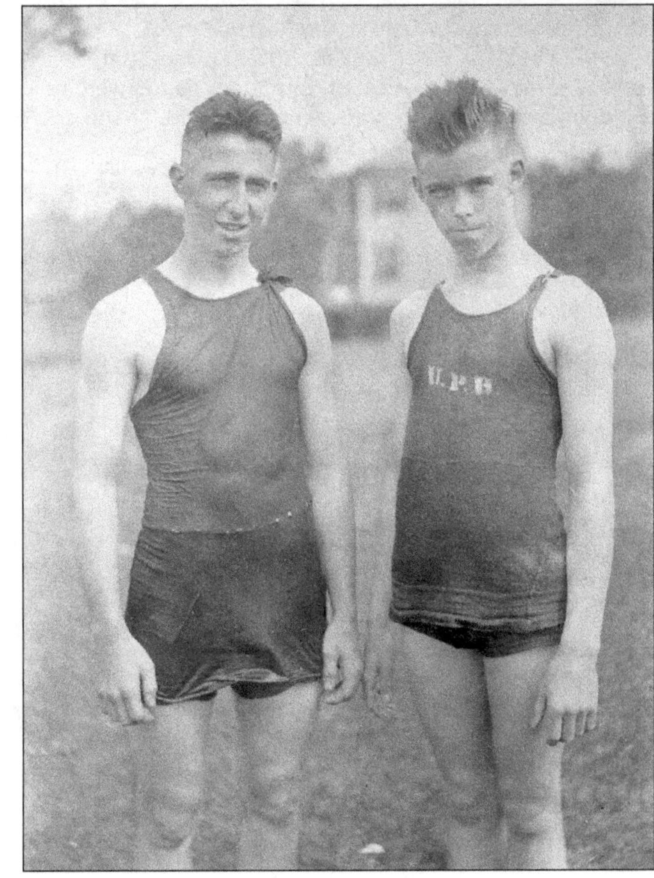

Two of the Underwood Pool lifeguards display the latest swimwear in 1912. By the summer of 1922, there was part-time supervision on all the school playgrounds, the town field, and Underwood Park. There were organized games, contests, storytelling, athletic feats, and handiwork. The season closed with pageants.

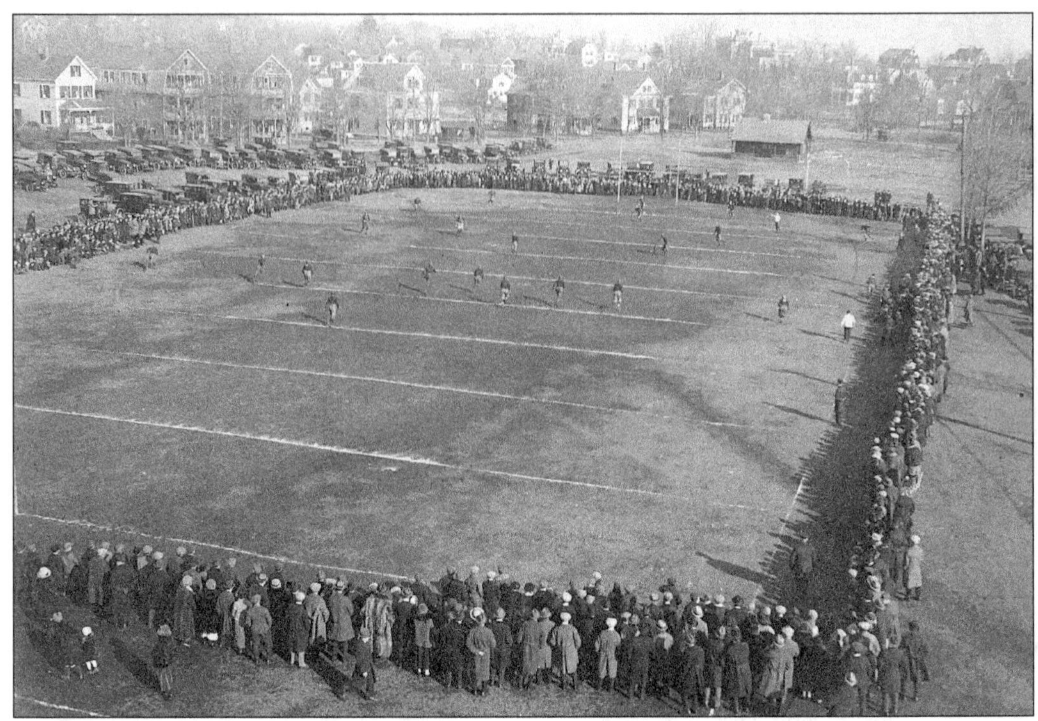

In 1902, land was purchased from the Harris Estate with contributions from private citizens, and the town field was created. Important games were held here, always with huge turnouts for the Belmont-Waverley games. The clubhouse at the end of the field was built by high school students in their manual training class.

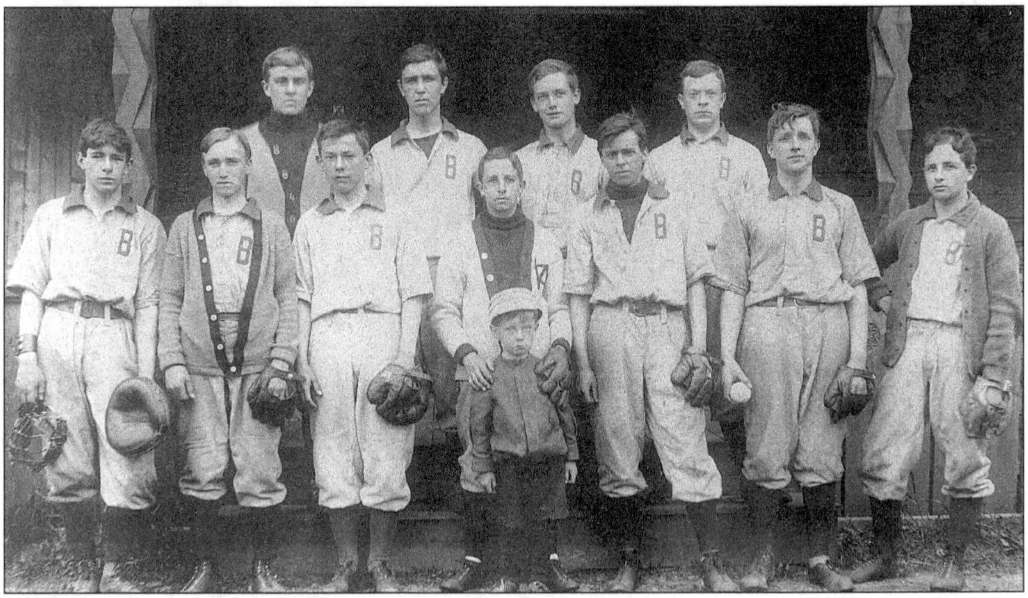

Standing in front of the clubhouse are members of the Belmont High School baseball team in 1908. They are, from left to right, as follows: (front row) F. Parker, H. Gibson, G. Robinson, W. Brown Jr., A. Husband, G. Simm, and J. Brown; (back row) W. Flett, H. Trafton, A. Blaike, and A. Poole. The mascot, Stewart, looks as if he would rather be playing ball than posing.

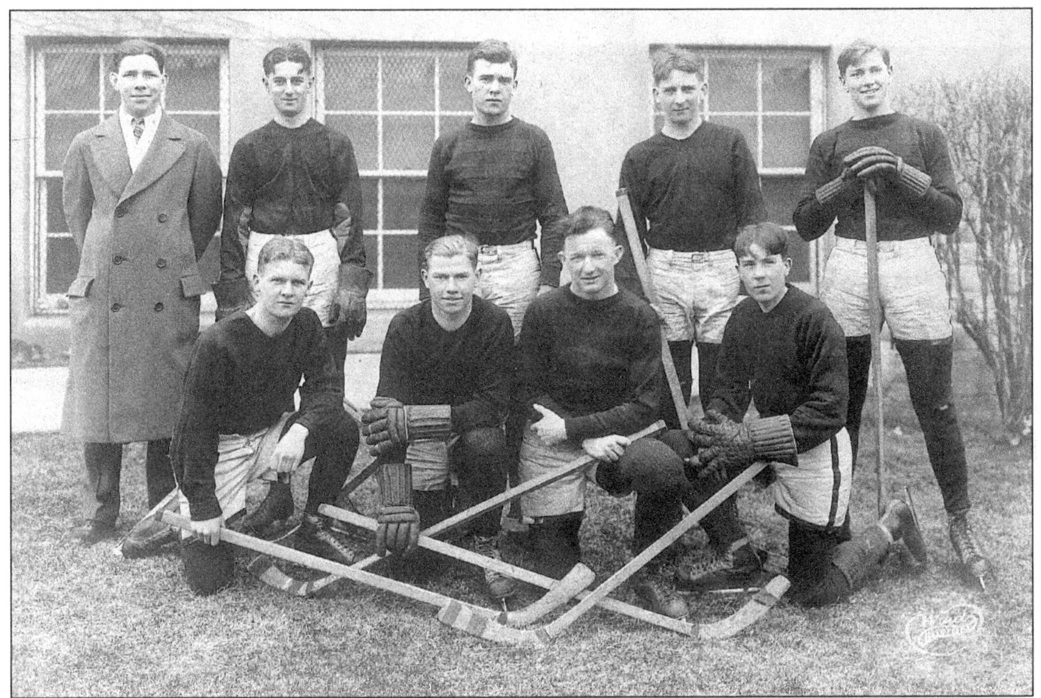

These stalwarts were members of the 1925–1926 hockey team at the high school. Michael Egan, later a popular teacher in Belmont, is third from the left in the front row.

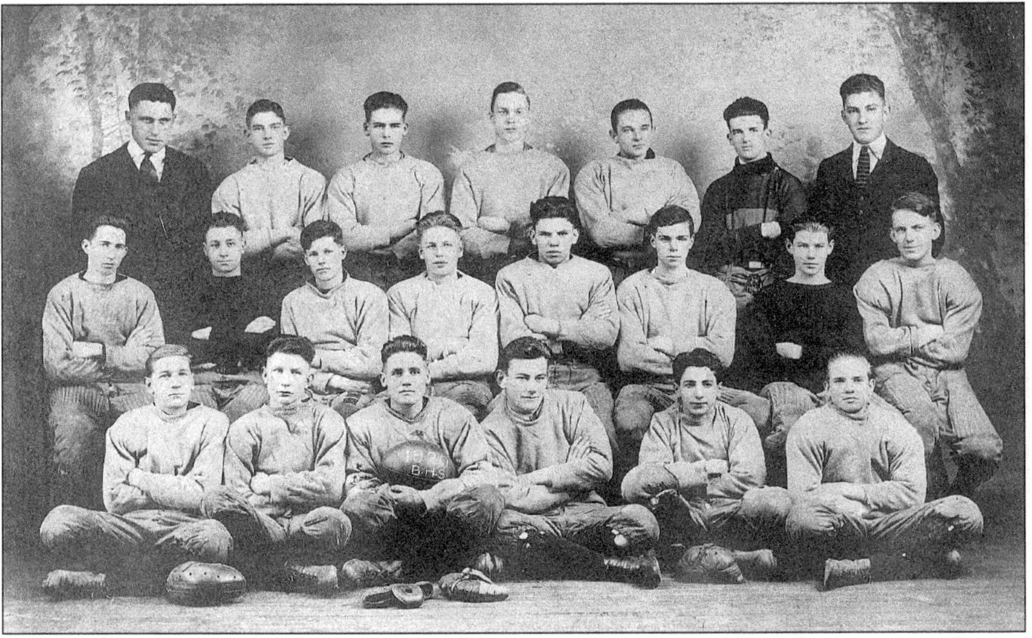

The Belmont High School football team of 1920 consisted of the following players, from left to right: (front row) E. Kellogg, E. Bailey, R. Peabody, V. Johnson, W. Nelto, and R.Sterritt; (middle row) H.O'Brien, V. Aimone, A. Marsh, C. Swanson, A. Cook, W. Jenney, unidentified, and E. Metcalf; (back row) Coach R. Ertel, two unidentified players, H. Jaynes, W. Johnson, A.. McLean, and manager J. Cody.

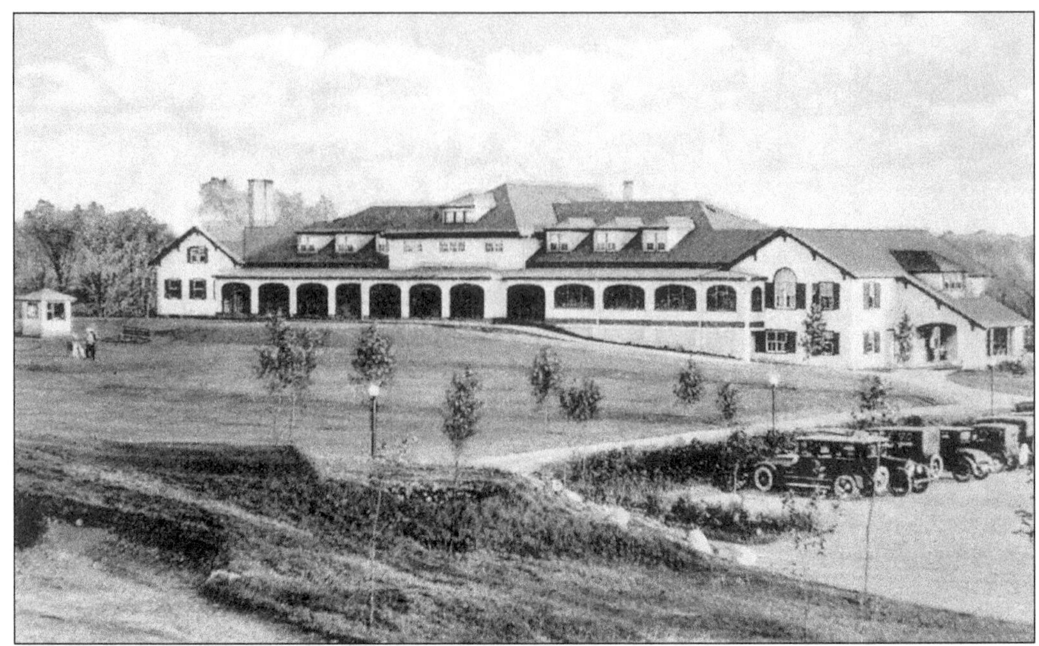

The Belmont Country Club was built in the early 1900s and, after World War I, reached a full membership of 550, with a long waiting list. During the 1930s and 1940s, crowds were attracted to watch tournaments with famous golfers. Belmont boys remember dashing from school to caddie here. Carrying a bag for 18 holes, in usually about four hours' time, they could collect $1 and possibly a 10¢ tip. (Courtesy of John Garrity.)

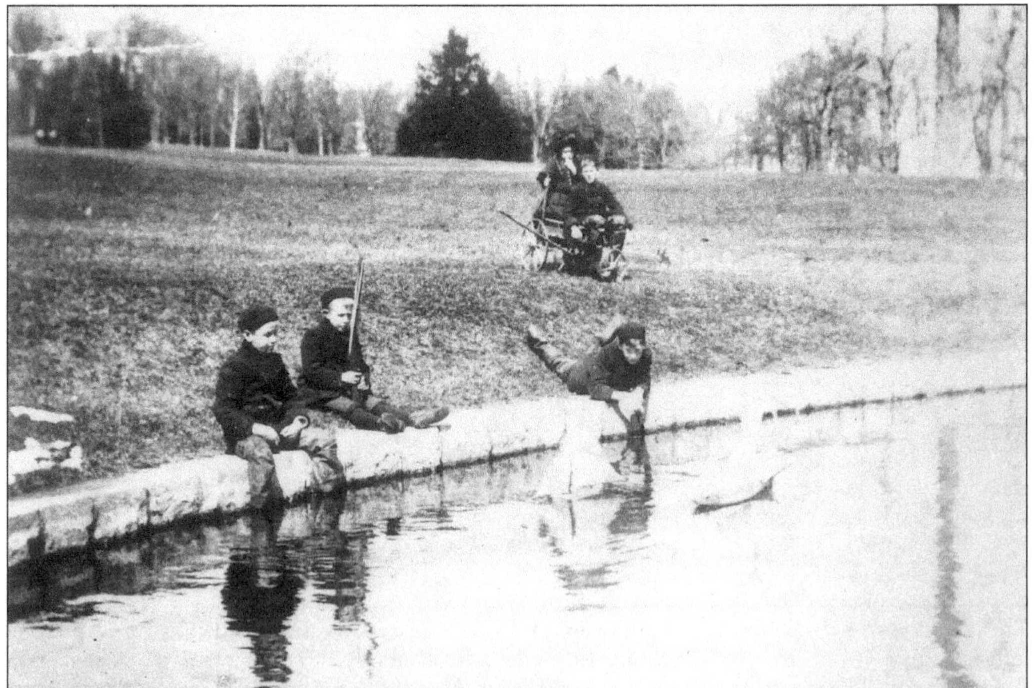

These children enjoy fishing and playing with toy boats on a pond at the Payson estate. The boy on the left, in the boots, was available to retrieve any boats that got away.

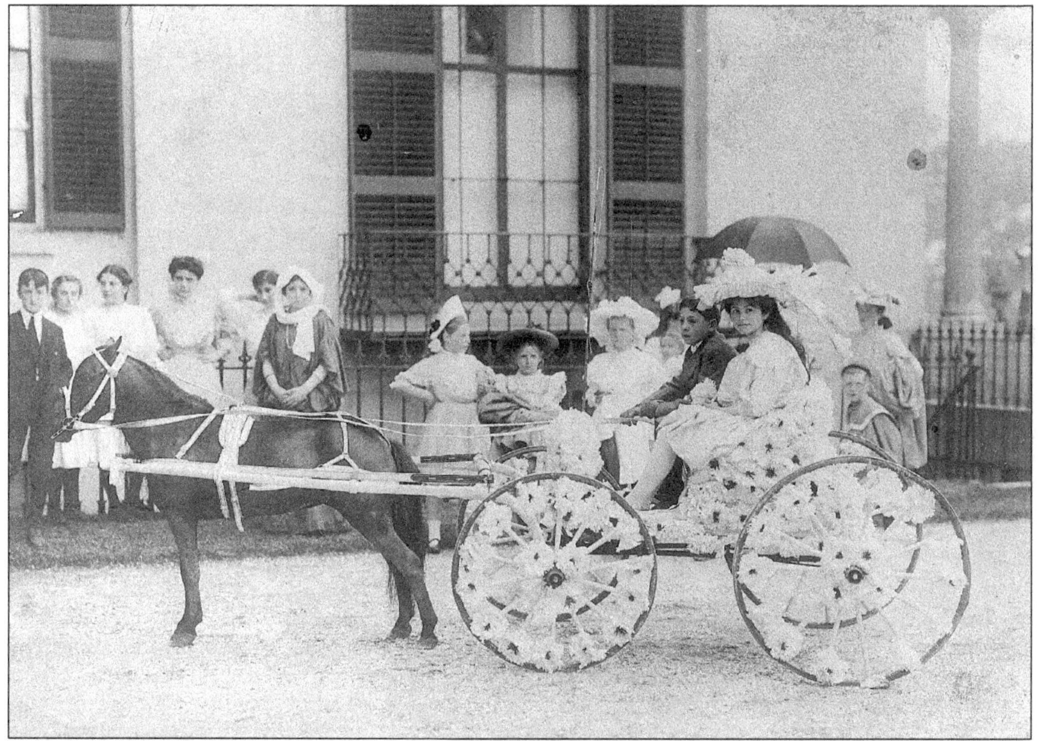

Tom and Elizabeth Harris rode in their decorated carriage at the Benton Estate in 1905. One of the preparations children enjoyed for holidays and parades was the decorating of carts, wagons, and bicycles.

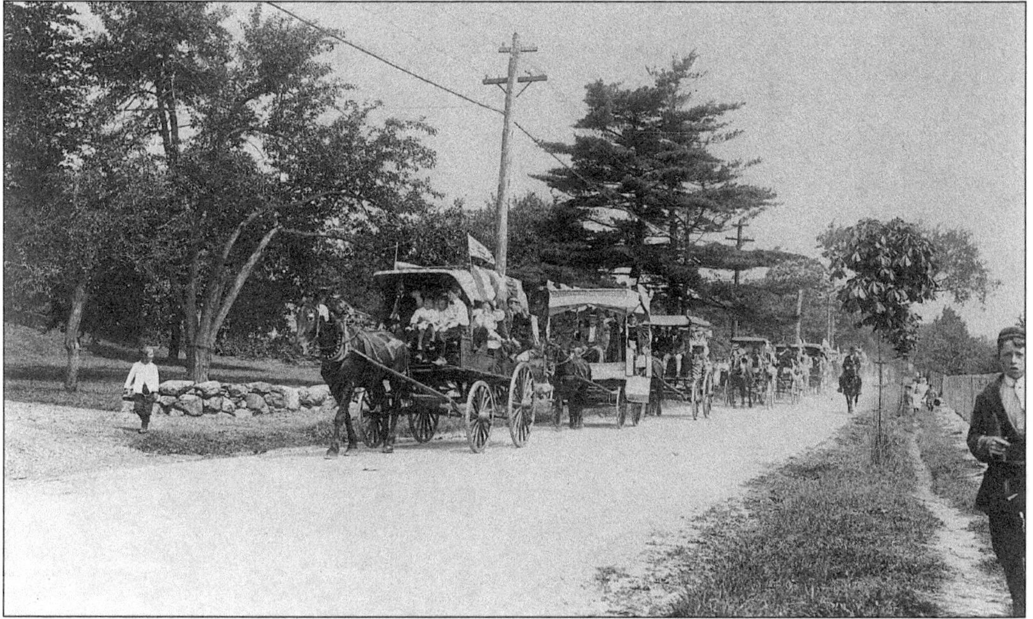

June 17, 1909, was a red-letter day, as Belmont celebrated its 50th anniversary. A salute of 50 guns was fired at sunrise. This photograph shows some of the local citizens taking part in the celebration.

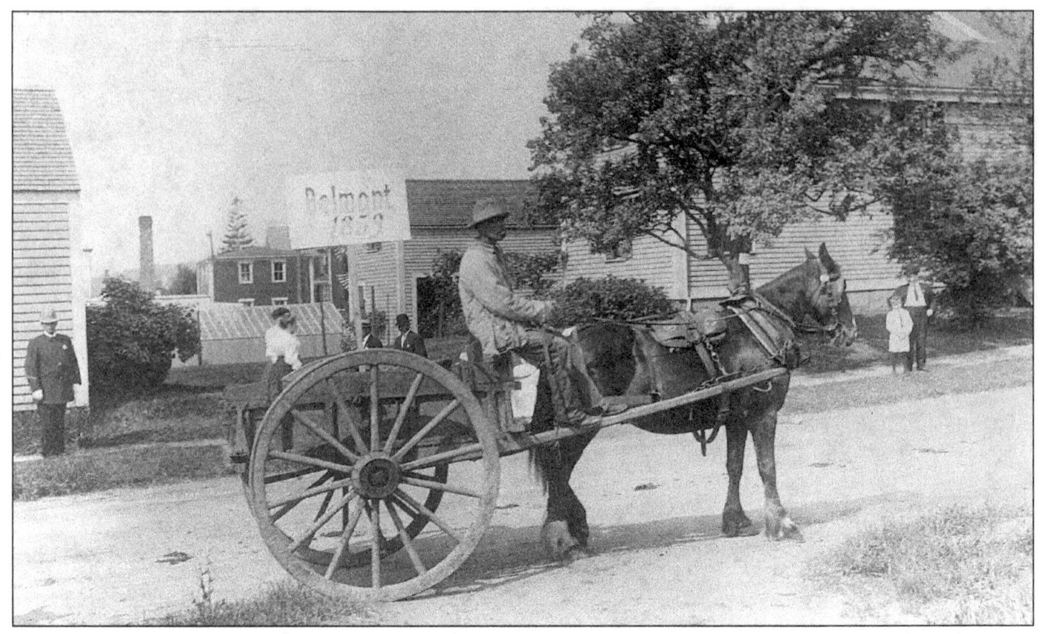

This rig from the Frost farm on Brighton Street is being prepared for the parade. The two harness bells took on a distinctive tone depending on the gait of the horses. Residents could identify the teams driven on Belmont roads.

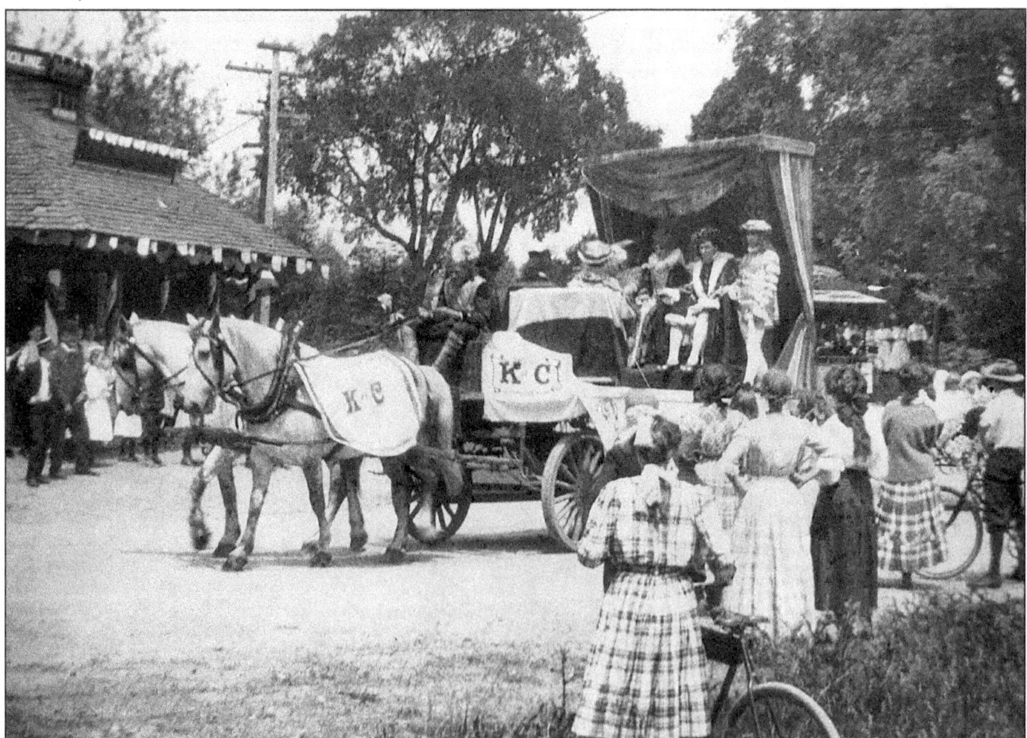

The Knights of Columbus float, pulled by a team of horses in the 50th anniversary parade, passes through Cushing Square. The store in the background was the country store operated by Charles F. Merrow, who sold everything from spring water to gasoline.

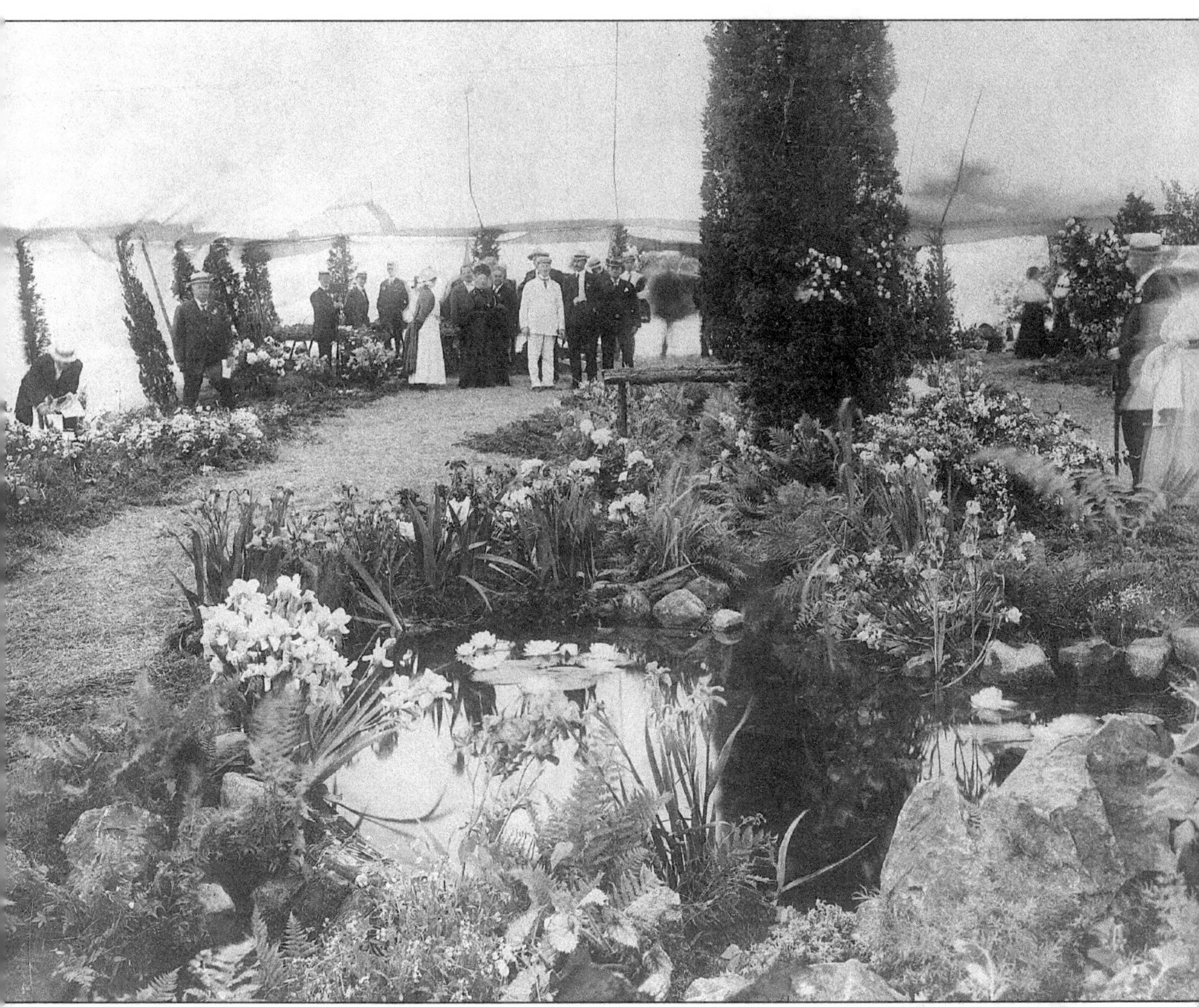

The chief feature of the day was a Strawberry and Flower Show, for which Belmont had become famous. This was set out in a large tent on the town hall grounds. A novel feature was a running stream, in imitation of a brook, flowing through the whole length of the tent and stretching into pools that were supplied with goldfish and water plants. Loring Underwood designed this display.

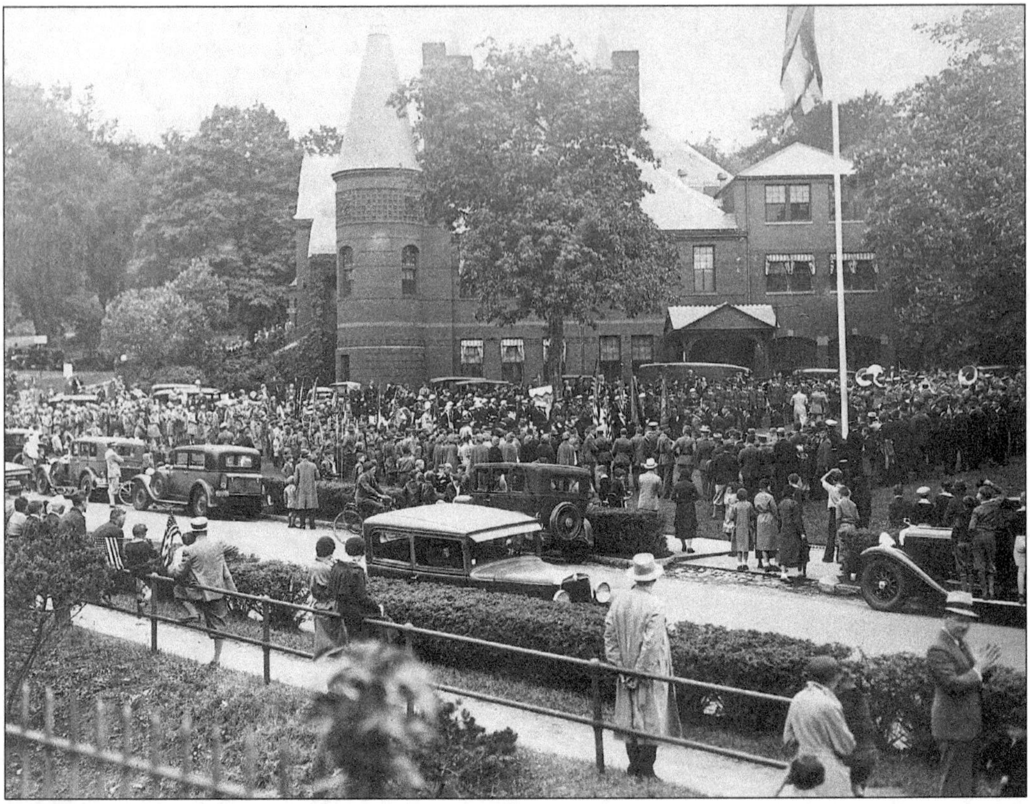

This is the town hall, *c.* 1920, probably on Decoration Day. The bands and parade groups are gathered around the flagpole for ceremonies. One is able to see the awnings on some of the windows and also the hedges on both sides of Concord Avenue.

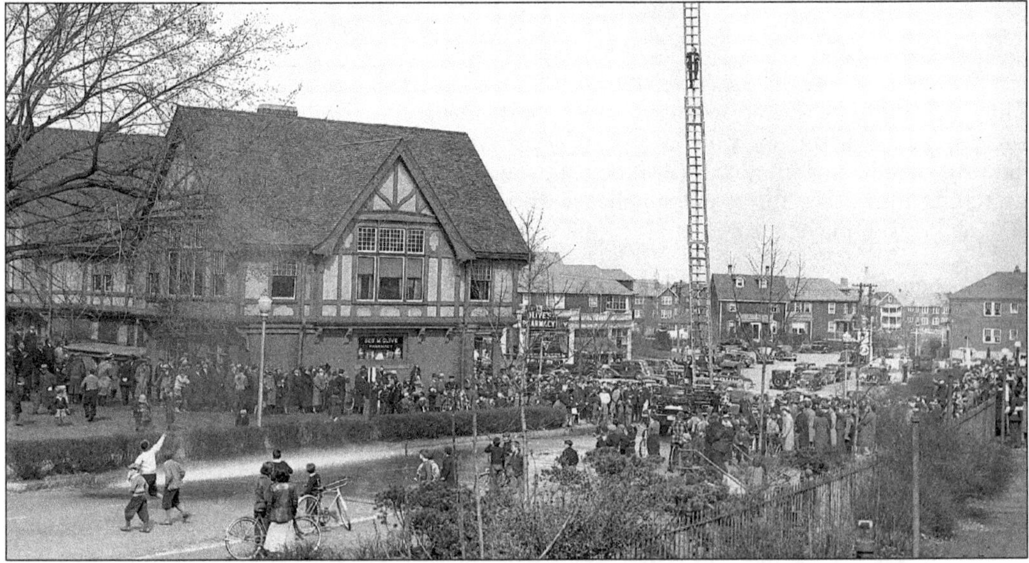

In 1937, the townspeople enthusiastically greeted the new 65-foot aerial ladder. This was to replace the 1918 ladder truck. The crowd cheered as the Seagrave Company demonstrated this wonderful $15,600 ladder truck.

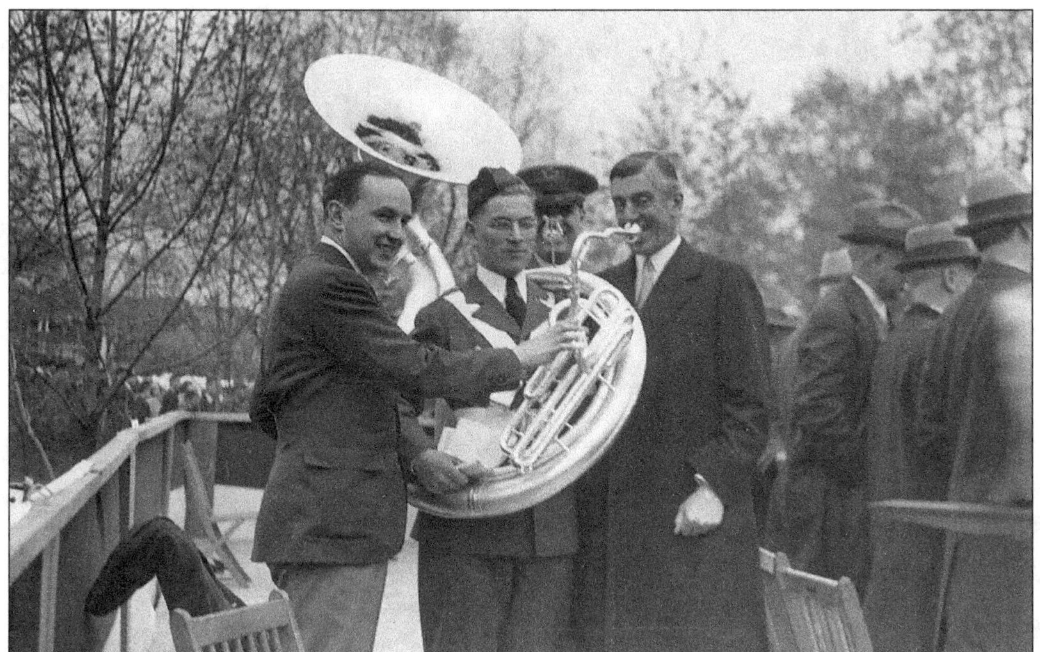

The statewide music festival took place in Belmont in 1939. Gov. Leverett Saltonstall, on the parade review stand, tries the tuba. The music director, Warren Freeman, stands on the left.

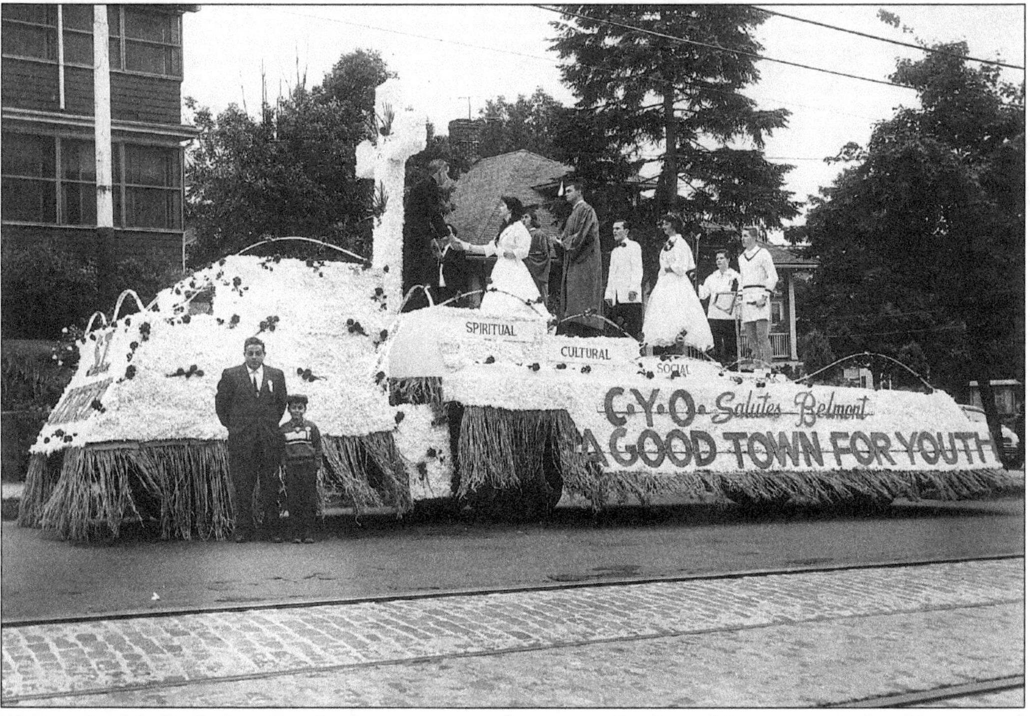

This colorful Catholic Youth Organization float was St. Joseph's entry in the Centennial Parade in 1959. James J. Castanino, superintendent of highways, is seen standing with his son Peter Castanino, who is the present superintendent. Notice the trolley tracks on Trapelo Road. (Courtesy of Peter Castanino.)

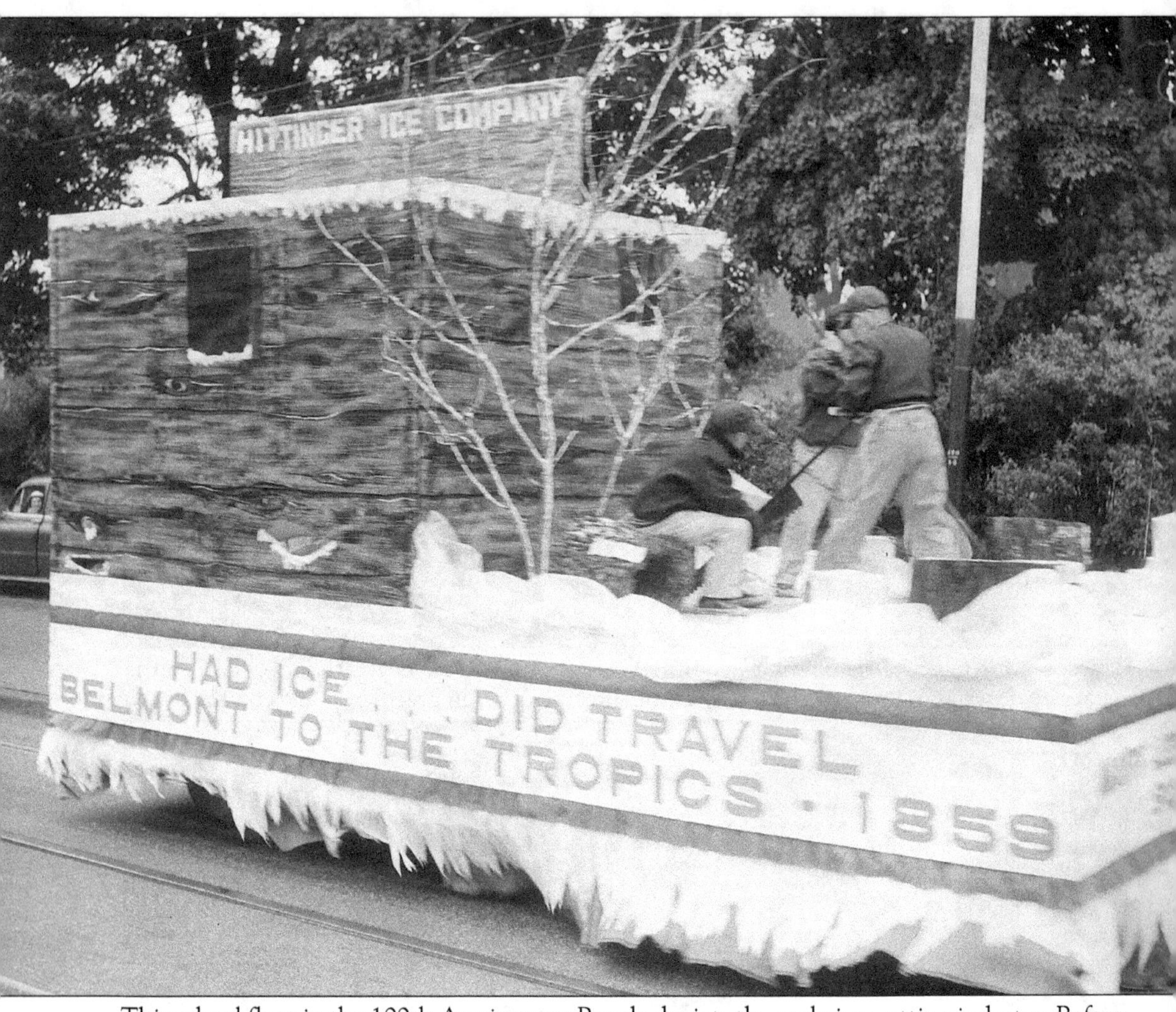

This school float in the 100th Anniversary Parade depicts the early ice-cutting industry. Before refrigerators came into use, the Hittinger Ice Company was an important business and shipped ice as far away as the Tropics.

The Centennial Celebration took place during four days in June 1959. The many activities included an art festival, a historical exhibit, a symphony, a band concert provided by the veterans organizations, and a square dance. On the final day, there was a grand parade with many floats and bands. The evening ended with a wonderful display of fireworks over Clay Pit Pond. Belmont's 100th anniversary was celebrated with a feeling of great camaraderie and a sense of pride for all Belmontians.

www.ingramcontent.com/pod-product-compliance
Lightning Source LLC
LaVergne TN
LVHW081530100826
845153LV00004B/245

9781531602895